WE HAVE THE MIND
OF CHRIST

Jerome M. Hall, S.J.

WE HAVE
THE MIND
OF CHRIST

The Holy Spirit and Liturgical Memory

in the Thought of Edward J. Kilmartin

A PUEBLO BOOK

The Liturgical Press Collegeville, Minnesota

A Pueblo Book published by The Liturgical Press

Design by Frank Kacmarcik, Obl.S.B. Cover photo: Edward J. Kilmartin, S.J., courtesy of Robert J. Daly, S.J.

Library of Congress Cataloging-in-Publication Data

Hall, Jerome M., 1950–
    We have the mind of Christ : the Holy Spirit and liturgical memory in the
    thought of Edward J. Kilmartin / Jerome M. Hall.
        p. cm.
    "A Pueblo book."
    Includes bibliographical references and index.
    ISBN 0-8146-6184-X (alk. paper)
    1. Kilmartin, Edward J. 2. Jesus Christ in the liturgy—Catholic Church—
History of doctrines—20th century. 3. Jesus Christ—Presence—History of
doctrines—20th century. 4. Holy Spirit—History of doctrines—20th
century. 5. Catholic Church—Liturgy—History—20th century. 6. Catholic
Church—Doctrines—History—20th century. I. Title.

BT575 .H35 2001
264'.02'0092—dc21
                                                                00-067165

Contents

Acknowledgments

This book was originally written as a Ph.D. dissertation for the School of Religious Studies of The Catholic University of America. Mary Collins, O.S.B., suggested that I explore Edward Kilmartin's work and generously guided the dissertation to its conclusion. Ed Kilmartin gave me the topic, saw me through the writing of an outline, and shared with me not only his papers and books but also much of his time in the last months of his life. Stephen Happel and William Loewe, readers of the dissertation, offered much helpful criticism. I thank my Jesuit brothers, both in the United States and in Rome, for their support; I am extremely grateful that I was encouraged to return to studies in the midst of a career as a pastoral minister. I thank my family, who have shaped my own outlook, and especially my parents, who taught me to love the liturgy. When I was very young, my parents took me to Mount Saviour Monastery, Pine City, New York, where I learned the mystery theology of Maria Laach. As a token of thanks this book is dedicated to them.

Introduction

In a thirty-five year career of teaching and writing in the area of liturgical theology, Edward J. Kilmartin, S.J. (1923–1994), became noted among Roman Catholic theologians for his emphasis on the activity of the Holy Spirit in Christian liturgy. At the time of his death his writing showed particular concern with the role of the Holy Spirit in the liturgical memorial, or anamnesis, of Jesus Christ. This book serves as an introduction to Kilmartin's work and argues that one particular concern, the relationship between Jesus' historical deeds and the liturgical celebration, lies at the heart of his theological project. His interest in this subject may be understood in light of the events that brought him to the field of sacramental and liturgical theology just before the Second Vatican Council.

OVERVIEW OF KILMARTIN'S MINISTRY

After graduating from Cheverus High School in Portland, Maine, Kilmartin entered the New England Province of the Society of Jesus on September 7, 1941. During the early years of his Jesuit formation, he volunteered for the New England Jesuits' mission in Iraq. After the required courses in philosophy, which he completed in 1948,[1] his further studies were directed toward advancing two projects through which his superiors planned to broaden the mission's impact. First, the Jesuits hoped to open a petroleum engineering school at their university in Baghdad. This school would educate not just Iraqis but also promising students from around the Middle East. Kilmartin was sent to study physical chemistry so that he would be able to join the

---

[1] Kilmartin's M.A. thesis seems to be the first expression of his concern for the construction of a systematic understanding of the world: Edward J. Kilmartin, "A System of Organic Synthesis" (M.A. thesis, Boston College, 1948). Degree awarded *magna cum laude*.

new engineering faculty. He earned the M.S. *summa cum laude* at Holy Cross College in 1950.[2] He showed some promise in the field; with his major professor he co-authored two articles on the surface energy of sugar,[3] which were important enough that even during his last illness he received occasional inquiries about that work.

His superiors' plans for a second project involved the field of theology and may have sparked Kilmartin's interest in the theology of the Eastern Churches. The Chaldean patriarch of Baghdad, head of an ancient Eastern Church in union with Rome, had expressed interest in having the American Jesuits replace the French Dominicans who taught in his seminary. In preparation for that work, Kilmartin, after his presbyteral ordination on June 19, 1954, and a fourth year of theology at Weston College, was sent to the Gregorian University in Rome, where he studied dogmatic theology, with an emphasis on theological controversy between Roman and non-Roman Christians.[4] Following his doctoral studies, Kilmartin did the year-long tertianship that completed his Jesuit formation, made his solemn final vows as a Jesuit on February 2, 1959, and was ready to teach in Baghdad.

The provincial of New England, however, asked the mission superior to lend Kilmartin back to the province for a short time to fill a sudden vacancy on the theological faculty of Weston College. The request was granted, so in 1959 Kilmartin found himself assigned to Weston to teach sacramental theology, an area in which his formal education did not go beyond the courses he would teach. In his first year he followed the manuals of neo-scholastic sacramental theology that he himself had studied at Weston. In 1960, his second year, he abandoned the manual approach and began to teach the sacramental theology of Karl Rahner. During that year his first published articles in theology reported on the work of various European scholars who were developing the scriptural and traditional basis for the approach

[2] Kilmartin, "Two Thermodynamic Relations of the System: Sucrose and Water" (M.S. thesis in Physical Chemistry, Holy Cross College, 1950).

[3] E. J. Kilmartin and Andrew Van Hook, "Heats of Crystallization of Sucrose from Water Solutions," *Sugar* (London, England) 45, no. 10 (October, 1950). Andrew Van Hook and Edward J. Kilmartin, "The Surface Energy of Sucrose," *Zeitschrift für Elektrochemie*. Berichte der Bunsengesellschaft für physikalische Chemie Band 56, Heft 4 (1952) 302–305.

[4] Kilmartin, "Eschatology and the Evanston Congress: A Study of Developments in Eschatology in the Twentieth Century, and Its Influence on the Theology of the World Council of Churches" (Rome: Gregorian University Press, 1958). S.T.D. awarded *summa cum laude*.

to sacramental theology that would be taken by the Second Vatican Council.

Kilmartin's short-term assignment to the Weston faculty lasted for fifteen years and set his career in a direction that neither he nor his superiors had foreseen. In the mid-1960s the American Jesuits, who never founded the petroleum engineering school nor took over the seminary, were expelled from Iraq by the new revolutionary government of the Baath party. The New England Jesuits who had been assigned to the Baghdad mission were reabsorbed into the New England Province. By that time Kilmartin was well established at Weston as a teacher of sacramental theology, as a participant in ecumenical dialogue between the archdiocese of Boston and the Orthodox and the Reformation Churches, and as a writer for scholarly and popular audiences on both sacramental theology and ecumenism.

Kilmartin remained at Weston until 1974, when he became director of the Ph.D. program in liturgical studies at the University of Notre Dame, a position he held for ten years. There his suggestions for dissertation topics matched his students' gifts and interests with questions that he was exploring as he articulated a post–Vatican II theology of liturgy.

In 1984 Kilmartin returned to Rome to teach the theology of liturgy at the Pontifical Oriental Institute. There he began to articulate a theological synthesis that attempted to bring together the insights of both East and West in a way that would help the Churches overcome the ancient disputes standing in the way of reunion. It was in the middle of the work of combining the Western theological tradition's strong Christological emphasis with the Eastern tradition's pneumatological stress that he was struck by multiple myeloma. As he fought this illness, he directed his diminishing energies toward outlining a systematic theology of liturgy that emphasizes the activity of the Holy Spirit in the Church's liturgical memorial of Jesus. Had he remained healthy, Kilmartin might have constructed a synthetic and systematic treatment of the Holy Spirit's role in liturgical anamnesis. As it is, his work on this subject, which many consider his most important contribution to the field of liturgical and sacramental theology, is fully accessible only through reading his many articles and through studying his papers and unpublished manuscripts.

Given the fact that he was in effect self-taught in his chosen field, Kilmartin set himself a daunting task in trying to replace the neo-scholastic system of sacramental theology that he had been taught.

One key to his progress toward this end was a combination of highly focused attention and great physical and mental vigor. From his youth he found that physical activity cleared his mind and helped him approach problems successfully. The style of Jesuit formation that he had experienced helped him develop the ability to focus on academic questions not just at his desk but while exerting himself outdoors. As his health failed in his final years, his tenacious pursuit of systematic understanding continued; he took a notepad to bed and, while resting, sketched out ways to relate the truths of the faith to one another.

Another key to his development was his persistent use of a gift for the study of languages. As a student at Weston, he supplemented the required reading in English and Latin with perusal of French and German journals. In this way, at a time when seminary education did not require Roman Catholic seminarians to delve deeply into scholarly conversations, Kilmartin became familiar with theological discussions being carried on by French and German scholars. He shared his knowledge of European authors and of the issues that concerned them not only through his own articles but also through more than one hundred book reviews for *Theological Studies* and other journals. Indeed, it was the European theologians, especially the Germans, who became his conversation partners as he developed a systematic theology of liturgical celebration.

THE QUESTION OF THE MYSTERY PRESENCE

Perhaps the most vigorous and most significant discussion in sacramental theology while Kilmartin was a theological student at Weston, from 1951 to 1955, concerned the manner of presence of Christ and his saving acts in the liturgy. This controversy had begun in the 1920s, and, especially in its early years, had occasioned great dispute between the German Benedictine Odo Casel and other monks of the Rhineland abbey of Maria Laach, on one side, and Jesuits at the Gregorian University, among others, on the other side. In 1947, in the encyclical *Mediator Dei*, Pius XII addressed the subject, affirming the presence of Christ and his saving acts in the liturgy, but he did not take a position on the disputed question of the manner of that presence. Spirited discussion of the subject continued right up to the beginning of the Second Vatican Council in 1962. Interest in the council's constitution on the liturgy, *Sacrosanctum Concilium*, promulgated in 1963, forced the disputed question into the background without its ever having been resolved.

Thus when Kilmartin was learning to teach sacramental and liturgical theology, the presence of Christ and his saving deeds in the Church's liturgy[5] had been a major topic of discussion in Roman Catholic sacramental theology for a good part of the twentieth century. The conversation was carried on through articles that were vigorous in their argumentation and insistent on the pastoral importance of a proper understanding of the Church's liturgy. The disputing theologians defended their positions by referring to Scripture, liturgical texts, and patristic literature as well as to scholastic theology and magisterial statements. As a young professor constructing his own courses in the theology of Christian worship, Kilmartin would have been compelled to treat the question of how Christ's saving acts are present in liturgical celebration.

Kilmartin applied his energy, attention, and scientific education to the subject of this controversy. In more than thirty years of debate, no theologian had proposed a solution that seemed satisfactory; indeed, many proposals seemed to raise more questions than they answered. That led him to think that the question itself was being formulated in an improper fashion. Over time he developed the elements of an explicitly Trinitarian approach to sacramental theology, an approach that he believed could explain the mystery presence in a more acceptable way than that of Casel and his interlocutors. Kilmartin found support for his position in the work of colleagues who were also developing Trinitarian theologies of liturgy.

At the same time, Kilmartin was quite aware that "the average modern Catholic theology" not just of the Eucharist but of liturgical celebration in general was still fixed on approaches which, by their inability to answer the question of the mystery presence, had proven to be "without a future."[6] Constructing Trinitarian theologies of liturgy that would capture the popular imagination by more satisfactorily treating the mystery presence while systematically relating the various truths of the faith to each other was, he believed, a major part

---

[5] Various prayers and other texts of the Eucharistic liturgy refer to the liturgical event as "celebration of the sacred mysteries"; texts of other liturgies also use the term "mystery." Following this usage, Casel called the liturgical presence of Christ the "mystery presence" (*Mysteriengegenwart*).

[6] Kilmartin, "The Catholic Tradition of Eucharistic Theology: Towards the Third Millennium," *Theological Studies* 55 (1994) 443.

of the task of liturgical theology at the beginning of the third millennium.[7] His illness and death, however, prevented him from assembling all the elements of his Trinitarian approach to the mystery presence into a unified presentation.

SCOPE AND STRUCTURE OF THE BOOK

This book gives a systematic and synthetic presentation of Kilmartin's approach to the presence of Christ and his saving acts in the liturgy that the Church celebrates in his memory. The liturgical memorial of Christ is frequently referred to using the Greek word *anamnēsis*, which means "calling to mind" or "remembrance." Theologians of the liturgy use this term in two senses. In a narrow sense it refers to the section of the Eucharistic Prayer immediately following the narrative of institution of the Eucharist, which states that the Church's prayer is offered in remembrance of Christ's death and resurrection. In a broader sense, the term indicates an essential aspect of all Christian worship: the Church's gathering, listening to Scripture, praise of God, and petition for continued blessings are all done in memory of God's saving deeds in Jesus Christ.[8] This book considers liturgical anamnesis in its broader sense.

The first chapter gives the *status quaestionis* in Roman Catholic theological reflection on the liturgical presence of Christ and his saving deeds at the time Kilmartin began his work. This chapter outlines the major positions taken during the controversy over the manner of that presence, points out the problems inherent in each position, and indicates the development of the Roman magisterium's teaching on the presence of Christ and his acts in the liturgy. All this has been thoroughly developed in secondary literature.

The second chapter describes Kilmartin's method of uncovering the theological content of the *lex orandi*, the Church's rule of worship, and lists the conclusions that he drew from liturgical text and practice.

The third chapter presents the principal elements of his proposed solution to the question of the liturgical presence of Christ in a thematic and systematic fashion, indicating the other theologians whom he cited as his most important conversation partners.

---

[7] Ibid., 457.

[8] Allan Bouley, O.S.B., "Anamnesis," in Joseph A. Komonchak, Mary Collins, and Dermot A. Lane, eds., *The New Dictionary of Theology* (Wilmington: Glazier, 1987) 17.

The fourth chapter details Kilmartin's synthesis of those elements, relating the prayer of the liturgical assembly to Jesus' acts through the personal activity of the Holy Spirit.

The fifth chapter uses the criticisms raised against the various positions outlined in chapter 1 as criteria for judging Kilmartin's proposed solution to the question of describing the mystery presence and considers his success in integrating the various themes presented in chapters 2 and 3 into a truly systematic theology of liturgical celebration.

Chapter One

Liturgical Anamnesis and the Mystery Presence of Christ's Saving Deeds: State of the Question at the Beginning of Kilmartin's Career

The Second Vatican Council taught that the Church's liturgy celebrates and proclaims the paschal mystery of Christ's death and resurrection. Through the liturgy Christians "are enabled to express in their lives and manifest to others the mystery of Christ and the real nature of the true Church."[1] The Council's emphasis on the paschal mystery, expressed in the postconciliar liturgical reform, was one of the fruits of a vigorous debate on the "mystery presence of the saving work of Christ" (*Mysteriengegenwart der Heilstat Christi*).[2] The controversy over the mystery presence began in the 1920s and continued until the opening days of the Vatican Council.[3]

---

[1] Vatican Council II, *Sacrosanctum Concilium: Constitution on the Sacred Liturgy,* (December 4, 1963; hereafter cited as *SC*) 2. English translation in Austin Flannery, O.P., *Vatican Council II: The Conciliar and Post Conciliar Documents,* vol. 1 (Collegeville: The Liturgical Press, 1975) 1–40.

[2] The compound word *Mysteriengegenwart,* usually translated as "mystery presence," has levels of meaning that do not survive the translation. "*Mysterien*" is the plural form of the noun *Mysterie*; the "presence" *(Gegenwart)* referred to is that of the mysteries of Christ's saving work, which include the liturgical mysteries that the Church celebrates.

[3] Philip Gleeson, O.P., "Mystery," in Joseph A. Komonchak, Mary Collins, and Dermot A. Lane, eds., *The New Dictionary of Theology* (Wilmington, Del.: Glazier, 1987) 690–691; Johannes Betz, "Die Gegenwart der Heilstat Christi," in *Wahrheit und Verkündigung: Festschrift M. Schmaus,* ed. L. Scheffczyk et al. (Munich: Schöningh, 1967) 1813–1815; Angelus Häussling, "Odo Casel—noch von Aktualität?" *Archiv für Liturgiewissenschaft* 28 (1986) 360, 386–387; Ghislain Lafont, "Permanence et transformations des intuitions de Dom Casel," *Ecclesia Orans* 4 (1987) 283–284.

One side of the debate was identified with Odo Casel, O.S.B. (1886–1948), and his fellow monks at the Abbey of Maria Laach, in the German Rhineland. Under the veil of the sacramental sign, according to Casel, the glorified Christ makes present the saving deeds that he accomplished on the cross. Through the mystery presence of Christ's saving deeds in the Church's worship, Christians are able to die and rise with Christ, and so share in the salvation that Christ won for them. Casel's "mystery theology" was opposed by various theologians, who insisted that Christ's presence in the liturgy is only a "virtual" presence. By his power *(virtus)* as the glorified Lord, the grace that resulted from Christ's sacrificial death is applied to the recipients of the sacraments. The glorified Christ is certainly present in the liturgy, these theologians argued, since it is his grace that is given to the worshipers. His saving deeds, however, are present only in their effects, that is, in the gift of grace to the recipient of the sacrament.[4]

For about forty years before the beginning of the Second Vatican Council, Roman Catholic sacramental theologians carried on a vigorous discussion about the nature of Christ's presence in the Church's liturgy. They did not, however, arrive at a consensus on the relationship between the liturgical memorial of Christ's saving acts and Christ's presence in the liturgy. Such a consensus still has not been achieved among Catholic theologians. The Roman magisterium has also taken no position, neither during the controversy nor in the years after the Second Vatican Council, on the question. Instead, the Church's official teaching that in the liturgy Christ is present with his saving deeds uses language acceptable to either side of the *Mysteriengegenwart* controversy. From this point of view, the controversy over the mystery presence of Christ and his saving acts has never been resolved.[5]

The continuing controversy over the mystery presence of Christ and his saving deeds in the liturgy seems particularly to have drawn Edward Kilmartin's attention when he began teaching sacramental theology in 1959. That this interest continued throughout his career is demonstrated not only in his writings but also in the notes and translations kept in his files. When he was moving from Rome only

[4] Theodor Filthaut, *Die Kontroverse über die Mysterienlehre* (Warendorf, Westf.: Schnellsche, 1947) 26–28.

[5] Franziskus Eisenbach, *Die Gegenwart Jesu Christi im Gottesdienst: Systematische Studien der Liturgiekonstitution des II. Vatikanischen Konzils* (Mainz: Grünewald, 1982) 753–754.

months before he died, he gave this author rough translations, on paper yellowed with age, of several articles reporting on the controversy, along with extensive notes on other articles and lectures about the presence of Christ in the liturgical mysteries. He kept photocopies of several articles to use while composing the last of his writings.[6] Among his written and computerized files there are also outlines of courses that refer to the *Mysteriengegenwart* controversy, including an entire course on Christ's presence in the liturgy that he developed while at the Pontifical Oriental Institute.

This chapter sets Kilmartin's understanding of the activity of the Holy Spirit in liturgical anamnesis in the context of the twentieth-century debate about the mystery presence. The first section indicates the major issues in the *Mysteriengegenwart* controversy at the beginning of Kilmartin's career. This presentation relies heavily on four secondary sources that he apparently found most useful. Three of those sources are descriptive and analytical. The first is Theodor Filthaut's comprehensive report of 1947, *Die Kontroverse über die Mysterienlehre*, which details the early stages of the controversy. Filthaut's book was published before Pius XII's encyclical on the liturgy, *Mediator Dei*, and before Casel's death. A second source is an article by Eloi Dekkers, O.S.B., "La Liturgie, Mystère Chrétien,"[7] published shortly after Casel's death. Dekkers both described the outlook of the mystery theology and summarized the principal points of dispute. In 1957 Jean Gaillard, O.S.B., summarizing the discussion over the mystery presence, organized the disputants according to the type of presence they affirmed.[8] Gaillard highlighted the contributions made by Edward Schillebeeckx's *De sacramentele Heilseconomie*.[9] The fourth secondary source is an article published in 1958, "Réactualisation des mystères rédempteurs dans et

[6] Kilmartin, "The Catholic Tradition of Eucharistic Theology: Towards the Third Millennium," *Theological Studies* (hereafter cited as *TS*) 55 (1994) 407–409, 450–452, refers to the *Mysteriengegenwart* controversy. Kilmartin's final work, *The Eucharist in the West* (Collegeville: The Liturgical Press, 1999), edited for posthumous publication by Robert J. Daly, S.J., treats the various issues of the controversy in its closing chapters.

[7] Eloi Dekkers, "La Liturgie, Mystère Chrétien," *La Maison-Dieu* 14 (1948) 30–64.

[8] Jean Gaillard, "Chronique de Liturgie. La Théologie des Mystères," *Revue Thomiste* 57 (1957) 510–551.

[9] Edward Schillebeeckx, *De sacramentele Heilseconomie: Theologische bezinning op Sint-Thomas' sacramentenleer in het licht van de traditie en van de hedendaagse sacramentesproblematiek* (Anvers: 't Groeit, 1952).

par les sacrements,"[10] in which Jean-Hervé Nicolas, O.P., offered a critique of the various positions in the controversy from the light of Thomist metaphysics. Nicolas's reflections on the issues raised during the controversy, together with a more recent analysis of Thomas Aquinas's teaching on the relationship of an instrumental cause (Christ's deeds) and its effect (the sacramental grace), are briefly treated in a second section of the chapter.

The third section of the chapter summarizes the Roman magisterium's response to the issues raised in the controversy, in the encyclicals *Mystici Corporis* in 1943 and *Mediator Dei* in 1947. The teaching of these encyclicals on the liturgical presence of the mystery of Christ offered theologians new categories in which to address the question of the mystery presence.[11] The chapter concludes with a brief summary of points that Kilmartin drew from this theological conversation.

NEO-SCHOLASTIC THEOLOGY'S APPROACH: SACRAMENTAL PRESENCE OF THE EFFECTS OF CHRIST'S PASSION

At the beginning of the twentieth century, according to Kilmartin's secondary sources, Catholic theology, catechetics, and spirituality commonly described the sacraments as means of grace. Jesus' acts were considered primarily as the cause of the grace given through the sacramental celebration.[12] Catholic theology had for centuries used the language of causality to describe the workings of sacramental grace. As Thomas Aquinas noted, God is the source or "principal cause" of grace, since "grace is nothing else than a certain shared similitude to the divine nature."[13] In the sacraments God gives grace by using two "instrumental causes." The first of these instruments is the humanity of Christ, which is joined to the principal cause through the hypostatic union of divinity and humanity in Christ. The second instrument is the sacrament itself. God communicates sacramental grace through the sacramental sign, the prayer of the Church, and the faith of the

---

[10] Jean-Hervé Nicolas, "Réactualisation des mystères rédempteurs dans et par les sacrements," *Revue Thomiste* 58 (1958) 20–54.

[11] Kilmartin, "Christ's Presence in the Liturgy," *Emmanuel* 82 (1976) 237–243.

[12] Gaillard, "Chronique," 538; Nicolas, "Réactualisation," 32.

[13] Thomas Aquinas, *Summa Theologiae* (hereafter cited as *ST*) IIIa, q. 62, 1, Responsio. English translation in Thomas Aquinas, *Summa Theologiae* 4 (New York: New Blackfriars, 1963) 53.

one receiving the sacrament. Aquinas carefully relates the effect of sacramental grace to the sacrament's character as sign of Christ's passion, for the passion is the cause of human salvation, of the gift of grace in the present, and of the promise of eternal life.[14]

A less nuanced approach than that of Aquinas seems to have been found in the neo-scholastic manual system of teaching sacramental theology that was still in favor when Kilmartin began his teaching career.[15] This system did not develop Aquinas's insight that the sacrament is sign of Christ's passion; instead, it stressed that the sacramental sign indicates the bestowal of grace. The theological manuals viewed Christ's humanity, and especially his passion, primarily as instrumental causes of grace. The liturgical anamnesis of Christ, then, was not emphasized; stress was instead placed on "the principle of the sacraments," their efficacy.[16] The sacramental celebration was seen predominantly as the instrumental cause of God's bestowal of grace upon the soul: through the sacraments God, in a juridical act, by extrinsic denomination, applies the merits of Christ's passion to the individual soul. Sacraments have their effect because of Jesus' redemptive deeds; those deeds, the instrumental cause of the sacramental grace, are present only in their effects.[17] While Aquinas had taught that the sacramental sign refers to Christ's passion, the manual system described the sign as a symbol juridically constituted by Christ to indicate the conferral of grace.

This approach, then, emphasizes the juridical effect of the sacrament and gives minimal reference to the sacraments as memorial of Christ's passion. Christ's passion has a "virtual" presence in the sacraments, for in them the power *(virtus)* deriving from the passion is present and active.[18] The relationship among the deeds of Jesus,

[14] *ST* IIIa, q. 60, 3, Responsio. A nuanced presentation of Thomas Aquinas's combination of the language of cause and that of symbol is given by Louis-Marie Chauvet, *Symbol and Sacrament* (Collegeville: The Liturgical Press, 1995) 9–20.

[15] Kilmartin, "Catholic Tradition," 406–407, distinguishes the teaching of Thomas Aquinas and that of "later thomistic schools."

[16] Nicolas, "Réactualisation," 22, 20.

[17] D. J. Kennedy, "Sacraments," in *The Catholic Encyclopedia* 13 (New York: Appleton, 1912) 295–305, shows a concern for the causes of grace and for establishing divine institution of the sacraments, with minimal treatment of the role of sacramental sign.

[18] Gaillard, "Chronique," 538. This interpretation seems not unreasonable in light of a manual on sacramental theology that Kilmartin may have used while a student at Weston: H. Lennerz, S.J., *De Sacramentis Novae Legis in Genere*, editio

the sacramental sign, and the bestowal of grace appears to be princi-
pally a juridical one.[19]

A NEW APPROACH:
THE MYSTERY OF SALVATION PRESENT
IN THE SACRAMENTAL CELEBRATION

Rather than describing the sacraments as juridically constituted
means of grace, Odo Casel and his fellow "mystery theologians"
taught that the Church's liturgy is the occasion of a saving encounter
with the person of Christ. Their sacramental theology involved "a
conception of the whole of Christianity, encompassing the entire
Christian life."[20]

Casel's key concept is that of "mystery," which he defined as "the
presence of divine salvation under the veil of a symbol."[21] The first
great mystery is that of God, who is present to the world through created realities. "Mystery is first of all *God in self*, God as the infinite
distance, the Holy and unapproachable."[22] God's salvation is present
above all in Jesus Christ and in the deeds by which he accomplished
human salvation; Christ and his saving deeds are the basic mystery
(Urmysterium). Christ, in turn, makes himself present with his saving
deeds in the liturgy. The mystery of worship *(Kultmysterium)* shapes

---

secunda (Rome: Gregorian, 1939). Lennerz devotes three pages to consideration
of the sacrament as sign of conferral of grace and fifty-five pages to the effects of
the sacrament. A later manual also among Kilmartin's books introduces the language of mystery in a short history of sacraments and then goes on to consider
sacraments as causes of grace: William van Roo, S.J., *De Sacramentis in Genere*, editio
secunda (Rome: Gregorian, 1960).

[19] Gaillard, "Chronique," 538; Filthaut, *Mysterienlehre*, 30. The definition of a
sacrament found in the Baltimore Catechism reflects this juridical emphasis: "A
sacrament is an outward sign instituted by Christ to give grace." A similar statement appears in the Catechism of the Catholic Church (no. 1084), but in the context of the liturgical celebration of the Trinitarian economy established in the
paschal mystery.

[20] Dekkers, "La Liturgie," 31, quoting Damasus Winzen, O.S.B., who represented the Abbey of Maria Laach at the 1938 Liturgical Week. All translations in
this book, unless otherwise indicated, have been done by its author.

[21] Casel, "Mysteriengegenwart," *Jahrbuch für Liturgiewissenschaft* 8 (1928) 145.

[22] Quoted in Gottlieb Söhngen, "Die Kontroverse über die kultische Gegenwart
des Christusmysteriums," *Catholica* 7 (1938) 114–115.

and constitutes the Church by conforming Christians to Christ's dying and rising.[23]

According to Casel's mystery theology, Christianity is not primarily a doctrine to be accepted by an intellectual act of faith but is rather "a deed, a history in which we can participate; a history which, in a fashion, becomes contemporaneous with all the generations to come."[24] Grace, from this viewpoint, is not simply the effect of Christ's actions, the divine power by which a person may live a virtuous life. Properly understood, "grace is Christ himself and his redeeming work in all its fullness, not just a fluid which flows forth and which a sacrament gives us almost 'as a medicine in a pill.'"[25] The grace given in sacramental celebrations elevates Christians to participate in the divine life by configuring the recipient of the sacrament to Christ.[26]

Sacraments have this effect because they are much more than juridically constituted signs of the conferral of grace; sacraments are reactualizations of the saving deeds of Christ. While those deeds are historically past, they are made present sacramentally, "in mystery," in the performance of the sacramental rite. Those who enter into the rite encounter Christ in his passion, join in his sacrifice, and are transformed by sharing in his dying and rising. Sacramental sanctification, then, consists in the worshipers' participation in Christ's saving deeds.[27] In contrast, the *Effektustheorie* of the manual system, speaking of grace as power juridically applied, seems to narrow the understanding of God's plan for human sanctification and to obscure the richness and beauty of the life "in Christ."[28]

Anscar Vonier's "Key to the Sacraments"

When Casel first proposed his theory in 1922, he offered little speculative grounding for his position. In 1925 the English Benedictine

---

[23] Dekkers, "La Liturgie," 42–43.

[24] Ibid., 32.

[25] Gottlieb Söhngen, *Symbol und Wirklichkeit im Kultmysterium* (Bonn, 1940) 58. Quoted by Dekkers, "La Liturgie," 40. Söhngen's books on the mystery presence were published in Germany during World War II and were not republished after the war, so they can be found in few American libraries.

[26] Filthaut, *Mysterienlehre*, 27.

[27] Gaillard, "Chronique," 510. Casel's initial formulation of this position was in *Die Liturgie als Mysterienfeier* (Freiburg i. B.: Herder, 1922).

[28] Filthaut, *Mysterienlehre*, 30.

Anscar Vonier provided a basis for the mystery theology from the Thomist[29] theological tradition.[30] Vonier emphasized the anamnetic or commemorative role of the sacramental sign in the sacramental theory of Thomas Aquinas.[31]

Aquinas teaches that the sacramental sign contains what it signifies. The sacramental sign effectively signifies Christ's passion, which is the cause of salvation and of the sacramental grace. Christ's passion, Vonier concluded, must be contained in the sign, made present in its substance, according to a sacramental mode of being, without the fetters of space and time. This presence is demanded by the commemorative nature of the sacramental sign:[32] the sacramental sign must not simply bring to mind the passion but must make it present to the worshiper in order for its power to be accessible in the celebration.[33]

It is the glorified Christ who acts in the sacrament, but he comes to the worshiper as the one who has suffered, as the *Christus Passus*. The Crucified One is present, however, not "in his natural condition, *sub proprie specie*,"[34] but in an atemporal sacramental mode of being, in order that the worshiper may by faith enter into Christ's passage to the Father. Thomas Aquinas's teaching on baptism, Vonier held, illustrates the importance of this sacramental mode of being: "to every one who is baptised the Passion of Christ is communicated for a remedy as if he himself had suffered and had died."[35] The passion is communicated to the one who is baptized through the sacramental sign, in and through which Christ is present. Through the sacramental sign, the liturgical celebration "links us up with Christ, historically as well as actually,"[36] conforming the worshiper to Christ's

---

[29] This presentation observes the distinction made in some philosophical circles between "thomistic philosophy and theology," which proceeds (and in some cases departs) from the work of Thomas Aquinas, incorporating the teachings of later commentators, and "Thomism," which attempts to return to Aquinas's own thought.

[30] Anscar Vonier, *A Key to the Doctrine of the Eucharist* (New York: Benziger, 1925).

[31] Filthaut, *Mysterienlehre*, 28–29, remarks that Vonier's interpretation of Aquinas was not universally accepted.

[32] Vonier, *Key*, 19.

[33] Ibid., 31–32.

[34] Ibid., 32.

[35] Ibid., 52, quoting *ST* III, 50, art. 2.

[36] Ibid., 43.

passion. "The sacrament is a representation of an historic fact,"[37] since that representation does not just signify but contains the immolated Christ; it brings worshipers into contact with the events that result in their salvation.[38]

In the Eucharist, for example, Vonier held that Christ's passion is sacramentally represented in the separate consecrations of bread and wine.[39] These signs represent the risen Lord, who acts in the sacrament as the sacrificed victim. In his death on the cross, Christ's blood was separated from his body; the separate consecrations of bread and wine, then, symbolically represent Christ at the moment of his death. Through the sign of the separation of the species, the glorified Christ is present in the sacramental mode as "the *Christus Passus* of Calvary, who is the one represented, applied, immolated, and contained in the Eucharistic sacrifice."[40] The symbolic representation of Christ's death makes his sacrifice present in its sacramental mode, enabling the faithful to join in that sacrifice.[41]

The sign of the separate consecrations, then, makes the glorified Lord whose power works through the sacraments present precisely as sacrificial victim and priest, as the *Christus Passus*.[42] The sacramental separation represents the effect of his passion, his death. In this way, Vonier argues, Christ's passion is present in the Eucharist not just as the instrumental cause of sacramental grace but also through the sacramental representation of the dead Christ.[43]

Casel's Theory: Presence of Christ with His Saving Acts

Casel, according to his interpreter Dekkers, disagreed with Vonier about the reality contained in the sacramental sign. Vonier held that it was sufficient for the sacrament to represent the *Christus Passus*, the effect of the passion. Casel, however, believed that for the sacramental celebration to conform the Christian to Christ's dying and rising, it must make present the passion itself, for the passion contains the mystery of redemption.[44] Christ's presence in the liturgy, then, must

[37] Ibid., 57.
[38] Ibid., 60, 61.
[39] Ibid., 111.
[40] Ibid., 133.
[41] Ibid., 123.
[42] Ibid., 131.
[43] Ibid.
[44] Dekkers, "La Liturgie," 45.

include the totality of the salvation that he accomplished in time. His saving deeds are not, however, present in the historical particularity of the crucifixion, with the hatred of Jesus' tormentors, with the sweat and the nails and the jeers of the onlookers. It is rather the kernel or essence of these acts, in a non-temporal mode of sacramental existence, that is present under the veil of the sacramental sign:

"The passion is not there according to its natural manner of being, as it was historically, *in tempore,* and also not merely *in signo,* but sacramentally. Because it is not *in tempore,* it is therefore present *secundum modum substantiae,* without historical 'before' or 'after,' precisely in its kernel as the salvific act of the God-man. Hence metaphysical hypotheses concerning time, concerning the impossibility of a renewal of historical acts and the like, *do not come up for consideration at all in the case of the sacrament."*[45]

In the sacrament, Casel argued, the salvation that Christ accomplished in time is present in a symbolico-real fashion, as supratemporal reality. The sacrament is that redemptive work made present in its substance by the glorified Christ himself.[46] The very purpose of the sacraments demands that Christ's acts be substantially present, "for the sacrament exists to enable the faithful to participate in the life of Christ, *as their redeemer,* for their own salvation."[47]

Through the sacramental rite, worshipers enter into and participate in the redemptive deeds that Christ makes present under the veil of the sacramental sign. By participating in the liturgy with lively faith, they join with Christ in his sacrificial self-offering.

Casel insisted that Christ's redemptive work is not repeated or multiplied when the sacraments of the Church are celebrated. Instead, the saving work, done once for all, is re-presented by Christ through the sacramental sign.[48] "The Christian liturgy is *the ritual performance of the redemptive work of Christ in and through the Church; hence it is the presence of the divine saving act under the veil of the symbol."*[49] In the rite the glorified Lord makes his redemptive work present in its essence, according to the sacramental mode of existence.

[45] Casel, "Mysteriengegenwart," 191.
[46] Dekkers, "La Liturgie," 48.
[47] Casel, "Mysteriengegenwart," 191; Dekkers, "La Liturgie," 49.
[48] Dekkers, "La Liturgie," 50; Söhngen, "Die Kontroverse," 121.
[49] Casel, "Mysteriengegenwart," 145. Emphasis in original.

Central to Casel's understanding is the idea that Christ's saving acts are "objectively" present in the liturgy; this presence is independent of and prior to its appropriation by the worshipers.[50] The objective presence of Christ's deeds evokes the worshipers' response of faith. In this way Casel makes clear that it is Christ, not the Church, who makes the redemptive work present in the Church's liturgy. Through the sacramental rite the Church cooperates with Christ's action, entering into his redeeming work by faith. The mystery of salvation, however, is present through Christ's action, not through that of the Church. Since Christ is present with his saving acts in the liturgical celebration, the worshiper meets Christ in his work of salvation. Entering into the rite with faith, the Christian can join with Christ in his redeeming sacrifice. "The *Mysterium* is a holy ritual action, in which the redemptive event becomes present under the rite. While the community of worship performs the rite, it takes part in the redemptive act and by that acquires salvation."[51]

The mystery presence of Christ and his saving deeds, Casel taught, permeates the Church's life of prayer. Christ's sacrificial self-offering and the Father's acceptance of his sacrifice for the world's salvation are, of course, most clearly present in the Eucharist, as his body and blood are substantially present under the forms of bread and wine. In each of the other sacraments, however, Christ's redemptive act has a proper mode of presence that is related to the purpose of the sacrament. Accordingly, each sacrament conforms the Christian to Christ's Pasch in its own particular fashion.[52] Furthermore, since Christ uses the entire liturgical life of the Church, with its cycle of feasts and seasons, to bring Christians to participate in his saving work, the mystery of salvation is present in the liturgy of the hours and in the cycle of the liturgical year.[53]

As grounding for his teaching on the mystery presence, Casel appealed to the history of religions, to Scripture, and to the Church Fathers.

---

[50] Gaillard, "Chronique," 533. Nicolas, "Réactualisation," 24–26, claims that by insisting on an "objective" presence, Casel avoided accusations of Pelagianism. If the sacramental presence of Christ were dependent on the sign's operation on the imagination of the recipient of the sacrament, salvation might be said to be a human achievement.

[51] Casel, *Das Christliche Kultmysterium*, 3rd ed. (Regensburg: Pustet, 1948) 102.

[52] Ibid., 200.

[53] Casel, *Kultmysterium*, 117–174 passim.

Casel believed that the Hellenistic mystery religions were the means by which God prepared humankind to participate in the mystery of Christ. He saw the Eleusinian mysteries and similar cults that celebrated the death and rebirth of a divine figure as providential preparation for popular acceptance of the Christian mysteries. Finding great similarity between the ritual and doctrine of the mystery cults and those of Christianity, he suggested that the Hellenistic mystery religions had contributed to the development of the Christian mysteries.

In response to this theory, scholars who engaged in more developed study of the Hellenistic mystery religions concluded that Casel had erred. He thought that Christian ritual developed under the influence of the Hellenistic mystery cults; it seems more likely that the late Hellenistic mystery rites were influenced by Christianity. The doctrinal similarities that Casel found so compelling also appeared, upon closer inspection, to be more superficial than substantial. Those who were initiated into the Hellenistic mysteries believed that they had been brought into a cycle of endless return that gave them a sort of immortality. Those initiated into the Christian mysteries, however, believed that they participated in the ultimate triumph of Christ over death.[54]

Casel sought the origin of the concept of mystery in the Hellenistic cults because he did not perceive the mystery quality of Old Testament religion; he saw Judaism as a formalistic religion, lacking in inspiration.[55] Scholars who traced the development of Christian liturgy, however, showed that Casel's evaluation of Old Testament Judaism was inadequate. They argued that the worship of Jewish communities in the intertestamental period had strong indications of a mystery character, and from these liturgies, especially from the Passover celebration, the Christian mysteries may easily have developed. Other scholars pointed to the elements of mystery found in the Hebrew Bible. Damasus Winzen, a young monk of Maria Laach, found the concept of mystery clearly articulated in the texts of the psalms that were sung in the liturgy of the Temple in Jerusalem. The psalm texts indicate that as the liturgical assembly sings its proclamation of

---

[54] Filthaut, *Mysterienlehre*, 86–98; Gaillard, "Chronique," 518–519, with reference to Louis Bouyer, "Le salut dans les religions à mystères," *Revue des Sciences Religieuses* 28 (1953) 16.

[55] Gaillard, "Chronique," 523.

God's past saving deeds, those deeds are renewed in their midst. "The world of the psalms," Winzen wrote, "is based on the fundamental idea of mystery."[56]

APPEAL TO SCRIPTURAL TEACHING

Casel found the clearest scriptural support for his thesis in the sixth chapter of the Letter to the Romans, where Paul writes about the Christian's being configured to Christ's dying and rising through baptism: "Do you not know that all of us who have been baptized into Christ Jesus were baptized into his death? We were buried therefore with him by baptism into death, so that as Christ was raised from the dead by the glory of the Father, we too might walk in newness of life" (Rom 6:3-4). Dying with Christ was Casel's key to understanding not just baptism but all the sacraments. If the believer is to die and be buried with Christ in baptism, he argued, Christ's dying must itself be sacramentally present in the performance of the rite.

Furthermore, baptism is only the first liturgical event in which the believer encounters Christ in his passion, dies with him to sin, and rises to new life in him. If the worshiper is to be sacramentally conformed to Christ, Casel held, Christ's passion and death must be really present not just in baptism but in every sacrament. This presence of Christ's passion ensures that the divinely willed effect of the sacrament—the conformation of the believer to Christ in his dying and rising—takes place in reality and not just in figure. Paul's teaching that the Christian dies and rises with Christ, then, indicates that not only in baptism but in all the Church's liturgy, Christ's dying and rising are really and objectively present. The presence of Christ's saving deeds, in a supra-temporal sacramental mode, guarantees the sanctifying power of the sacrament.[57]

New Testament scholars subjected Casel's interpretation of the Pauline texts to heavy criticism.[58] They pointed out that Paul does not specify precisely how configuration to Christ takes place; it is the configuration to Christ risen that is the effect of the baptismal "dying with" Christ.[59] The text from the Letter to the Romans certainly

---

[56] Damasus Winzen, "Note complémentaire et réponse à quelques critiques," *Les Questions liturgiques et paroissiales* 24 (1939) 111.

[57] Casel, "Mysteriengegenwart," 174. Cf. Söhngen, "Kontroverse," 130–131.

[58] Filthaut, *Mysterienlehre*, 81–85.

[59] Gaillard, "Chronique," 524.

affirms that Christians show their moral and spiritual conformity to Christ in their attitude toward God and toward men and women as they "walk in newness of life." It is not at all obvious from the text that Paul holds a developed sacramental theology of perennialized acts.[60] It seems, then, that Casel was reading his interpretation into the scriptural texts.

Casel's interpretation of the Pauline texts also finds no support in the writings of Thomas Aquinas, whom Casel claimed to be following. Aquinas's commentary on the Letter to the Romans, Gaillard writes, makes no reference to the mystery presence that Casel finds so clearly in the letter.[61]

APPEAL TO PATRISTIC TEACHING

All the Fathers of the Church, Casel claimed, taught that in the liturgy Christ's temporal deeds are actively present, according to a sacramental mode of existence.[62] The authentic patristic teaching on the sacraments, he held, included the objective and actual presence of Christ's Pasch. This doctrine was forgotten, however, under the influence of late scholasticism, which replaced the patristic mystery theology with the *Effektustheorie* and treated the sacraments as means of grace.[63]

Casel's evaluation of the patristic evidence was challenged by scholars like Gottlieb Söhngen and Johannes Betz, who distinguished between the affirmation of Christ's presence and the theological interpretation of that presence. The Church Fathers, they wrote, do indeed teach that liturgical celebration involves some sort of reactualization of Christ's saving work, but they do not propose any unified explanation of the mode of that reactualization.[64] Spurred by the controversy over Casel's teaching, monographs on the concept of mystery in the Greek Fathers began to show that patristic teaching was not at all as simple or as clear as Casel thought. Though the Church Fathers "affirm the *fact*, they do not explain the *how*. This active presence of the

---

[60] Gaillard, "Chronique," 524–525; Söhngen, "Kontroverse," 132.

[61] Gaillard, "Chronique," 525.

[62] Filthaut, *Mysterienlehre,* 73–80.

[63] Söhngen, "Kontroverse," 127; n. 17 of this address to the 1938 Liturgical Week at Mont César remarks on the parallels between Casel's criticism of neo-scholasticism and those of the French Dominicans who, at this time, attempted to reform theological education. See Marie-Dominique Chenu, "Le Saulchoir," in *Une École de théologie: le Saulchoir,* ed. G. Alberigo et al. (Paris: Cerf, 1985).

[64] Gaillard, "Chronique," 526; Filthaut, *Mysterienlehre,* 77–80.

14

mysteries of Christ under the veil of the cultic symbols may be understood entirely differently from the way of Casel's system."[65]

By and large, the Church Fathers, dealing in the Platonic worldview of their time, seem to speak of the Christian life and the sacraments as participation in Christ and his saving deeds. Since the sacraments give the recipient some participation in Jesus' new life, Christ's redemptive acts are, in some fashion, present in the sacraments. The patristic teaching moves from the effect of participation in Christ's life to speaking of a presence of his saving deeds. Casel, however, argued in the opposite direction: participation in Christ's new life is possible because the redemptive acts themselves are present.[66]

UNANSWERED CRITICISMS OF CASEL'S PROPOSAL

Casel's theory, which claimed to reproduce the teaching of Thomas Aquinas, was strongly criticized as contradicting basic Thomist principles. According to Thomist metaphysics, actions exist only in space and time. An event or act has no essence; an action is an accident, which exists only under the dimensions of time and space and cannot be freed from their constraints.[67] Casel, however, taught that there is an essential kernel of Christ's deeds that has been freed from the bonds of space and time, being given a separate existence in a sacramental mode. Claiming that he was following Aquinas's teaching on the sacraments, he insisted that Thomist metaphysics simply does not apply to the sacramental mode in which the saving deeds of Christ exist. His opponents responded that according to Aquinas, an act has no essence that could be separated from space and time. Casel's proposal, they said, must be rejected on metaphysical grounds.

Casel rejected this criticism again and again, claiming that metaphysics has nothing to do with the sacraments. In the sacramental mode of being, he said, Christ's saving deeds have a perennial existence, freed from the accidents in which they were originally clothed. Perhaps because of his distrust of scholastic theology,[68] he never

[65] Gaillard, "Chronique," 526. Cf. Louis Monden, S.J., *Het Misoffer als Mysterie, Een studie de heilige mis als sacramenteel offer in het licht van de mysterieleer van Dom Odo Casel* (Roermond-Maaseik: Romen & Zonen, 1948) 78–84.

[66] Gaillard, "Chronique," 527; See n. 1, remarking on Winzen's admission in 1939 that Casel's interpretation of the patristic texts proceeded from an *a priori* judgment of their content.

[67] Filthaut, *Mysterienlehre*, 62–72; Söhngen, "Kontroverse," 126–127.

[68] This is the judgment of Söhngen, "Kontroverse," 127–128.

addressed the philosophical question of how an act could exist apart from space and time. Yet, to understand fully his proposal, it seems necessary to ask how to distinguish between an act, which is by nature historical, bound to time and space, and its supra-historical substance. Casel's inability to make this clarification calls the intelligibility of his proposal into question. Since no satisfactory explanation was offered over the protracted course of the *Mysteriengegenwart* controversy, it may well be thought that no such explanation exists.[69]

Casel was also criticized for not specifying the way in which the mystery presence of Christ with his saving acts brings salvation to the worshipers. It is not enough to identify grace with the presence of Christ and to describe sacraments in terms of his presence. "That is not false, but when Christ lived on the earth and worked there for the salvation of the world, all saw him, all heard him, and all did not believe him, all were not saved; today his sacramental presence does not suffice to assure faith and salvation for all those who might benefit from it."[70] Indeed, Casel affirmed that in the sacramental celebration Christ is present with his saving deeds in order to unite Christians with himself by faith through the performance of the rite. A sufficient explanation of Christian sanctification should, however, connect the mystery presence to its effective acceptance by the worshipers. Casel did not make that connection but simply asserted that it exists.[71]

RESPONSES TO CASEL:
MODES OF PRESENCE OF CHRIST'S ACTS
IN THE CHURCH'S MYSTERIES

As the controversy continued, from Casel's initial publication in 1922 up to the time of Vatican Council II, various theories were advanced to explain how Jesus' historical acts are related to the sacraments of the Church.[72] Those proposals that are stressed in Kilmartin's notes and addressed in his writings have been selected for summary here.

[69] Nicolas, "Réactualisation," 27–28.

[70] Ibid., 26.

[71] Ibid.

[72] Gaillard, "Chronique," 534, organizes these into three groups: those who claim an actual presence of Christ's deeds, those who affirm a virtual presence, and those who attempt a synthesis by proposing a perennialization of some aspect of those deeds. Kilmartin follows Gaillard's method of organization in chapter 9, "Twentieth-Century Contribution," in *The Eucharist in the West*, 268–290.

WARNACH: CHRIST'S *TRANSITUS* AS METAPHYSICAL ACT

Victor Warnach, like Casel a monk of Maria Laach, approached the question of how Christ's historical acts could be freed from the bonds of space and time by using the classical distinction between *chronos*, or worldly time, and *kairos*, the time of God's saving acts. The salvation accomplished by Christ frees believers from the repetitiveness and hopelessness of *chronos*, which leads only to death. In Christ, human persons are offered the way into God's time of salvation and receive eternal life in God. The opening from human time to God's time has happened once for all in the Pasch of Jesus, his *transitus* to the Father. The historical actions by which Jesus passed to new life are locked in history, "but the true event of the history of salvation, the 'christic' event, is the Pasch, i.e., the 'metaphysical' act by which Christ passed from suffering to eternal glory; that is the transformation of the earthly existence of Jesus into the majesty of the Kyrios. The Pasch of the Lord is the human-divine act that has broken the limits of time, that has broken its power, freeing those who were held captives of time."[73]

In Warnach's understanding, then, the transformation of Jesus' own life, his *transitus* to the Father, is a metaphysical fact; it has become part of the structure of reality and exists without temporal limitations. The passage from this life to divine glory is the content of the *mysterion*. This inner meaning of Jesus' historical acts is not locked in time as the acts themselves are. The mystery of Christian worship allows believers "to break away from the bondage of time in order to join this supra-temporal act, and assures our common destiny with Christ dead and risen."[74] Through the liturgy Christ's *transitus* from *chronos* to *kairos* is manifested, made truly present to the worshipers.[75]

Warnach does not, according to the commentators, develop the necessary grounding for his position. He affirms the Lord's entry into glory as a metaphysical fact, and liturgy as the Christian's means of contact with Christ's saving mystery. He does not, however, indicate

---

[73] Gaillard, "Chronique," 535. See Filthaut, *Mysterienlehre*, 60–61.

[74] Gaillard, "Chronique," 535, with reference to Victor Warnach, *Agape: Die Liebe als Grundmotif der neutestamentlichen Theologie* (Düsseldorf, 1951) 389. See Dekkers, "La Liturgie," 44.

[75] Gaillard, "Chronique," 536.

the manner in which the sacrament provides contact with Christ's *transitus* and frees the worshiper from the domination of time.[76]

SÖHNGEN: THE PRESENCE OF CHRIST'S ACTS
IN THE RECIPIENT OF THE SACRAMENT[77]

Gottlieb Söhngen, who was a participant in as well as a reporter on the controversy,[78] described the nature and content of the mystery in a way that does not conflict with Thomist metaphysics. If they are truly human actions, Jesus' historical acts must be considered as locked in time and inaccessible to believers; like all human actions, they are temporal by nature and cannot be perennialized. The content of the mystery is the supernatural reality accomplished in these acts: the transformation of Christ, the Church, and individual believers. The mystery present in the sacramental celebration, then, is not Christ's acts but the configuration of the worshipers to the likeness of Christ, crucified and risen.[79] This transformation, which is the effect of Jesus' acts, is made available to the believer through faith and sacrament.

Söhngen explicitly rejected Casel's idea that the sacramental representation of Christ's Pasch is "objective," existing in and by itself before its appropriation by the faithful. The sacramental representation, he insisted, includes the sacrament's effects in the faithful: "Sacramental imitation is not a representative image which exists in itself and for its own sake, something which stands between the death on the cross and its effects in the Church. Rather, that image exists in and with the sacramental effects in the faithful; it has no essence or substance except that of something dynamic and spiritual, the fluid existence of a spiritual power."[80] An "objective" sacramental presence of Christ's saving acts, Söhngen argued, would contradict the basic truth that a sacrament is not a thing but a dynamic event.[81] The

---

[76] Ibid.

[77] Gaillard puts Söhngen among the proponents of a virtual, not actual, presence of Christ's deeds. In this he follows Casel and Warnach in their judgment of Söhngen. Kilmartin agreed with Söhngen that he was teaching an actual presence of Christ's deeds. Since Kilmartin found Söhngen's position to be the most helpful in working out his own understanding of the mystery presence, this position is given lengthy consideration here. Kilmartin, *The Eucharist in the West*, 284–290.

[78] Filthaut, *Mysterienlehre*, 26–61.

[79] Söhngen, "Kontroverse," 132.

[80] Söhngen, *Symbol und Wirklichkeit im Kultmysterium*, 100. Quoted by Dekkers, "La Liturgie," 53.

[81] Gaillard, "Chronique," 42; Filthaut, *Mysterienlehre*, 41, 58–59.

sacrament effects itself in the worshiper, acting through faith. It exists essentially *in applicatione materiae*, in the use of the sacramental sign. Christ's saving deeds must be present in that *applicatio*; an objective presence that precedes the use of the sign would distort the very nature of the sacrament. The whole reality of the sacrament, Söhngen insisted, consists in its celebration in the faith of the Church and includes the sacramental grace of configuration to Christ, increased faith and new life in him. This grace must not be understood quantitatively or vaguely as the power of God, but dynamically, as the new life given in Christ present and active in his Church through faith.[82]

For Söhngen, then, the mystery of worship is Christ's transformation, his dying and rising, reproduced or realized in the worshiper through the sacrament. For Casel, the mystery is the redemptive act itself, rendered present in order that Christians may partake of it; this mystery is made present under sacramental signs, just as Christ himself is present under the eucharistic species.[83]

According to Söhngen, the transforming effect of Jesus' historical acts is represented in the Christian by faith. Christ's Pasch is not made "objectively" present on the altar in the Mass prior to its real presence in the worshipers, nor is his dying and rising "objectively" present in the act of baptism prior to its presence in the baptizand. Instead, Christ's Pasch is truly reproduced in the Christian by grace, through the faithful celebration of the sacrament. "If we want to speak of a presence, then, we can say at all events what the Fathers said: in and through the mystery of worship the saving death of Christ becomes a true presence, which accomplishes in us sacramentally or in mystery the same death which was accomplished actually or in historical fact in Christ."[84] From this viewpoint, the sacramental sign expresses the inner reality of the person's conformity to Christ. Christ's mystery presence is effected in the Church and in the Christian through the sacramental celebration. The mystery presence is found in the recipient of the sacrament rather than "objectively" in the sacrament before its appropriation by the faithful.

The Eucharist, for example, is sacrament of the sacrifice of Christ; it makes the one sacrifice of Christ present and active in the believers who offer it. In the Eucharist Christ is really and actively present in

---

[82] Dekkers, "La Liturgie," 54.
[83] Ibid., 55.
[84] Söhngen, "Kontroverse," 134–135.

the members of the Church. He conforms them to his own likeness, representing his one sacrifice in their lives through faith. Because Christ's sacrifice is really present in the members of the Church through the sacramental anamnesis of his saving death, it is really present in the eucharistic species. "In this case the sacramental sacrifice of Christ does not preexist the sacrifice of the Church, but the sacrifice of Christ on the Cross is sacramentally present precisely through (the sacrifice of the Church), so that Christ makes his sacrifice as sacrifice of his Church."[85] The objective real presence of Christ's sacrifice in the eucharistic elements is sacrament of the presence that Christ effects first in the liturgical assembly as a whole and in its individual members, rather than having prior objective existence on the altar, as Casel held.

Casel believed that Söhngen's proposal obscured the action of Christ in the sacraments. He considered Söhngen's position as a retreat to the *Effektustheorie* and a treatment of the sacraments simply as means of grace. Söhngen's treatment of the mystery presence, however, seems to respect the demands of Thomist metaphysics in a way that Casel's does not. He does not attempt to separate the essence of an act from its temporality, nor does he appear to confuse time and eternity, as some others in this controversy did. He also makes the important point that a sacrament is not a thing that exists prior to the use of the sign but is rather a symbolic action in which Christ acts. His description of the mystery presence is consistent with the nature of a sacrament and clearly has pastoral utility. It is not clear, however, that he offered an explanation of the way in which the liturgy effects the reproduction of the sacrifice of Christ in the faithful worshiper.

Perennialization of Some Element of Christ's Temporal Acts

When Casel was asked how Christ's temporal acts could have an essence that can be made objectively present in the liturgy, he simply denied the relevance of philosophical objections. Following Vonier, he appealed to a sacramental mode of being in which the laws of space and time do not apply. Some theologians who approved of Casel's basic insight offered proposals that attempted to avoid the philosophical problems contained in his theory. They also sought to clarify the relationship between the objective mystery presence of Christ's saving actions and the Church's sacramental participation by

[85] Ibid., 138.

faith in Christ's sacrifice.[86] These proposals claim that some element of Jesus' acts has been perennialized and attempt to give some point of entry for the Church's participation in Christ's saving deeds.[87]

INTENTION OF CHRIST'S WILL

It is the intention of Christ's will that gave salvific value to his temporal acts. The Dutch theologian Pieter Smulders, S.J., proposed that, with Christ's glorification, this intention has been given some participation in eternity. Through this same intention Christ instituted the sacraments so that the salvation accomplished through his temporal deeds might be accessible to people of every time and place. Christ applies that saving will to the worshiper through the sacramental celebration.

The passion of Christ is present, then, inasmuch as the will that expressed and consummated itself in the passion operates in the sacraments. Smulders calls this a real and efficacious presence of the essence of the temporal deeds of Christ. In his understanding, the essence of Christ's saving deeds is the salvific will of Christ. This will, he claimed, exists separately from the acts that it governed in space and time.[88]

---

[86] Gaillard, "Chronique," 548, n. 5, refers to Monden, *Misoffer als Mysterie,* 161–164, 191; Johannes Betz, *Die Eucharistie in der Zeit der griechischen Väter,* I/1 (Fribourg: Herder, 1955) 249; Joseph Jungmann, *Missarum Solemnia,* vol. 1 (Paris: Beauchesne, 1951) 229–230; Charles Baumgartner, "Bulletin d'histoire et de théologie sacramentaire," *Recherche de Science Religieuse* 44 (1956) 282, 293–294; and Filthaut, *Mysterienlehre,* 53, n. 1.

[87] Gaillard, "Chronique," 549.

[88] Pieter Smulders, "Tractatus de Sacramentis in Genere, editio altera emendata, 1949," Course notes for distribution, 211–212. Since these notes, which Smulders gave Kilmartin, are not available in most theological libraries, the text is given here in translation from the Latin original:

"The acts of Christ which pertain to the essence of the redemptive work, while they were performed once in time, have been elevated through his exaltation to the order of eternity, and they enjoy a certain participation in eternity, so that they may be present to every time; for Christ is exalted as Redeemer, and together with him all the intentions of that will which pertain to the essentials of the redemptive work. For truly the intention of the will of Christ by which he willed that individual persons be saved through these external signs pertains to the essence of the redemptive work. Therefore the intention by which Christ instituted the sacraments, while historically past, is present to all times and places. And thus whenever the sacraments are administered to any person, through them and in them the efficaciously sanctifying will of Christ is applied to them. In

Louis Monden, S.J., and Edward Schillebeeckx, O.P., attempted to find an eternal quality in Jesus' salvific acts by virtue of the beatific vision, which was traditionally considered to belong to Jesus by virtue of the hypostatic union. In the beatific vision his attention is fixed on the Father in the unchanging or immobile oblation of divine charity in which the Word gives self eternally to the Father. All his temporal acts are informed by the love and knowledge contained in the beatific vision; he is considered "at the same time *viator* and *comprehensor*."[89] Because it is the eternal action of the Word, the immobile offering of love is the content of Jesus' redemptive sacrifice and, indeed, of all the mysteries of his life. The immobile oblation of the beatific vision, the content of Jesus' actions, is not bound to space and time but partakes of the divine eternity. This is the perennial element of the temporal acts by which Jesus offered himself to the Father. Because of its eternity, it is separable from the historical particularity of the acts themselves.[90]

THE DIVINE WORD'S ACTUALIZATION IN TIME AND SPACE

In Jesus there is not a fully constituted human person but rather a particular humanity united to the Person of the Word. This is the ground for another argument, which was proposed by Schillebeeckx and embraced by Betz. The divine Word personalized self through Jesus' human actions; Jesus' sacrifice on the cross is the highest peak of that personalization. Jesus' temporal actions, then, are the personal self-expression of the Word in Jesus' humanity. Because of the hypo-

---

this sense we can concede to Dom Casel that the passion of Christ is present in the various sacraments: not, however, absolutely and through its own power, but insofar as the sanctifying will of Christ, which was fulfilled in the passion, operates now in the various sacraments.

"You may say that our thought makes a parallel between the sacraments and the external acts of Christ in his earthly life, as far as theology allows. For the deeds of Christ did not merit sanctification except insofar as they were vehicles of his mental intention. For since the sanctifying grace of Christ was immediately governed by his soul, and since all communication of this grace necessarily is free and loving (for it is 'grace'), contact with the Body of Christ cannot efficaciously sanctify, except insofar as through this contact Christ wanted to communicate other treasures of his soul."

[89] Gaillard, "Chronique," 540.

[90] Ibid., 541.

static union, these human actions participate in the eternity of the divine Word; "they are eternally actual and enduring."[91] Since they have a perennial character, Jesus' acts can be present to all time.[92] They are present most certainly in the Christian's encounter with Christ in the sacraments, where they elicit the worshiper's personal response of faith and result in the grace of sanctification, conformity to Christ.[93]

THE PROBLEM WITH THEORIES OF PERENNIALIZATION
OF TEMPORAL ACTS

None of these suggestions about the perennialization of some element of Christ's temporal acts is acceptable from the viewpoint of the realist metaphysics of Thomas Aquinas.

First, the interior element of an act cannot be separated from its exterior and temporal elements; the act itself has an integrity that may not be broken. An action is an inseparable complex of the agent's will and intention and the deed that expresses or fulfills that will. Jesus' historical acts include the individual decisions and intentions that he made in the particularities of time and space. The decision or intention that gives meaning to the act cannot be separated from the action that expresses it.

Second, each action expresses a particular intention of the will, which must be distinguished from the fundamental option that guides a person's life. Jesus' fundamental option of love for the Father, his sacrificial intention of love of the Father, inheres in his Person and is present wherever he is. This fundamental option is not identical with the decisions and intentions that guided and gave value to his individual acts. By the same token, the divine charity does not essentially inform Jesus' human acts, although that charity is the ultimate aim of his actions. Each act is informed and valorized by a particular decision, not by the fundamental option that gave shape to his life.

Third, the beatific love cannot be extended to temporal objects but has its source and its fulfillment in the vision of God in eternity. The act of self-offering in love contained by the beatific vision is, indeed, immobile; it does not result in acts in space and time.[94]

---

[91] Edward Schillebeeckx, *Christ the Sacrament of the Encounter with God* (New York: Sheed and Ward, 1963) 57.

[92] Betz, "Gegenwart," 1821–1822, and n. 27, referring to Schillebeeckx, *Christus—Sakrament der Gottesbegegnung.*

[93] Schillebeeckx, *Christ the Sacrament,* 59–63.

[94] Nicolas, "Réactualisation," 28–31.

THOMIST CRITIQUE OF THE THOMISTIC *EFFEKTUSTHEORIE*

The controversy over the mystery presence led to a reevaluation of the Thomistic theory that in the sacraments Christ's past deeds are present through their effects. From the beginning, Casel had claimed that the *Effektustheorie* contradicted Thomas Aquinas's teaching about the commemorative nature of the sacramental sign. In time this theory came under heavy criticism from the viewpoint of Thomist metaphysics.

In his study of Thomas Aquinas's writings on the relation of sacramental efficacy and the saving deeds of Christ, Nicolas gives two reasons to join in Casel's rejection. A third reason was laid out by the Irish theologian Brian McNamara, S.J., whose transcendental Thomist treatment of the mystery presence Kilmartin found useful.[95]

The sign contains the thing signified

The formulation of the *Effektustheorie* that Casel rejected was a late thomistic position that descended from Cardinal Cajetan (Tommaso de Vio, Dominican theologian, 1469–1534) and Francisco Suarez (Jesuit theologian, 1548–1617). Cajetan and Suarez treated the divine decision to give sacramental grace through signs as merely juridical. The particular sacramental sign, by Christ's authority, indicates God's offer of grace and invites the recipient to believe and accept that gift. In this system the sign simply refers to the effect of the sacrament, and the commemorative nature of the sign is not developed.

In contrast, Thomas Aquinas taught that signification is of the essence of the sacrament. In his epistemology the thing signified is present in the sign and so becomes accessible to the imagination and the mind. In the sacraments the sign does far more than indicate the effect of the sacrament. It not only spurs the imagination but also produces a true presence of the thing signified. The sacraments signify and make truly present not just the grace won by Christ's saving acts; they signify both the glorified Christ who acts in the sacraments and the suffering Christ to whom the recipient is configured. The thomistic *Effektustheorie*, then, ignores the *Summa*'s clear teaching

[95] Brian McNamara, "Christus Patiens in Mass and Sacraments: Higher Perspectives," *Irish Theological Quarterly* 42 (1975) 17–35. Kilmartin summarizes McNamara's position twice: *Christian Liturgy: Theology and Practice* (Kansas City: Sheed and Ward, 1988) 342–347; *The Eucharist in the West*, 312–319.

about the character of the sacramental sign. Furthermore, denying that the sign makes present the thing signified causes obvious problems in the case of the Eucharist, in which the effects of the passion are communicated through the glorified Christ's real presence under the signs that refer to his passion.[96]

Instrumental efficient causality

The *Effektustheorie* presented in the neo-scholastic theological manuals misstates the workings of an instrumental efficient cause. The instrument must come into contact with the patient—the one acted upon—either directly or through a chain of other instrumental causes. Such a chain of instrumental causes may explain how an act in one place can cause an event in another place. Instrumental efficient causality, however, cannot relate an act at one time and an event at another time; the remove in time breaks the chain of instrumental causes. Indeed, the act occurs in time and then ceases to be. Once it ceases to exist, the act cannot be an instrumental cause, for action depends on existence. According to Thomist metaphysics, then, for the deeds of Christ to be instrumental efficient cause of sacramental sanctification, they must come into contact with the recipient of the sacrament. If those deeds have ceased to exist, as the *Effektustheorie* claimed, they cannot act as instruments.[97]

Time and eternity

Attempts to overcome the temporal break in the chain of instrumental efficient causality by claiming that Christ's actions done in time have been perennialized, and so operate at all times as instrumental efficient cause, confuse the relationship between time and eternity. For Aquinas, eternity is not endless duration, "but rather a successionless *nunc stans*,"[98] and divine acts in time and space are consequent terms of God's timeless knowing and willing. The temporal deeds of Christ that effect human salvation are themselves consequent terms of God's eternal knowledge and will.

If there were temporal succession in God, if God were perpetual rather than eternal, and if God and the world were parallel successions, then one might attempt to explain a perennialization of

[96] Nicolas, "Réactualisation," 32–35.
[97] Ibid., 39–40.
[98] McNamara, "Christus Patiens," 22.

Christ's temporal acts. But according to Catholic theological tradition, the divine knowing and acting is not successive, so "because of the radical distinction between a time-conditioned event and the a-temporal Designer, no occurrence in this world can become timeless. To offer as a solution to the Mystery-Presence problem with reference to the Mass that the sacrifice of Calvary becomes timeless in God is to sidestep the effort to understand by appealing to what can only be an admission of the failure to grasp the difference between eternity and time."[99] Theories about Christ's mystery presence that involve any perennialization of Christ's actions should therefore be dismissed because they confuse time and eternity. This applies no less to formulations of the late scholastic *Effektustheorie* than to Casel's own proposal.

THOMIST REFLECTIONS ON MYSTERY PRESENCE

Nicolas's reflections on the *Mysteriengegenwart* controversy included not only criticism of the various positions raised but also an explication of an approach that he considered acceptable from the point of view of Thomist metaphysics. His ideas were expanded upon by McNamara, who approached the subject as a transcendental Thomist. Since Kilmartin found McNamara's treatment compelling, his reflections on the presence of Christ in the sacramental event, as well as those of Nicolas, are summarized here.

Nicolas: Faith in the passion and the power of the risen Christ

Nicolas traced the development in Thomas Aquinas's thought on the causal interrelation of the *mysteria carnis Christi* and the efficacy of the sacraments in order to offer some suggestions on the description of the mystery presence.

While Aquinas treats the passion, death, and resurrection of Christ as a single saving act that is cause of human salvation, he emphasizes that these mysteries are not meritorious in themselves. There is no merit earned by Christ's death, for death is not an action of the soul, and only an action of the soul can be meritorious. The resurrection of Christ, though an action, does not happen while Christ is *in statu merendi*, so there is no merit gained by his resurrection.[100] Aquinas says clearly, however, that Christ's humanity is the instrumental effi-

---

[99] Ibid., 23.
[100] Nicolas, "Réactualisation," 42.

cient cause of human salvation. That humanity exercises its efficiency through Christ's saving acts.[101]

Aquinas also says that Christ's resurrection is cause of the saints' resurrection: Christ, raised by virtue of his divinity, causes others to participate in his resurrection, just as they participate in his grace.[102] The efficient cause of the resurrection of the just, then, is actually the risen Christ.[103]

Although the one who acts in the sacraments is the risen Christ, however, the sacraments receive their power from Christ's passion, and this power operates in the recipient through faith in Christ's passion. Nicolas uses these affirmations in his argument that faith and sacrament together bring a true, or effective, and real presence. "Faith is an act of the soul through which that which is not yet can be made present: the presence which it guarantees is true, but not real. The sacraments, on the other hand, are real actions."[104] In the sacramental event, the sacramental sign creates a true presence by faith in the recipient's imagination. At the same time, the glorified Christ makes himself really present in the soul. Exercising the gift of faith, then, the recipient appropriates a real and true presence of Christ and so is conformed to his passion.

Thomas Aquinas clarifies the connection between faith and sacrament a bit more, Nicolas remarks, when treating the distinction between the institution and the power of baptism. According to ancient tradition, the sacrament of baptism was instituted at Christ's baptism in the Jordan. The power of baptism as a sacrament of the New Law, however, comes not from Christ's baptism but from the passion, which was prefigured by it. That power is appropriated by the baptizand through faith, not in Christ's baptism, but in his passion.[105]

Aquinas also taught that when Christ descended into the underworld, he brought life to the dead in a way similar to the way he brings life to the living who are baptized, *in virtute passionis*. The dead who entered into beatitude with the glorified Christ did so by accepting his passion as liberating and life-giving. "In reality it is Christ who has acted, but the requisite disposition for benefiting from this action is configuration to Christ through faith and charity."[106] Faith in

---

[101] Ibid., 43.
[102] Ibid., 45.
[103] Ibid., 46.
[104] Ibid., 47.
[105] Ibid., 48.
[106] Ibid.

Christ's passion is expressed in the reception of the sacrament. The sacramental sign indicates the attitude required in order for the recipient to be configured to Christ crucified, dead, and risen, who is the cause of the sacrament's power.[107]

In this way Nicolas argued that although the saving acts of Christ are truly past, the sacramental event is connected with them, on both the level of signification and that of efficacy. It was through the passion that Christ came to glory; in this sense his humanity is instrumental cause of his own glorification and of Christians' justification and glorification. But human persons separated from Christ in time and space need to be brought into contact with the one mystery, the one act by which they are saved. Through the sacramental sign the risen Christ gives the worshiper the grace of being conformed to his passion, death, and resurrection. It is in this regard that the presence of his saving mysteries is both real and active.[108]

Nicolas's clarification of Thomas Aquinas's teaching on the causality of Christ's humanity and on the connection of sacramental signification and faith demonstrates a way to speak about the mystery presence without contradicting the scholastic reflection on sacraments. Nicolas's presentation is also valuable for its affirmation that the sacramental liturgy, as event of faith in Christ's passion, configures the recipient of the sacrament to Christ. Like the other theologians considered here, however, he offers no developed explanation of how this configuration takes place.

McNamara: Presence of Christus Patiens *metaphysically affirmed*

Eighteen years after Nicolas's article, the Irish Jesuit Brian McNamara revisited the question of the mystery presence from the viewpoint of Thomist metaphysics. McNamara both offers a reflection on the various viewpoints from which Christ's temporal actions may be considered and reviews the Thomist understanding of efficient causality.

McNamara not only points out the danger of confusing time and eternity but also observes that there are various levels from which the divine action may be perceived. First is the commonsense experience of temporal succession marked by the clock; though there are similarities between events, no event is repeatable. According to this experiential perspective, the passion of Christ is not in any way repeated in the cele-

---

[107] Ibid., 49.
[108] Ibid., 54.

bration of the Eucharist. By the same token, each liturgical celebration is unique; today's eucharistic celebration is not the same as yesterday's.

Second, there is a salvation-history perspective, in which the plan of God, the Pauline *mysterion*, is gradually revealed and accomplished. Biblical and liturgical languages speak from this perspective. Christ, glorified through the cross, is present and active in the Church without being limited by space and time. His historical mysteries are past but are renewed in their sacramental celebration.

Third is the view of speculative theology, which considers the divine plan revealed in Christ and its time-conditioned realization. From the viewpoint of timeless knowing, the life of Christ is not successive, as it is from the experiential or biblical-liturgical viewpoints, but a unity. Indeed, from this "higher" viewpoint, the intelligibility of the world rests on the single act of divine knowing and willing that is Christ's incarnation and *transitus* to the Father. The meaning of the created world, from this viewpoint, is that movement back to the Father. From the temporal viewpoint, the movement began with the first created being, reached its climax with the life of Christ, and is being worked out in the "age of the Church." From the divine viewpoint, however, there is no temporal succession, but only the timeless divine knowing and acting. It is this viewpoint, reached through reflection on the biblical and liturgical expression of God's revelation, that speculative theology embraces.[109]

McNamara's explanation of efficient causality lays forth five basic statements:

"1. Agent and effect are simultaneously present one to the other. . . .

2. Action as intelligible is neither in the agent nor between agent and effect but is identical with the effect. . . .

3. The power that experientially effects the action *(virtus)* is not a different reality from the action itself and is therefore also identifiable with the effect.

4. The instrument used by the agent is itself an agent acting, however, only insofar as it is used by the principal agent. This statement implies that the intelligibility of action is not to be sought within the instrument.

---

[109] McNamara, "Christus Patiens," 25–28. McNamara acknowledges his dependence on Bernard Lonergan for this understanding: 23, n. 14.

5. Efficient causality, therefore, is the relation of effect to cause and its reality is to be found in the effect as proceeding from cause. The agent of efficient causality is not changed by acting notwithstanding the experiential distinction between acting and not acting, for the change *is* the effect."[110]

These conditions, according to McNamara, are found in any case of efficient causality.

Considering the action of God through the sacraments, then, McNamara came to these conclusions:

"1. God is present to human persons by acting on them through the instrumental agency of Christ's humanity. The human nature of Christ as a unity and the entire *transitus* of Christ through which God acts are, then, present in the sacraments.

2. Sacramental action occurs in the human person who receives the sacrament, not between God and the person. Since the effect of the sacrament is the configuration of the person to Christ through "dying and rising with Christ," his *transitus* is present as form of the effect.

3. The power of Christ's passion is the power of God who acts on the world through the humanity of Christ. This power is identifiable with the effect of configuring human persons to Christ.

4. The life of Christ as instrument of the divinity can be understood only in light of the divine plan, the *mysterion*, which is revealed in Christ's *transitus* and which itself reveals the mind of God.

5. The divine action in the sacraments relates the recipient of sacramental grace to God. Every sacrament either establishes or increases the interpersonal relationship between the Father and the human person. This relationship brings about a change in the human person, not in God."[111]

From these principles McNamara described the mystery presence, respecting the relation of time and eternity as well as the principles of causality.

God is the principal agent, acting through Christ's humanity to transform the world through Christ's *transitus*. The instrument of this divine action is the human living of Christ: *Christus Patiens*, not *Christus Passus*. Christ's human living must be said to be present in sacramental action, since it is the instrument through which God acts.

[110] Ibid., 29.
[111] Ibid., 30.

The historical mysteries of the life of Christ are, then, present in their effect, in the human recipient, as metaphysically affirmed. While in biblical and liturgical language one distinguishes between the objective redemption already accomplished and the subjective redemption that is still in progress, that distinction disappears from the perspective of the divine plan in God, "for the ultimate intelligibility of the plan is the identity of one to the other."[112]

The effect of the presence of the historical mysteries of Christ's life is also intelligible in the light of the divine plan. God intends that all persons pass, in Christ, to the pneumatic life of the resurrection. "The effect of the presence of the historical mysteries of Christ's life to us must be some modification of the configuration to Christ which is significantly expressed in the Pauline *cum Christo convivere, conresuscitari, conglorificari.* . . . It signifies a 'putting on of the mind of Christ,' a real participation in the attitude of Christ expressed in the historical actions and passions of his earthly life."[113] Participation of Christians in the attitudes of Christ, then, is the key to understanding the mystery presence of Christ's deeds in the liturgy.

SUMMARY: MYSTERY PRESENCE, FAITH AND SIGN

Nicolas and McNamara correct many of the misconceptions found in various descriptions of the relation between the temporal acts of Christ and the sanctification given through liturgical anamnesis of his deeds. Their explanation of instrumental efficient causality makes clear that from a metaphysical perspective, the *mysteria carnis Christi* may be said to be present whenever Christian worshipers are configured to Christ through the celebration of the sacraments. Both theologians argue that the sacramental sign indicates the attitude necessary for the worshiper to receive the configuration that God intends to confer. Nicolas's distinction between true presence, caused by the operation of the sign in the imagination, and real presence, caused by the risen Christ, attempts to explain how the sacramental sign operates. By identifying the mystery presence with the Christian worshiper's participation in Christ's attitudes, both theologians point to the need for further development of how the sacramental celebration communicates those attitudes.

[112] Ibid., 34.
[113] Ibid.

MAGISTERIAL TEACHING:
MEDIATOR DEI AND THE MYSTERY PRESENCE

Pius XII's encyclical *Mediator Dei*,[114] published in 1947, was seen by some of the proponents of the *Mysterienlehre* as vindication of Casel's teaching, "an official consecration of the theological renewal begun in the area of liturgy by Dom Herwegen and Dom Casel."[115] The encyclical does, indeed, give indications that the biblical and patristic concept of mystery had gained the attention of the Roman magisterium.

The earlier encyclical *Mystici Corporis* (1943)[116] had begun the incorporation of "mystery" language into magisterial documents: "Sanctification does not come to [people] independently of the historical fact of Christ's life, death, and resurrection by which redemption was objectively realized. It is through the mystery of the Cross that [people] are joined to Christ" (*MC* 206). In this letter Pius XII taught that the glorified Christ communicates himself to the Church in such a way that the Church lives in his image. Because of this bond between Christ and the Church, his Body, and in order to fulfill the mission given Christ by the Father, "it is he who, through the Church, baptizes, teaches, governs, absolves, binds, offers, sacrifices" (*MC* 206).[117]

Mediator Dei defined liturgy as "the worship rendered by the Mystical Body of Christ in the entirety of its Head and members" (*MD* 20). In one sense this definition parallels Casel's "mystery of worship of Christ and the Church."[118] The encyclical's approach, however, is far removed from that of Casel; *Mediator Dei* treats worship first of all as the exercise of the virtue of religion. The person's proper turning to God consists in acknowledging "his supreme majesty and supreme authority" (*MD* 13; *DS* 3842).[119] Since the human person is

---

[114] Pius XII, *Mediator Dei* (November 20, 1947; hereafter cited as *MD*), *Acta Apostolicae Sedis* (hereafter cited as *AAS*) 39 (1947) 528–595. Quotations are taken from the Vatican Library translation, published by Daughters of St. Paul (Boston, 1947).

[115] J. Hild, "L'encyclique 'Mediator Dei' et le mouvement liturgique de Maria-Laach," *La Maison-Dieu* 14 (1948) 15. Ildefons Herwegen was abbot of Maria Laach, and himself a major figure in the German liturgical movement.

[116] Pius XII, *Mystici Corporis* (June 29, 1943; hereafter cited as *MC*), *AAS* 35 (1943) 200–250.

[117] Henricus Denzinger and Adolphus Schönmetzer, eds., *Enchiridion Symbolorum* (hereafter cited as *DS*) 26th ed. (Barcelona: Herder, 1976) 174–175, no. 3806: ". . . ipse est, qui per Ecclesiam baptizat, docet, regit, solvit, ligat, offert, sacrificat."

[118] Hild, "Mouvement liturgique," 16.

[119] *MD* 7.

both corporeal and spiritual, true worship involves both body and soul; the body/spirit complex is the basis for sacramental worship. Liturgy is primarily the upward movement of human persons offering worship to their Creator, not the downward movement of the divine reality that makes itself present under the veil of the symbol in order to draw all things to itself.[120]

Casel and his followers had taught that the mysteries of Christ's life are present not only in all the sacraments but in the representation of Christ's mysteries through the liturgical year. The French monk Jean Hild summarized their claim: "Christ lives and prays in the Church which celebrates the divine liturgy. He makes his saving mysteries come alive in her in order to involve us all in his eternal eucharist."[121] The encyclical seems to accept Casel's position, describing the liturgical year as the Church's progress through the mysteries of Christ's life. Through their celebration of the liturgical year, the faithful are, over time, transformed and configured to Christ (*MD* 165; *DS* 3855).

The heart of the mysteries, the encyclical taught, is the passion of Christ represented in the liturgical celebration. This mystery is found at the center of divine worship, is represented and renewed in the celebration of the Eucharist.[122]

In light of the encyclical's treatment of the liturgy, especially the Eucharist, the defenders of Casel's theory claimed that the Roman magisterium had embraced their position. Twenty-five years earlier, Casel had considered the Mass "not as sacrament of the *Christus Passus*, but as that of the *Passio Christi*, of Christ *in statu victimae*."[123]

What is the mode of presence of Christ's passion? The encyclical teaches that Christ is present, along with the Church, in every liturgical function (*MD* 20; *DS* 2297). It goes on to list the principal modes of this presence (*MD* 20; *DS* 3840): "Christ is present in the august sacrifice of the altar, both in the person of his minister and above all under the Eucharistic species; He is present in the sacraments, infusing into them the power that makes them ready instruments of sanctification; He is present finally in the prayer of praise and petition we direct to God, as it is written: 'Where there are two or three

---

[120] Betz, "Gegenwart," 1813–1815.
[121] Hild, "Mouvement liturgique," 17.
[122] Ibid., 18.
[123] Ibid., 19.

gathered in My Name, there am I in the midst of them' (Matt 18:20)."[124] According to Pius XII, then, Christ himself is indeed present and active; in the sacraments he is present "by his power," which makes them instruments of sanctification.

Despite Casel's claims that the Pope had vindicated his teaching, however, the text affirms only that the passion is present in the sacraments as the efficient cause of their power and grace. There is no echo of Casel's teaching that the kernel or essence of Christ's deeds is objectively present.[125] In fact, the Holy Office complained that the German translation of the encyclical implied a papal endorsement of Casel's theory, when no such approval was intended.[126]

Summary: Status Quaestionis

At the time Kilmartin began his work as a theologian of the liturgy, according to the data in the secondary sources that he relied upon, no fully satisfactory explanation had been offered for the relationship between the temporal deeds of Christ and the Church's liturgical celebration. The years of theological controversy, however, had resulted in increased awareness that the Church's liturgy, by its symbolic language of faith, is a preeminent means by which Christians are configured to Christ in his dying and rising.

Casel sought to explain how the liturgy configures the Christian worshiper to Christ's dying and rising. He postulated the perennialization of the kernel or essence of Christ's temporal acts, the objective presence of that essence of Christ's acts under the veil of the sacramental symbol, and the worshiper's access to the mystery that those acts contain through the faithful performance of the sacramental rite. As the defenders of Thomist metaphysics pointed out, however, actions done in space and time have no essence that can be separated from the situation in which they were performed. For this reason Casel's proposal must be disallowed.

Furthermore, as Söhngen asserted, a sacrament has no objective existence prior to its application to the recipient. Rather, the sacrament is constituted in the performance of the rite, or the use of the sacramental sign vis-à-vis the recipient of the sacrament. Casel's

---

[124] *MD* 10.
[125] Hild, "Mouvement liturgique," 24.
[126] *DS* 3855, fn. 1; Kilmartin, "Catholic Tradition," 422.

theory of an objective presence of Christ that is prior to the engagement of the worshiper with the sacramental sign must be rejected on these grounds.

The controversy over Casel's *Mysterientheologie* resulted in general acceptance of his insight that through performance of the sacramental rite the worshiper, by faith, is configured to Christ in his dying and rising. Yet, although Casel insisted that the power of the sacramental sign configures the Christian to Christ, he appears to have offered little explanation of how the symbol operates.

The later thomistic *Effektustheorie*, as described in the secondary sources that Kilmartin used, claimed that although Jesus' acts are past and no longer exist, they continue to operate as instrumental cause of the grace that God applies to the recipient of the sacrament. This position must be rejected because there is no unbroken chain of instrumental efficient causes in space and time to connect Jesus' acts to the recipient of sacramental grace. According to Thomist metaphysics, such a chain of causes must exist in order for a past act to be cause of an effect in the present.

Gottlieb Söhngen argued that Christ's *transitus* is represented in the worshiper through faith and the performance of the rite. He held that there is a real presence of Christ and his saving deeds in the recipient of the sacrament. By means of this presence the Christian is configured to Christ, fulfilling the purpose for which the sacraments were instituted. Söhngen's proposal meets the demands both of Thomist metaphysics and of sacramental theology's teaching that the sacrament is constituted by the *applicatio materiae*. From the literature in Kilmartin's files, however, it does not appear that he found in Söhngen's work an explanation of how the sacramental rite operates to configure the worshiper to Christ's *transitus*.

Nicolas and McNamara insist that the effect of the sacramental celebration is the worshiper's reception of the mind of Christ. There is, they point out, a link between the sacramental sign and the Christian's imagination. The symbolic nature of the sacramental event is the key to the acceptance of the sacramental grace of configuration to Christ. Nicolas suggests that the real presence of Christ in the sacrament *(ex opere operato)*, together with the true or effective presence of Christ spurred by the symbol through faith in the recipient's imagination *(ex opere operantis)*, makes a sacramental presence that is both real and true. This formulation points to the symbolic nature of the sacrament as the link between the deeds of Christ and the liturgical celebration. Neither Nicolas nor McNamara, however, grounds such an explanation in the human sciences and in sacramental theology.

The developing teaching of the Roman magisterium on the modes of presence of Christ in the liturgy indicates several directions for theological inquiry into the mystery presence. *Mediator Dei* affirms that there are various modes of liturgical presence of Christ, not simply an objective presence of Christ and his deeds under the veil of the symbol, as Casel taught. This more nuanced teaching makes clear that Christ's liturgical presence is multifaceted and that the modes of mystery presence are interrelated. The interrelationship of the modes of Christ's presence indicates that there is a dialogic nature to the mystery revealed in the liturgy. The Second Vatican Council would further develop that characteristic of the mystery presence.

SUMMA SUMMARUM

The materials in Kilmartin's files indicate several points that he would investigate as he sought to bring further clarity to the question of the mystery presence. These may briefly be summarized.

Of the positions advanced during the *Mysteriengegenwart* controversy, only Söhngen's contained no internal contradictions. Following Söhngen's lead, Kilmartin would look for the representation of the mystery of Christ and his saving deeds in the worshiper.

No proposal reported on in the secondary literature gave sufficient grounding for the relationship between Christ's deeds and the liturgical celebration. Kilmartin would have to develop the facets of that relationship in order to offer a satisfactory approach to describing the mystery presence.

In the theological conversation, three areas emerged for possibly fruitful reflection. First was the relationship between the sacramental symbol and the imagination of Christians at worship. Kilmartin would, in large part, treat that relationship under the category of human celebration. Second was the interrelationship of the modes of Christ's liturgical presence. Kilmartin would address this task through consideration of the liturgy as action of the Christian assembly and through examination of liturgical rites and prayer texts. Third was the dialogic character of the mystery that the liturgy celebrates. Kilmartin would make the investigation of the Trinitarian self-communication and of the human response of self-offering a central concern of his work. In that investigation he considered the response of Christ in his humanity to the divine self-communication, seeking to connect the life of faith of Christ, of the Church, and of the Christian.

Following these directions of inquiry, Kilmartin gradually constructed the elements of his own approach to describing the mystery presence of Christ's deeds in the liturgical celebration. The second chapter of this book treats Kilmartin's early writings and his attempt to appropriate the Vatican Council's treatment of Christian liturgy through analysis of classical liturgical texts. The rule of prayer that he discovered in textual and historical studies served as the foundation of the systematic theology of liturgical celebration that he constructed over the rest of his career. Elements of his theological system are considered in a systematic and synthetic manner in the third chapter.

Chapter Two

Early Writings, Vatican II, and the *Lex Orandi*

Early in his theological career Kilmartin began the task of describing the mystery presence. This chapter's three parts outline the development of his approach. The first section treats two short works published in 1962, before Vatican Council II, that indicate the basic orientations found throughout his life's work. In a pamphlet on the Church's sacraments, he emphasizes the dialogic nature of the New Covenant and touches on the modes of Christ's presence in the liturgy and on the role of symbols in forming Christian imagination. The second piece traces the Church Fathers' description of sacramental sanctification during the first four centuries of the Church's life. This article notes the Eastern Church's understanding that in the liturgy the Holy Spirit sanctifies Christians by conforming them to Christ's dying and rising.

These two works demonstrate that even before the Second Vatican Council Kilmartin had begun to describe the mystery presence in a way that included the personal activity of the Holy Spirit. The approach that he took in these early pieces would be congenial with Vatican II's teaching on the Church and the liturgy.

The second section of this chapter considers the challenge presented to theologians by Vatican II's treatment of the liturgy. *Sacrosanctum Concilium* not only repeats *Mediator Dei*'s listing of the modes of liturgical presence of Christ but also sheds new light on the Church's experience of the liturgy. It emphasizes the significance of the liturgical assembly and indicates that the assembly's conscious and active participation in the liturgy is the key to its members' configuration to Christ. The stress of the Constitution on the Sacred Liturgy on the liturgical celebration highlights the concept that the Church's liturgy is a source of theology. Full reception of the Council's teaching, however, can come only with the reintegration of the "rule of belief" into the Church's "rule of prayer." In order to bring the two rules together, there must be a clear understanding of what the rule of prayer actually teaches.

The third section of the chapter, therefore, considers Kilmartin's method of discovering the content of the Church's rule of prayer. He went about this work through articles and books that treat the Eucharistic Prayer as a literary and theological unit oriented toward the sacramental communion of the liturgical assembly. A brief description of Kilmartin's investigation into the Eucharistic Prayers of the ancient and undivided Church is followed by some of his conclusions about the rule of prayer and the mystery presence. Among the most important of these is that the official prayers of the Church, especially the Eucharistic Prayers, contain a systematic theology, that is, they relate the various truths of the faith to one another. The section closes with a brief listing of the elements of such a systematic theology.

EARLY APPROACHES TO THE MYSTERY OF WORSHIP

Two of Kilmartin's earliest works demonstrate approaches he would take in describing sacramental participation in the mystery of Christ throughout his career.

Sacraments, Signs of Christ:
Divine Self-Communication and the Human Response

For the Paulist Press Doctrinal Series, used in schools and in parish discussion groups, Kilmartin presented the Church's teaching on the sacraments in a way that is clearly influenced by the work of Karl Rahner.[1] He begins with the divine work of self-communication that reaches its height in the human living of Jesus Christ, the absolute bringer of God's salvation to the human race and to the world.[2] God communicates the divine self in humanly accessible fashion both in Jesus' earthly life and, after Jesus' death, in the Church. In Christ human persons meet God not merely in a spiritual fashion, but in a way that invites a fully human acceptance and response, embodied in history.[3]

The shape taken by God's self-revelation in Jesus Christ and in the Church makes clear that redemption involves a personal encounter

---

[1] Edward J. Kilmartin, *The Sacraments: Signs of Christ, Sanctifier and High Priest* (Glen Rock, N.J.: Paulist Press, 1962).

[2] Ibid., 3.

[3] Ibid., 5.

between God and the human person. That encounter—both God's invitation and a grace-filled human response—is realized in Jesus' embodiment of the New Covenant and continues in the covenant community, the Church.[4] "A corporeal encounter with the glorified Christ, and in Him with the Trinity, remains possible in the sacramental Church, which is the earthly, visible, redemptive organ of the living, invisible *Kyrios.*"[5]

Through the celebration of word and sacrament, "the two ways by which the Church actualizes herself as the medium of salvation,"[6] Christ and his saving work are made present in a humanly accessible way. "Without the sacraments, our contact with Christ would be only in faith. The human dimension of the *Incarnate* Lord would be lost. But God . . . offers the Kingdom of God in earthly form: in the sacraments of the Church—the place where [one] obtains personal communion with Christ and, in Him, with the Trinity."[7] In all its living, but especially in the liturgical celebrations that consciously express and celebrate its life, the Church "re-presents the redemptive work of Christ" and is shown to be the sacrament of Christ's humanity.[8] Inspired and accompanied by grace, the Church's celebration of word and sacrament is itself an expression of faith[9] that preaches the gospel of Jesus Christ. That preaching, in word and action, evokes a response of faith on the part of the hearers: their personal acceptance of the grace of divine self-communication.[10]

The sacraments, then, continue the offer and acceptance of the divine self-communication definitively accomplished in Christ. They not only are the result of Christ's redemptive work[11] but also continue his earthly worship of his Father.[12] That worship, in which Christ responded to the Father's love by giving his whole self back to the Father, is represented in the Church's sacramental celebrations; in them the Church builds itself up and is manifested as the community of faith that lives Christ's worship. In these celebrations Christ's

[4] Ibid., 4–6.
[5] Ibid., 6.
[6] Ibid.
[7] Ibid., 7.
[8] Ibid.
[9] Ibid., 12.
[10] Ibid., 6.
[11] Ibid., 14.
[12] Ibid., 16.

acceptance of and response to the divine self-communication becomes accessible for personal appropriation by the members of the liturgical assembly.[13] The context of the liturgical celebration, then, is the faith of Christ and the Church; worshipers proclaim this faith as they receive the Church's sacraments.[14]

Celebration and reception of the sacraments demand personal engagement on the part of all participants: "The sacraments . . . have the existence of interpersonal signs—of acts by which one person communicates with another. Involved in the sphere of personal encounter, they demand a human response by the one to whom the sign is directed. Moreover, because the reception of the sacraments is the decisive, crucial act of the Christian as Christian, there is demanded, in the ordinary course of events, an acute awareness and fervent devotion on the part of the subject."[15] By entering into the sacramental celebration in faith, the worshipers accept the grace of configuration to Christ; they willingly receive the participation in Christ's own life, which is their salvation and which will be their glory in heaven.[16]

If the sacraments are understood in this way, fruitful reception will demand far more from the worshiper than the dispositions of individual awareness, contrition for past sins, and pious devotion. Christians receive the grace of the sacraments by entering into the communal action of the liturgical celebration. They accept the gift of communion through Christ with the eternal Trinity by acting in communion with the other members of Christ's Body. In order fruitfully to receive the sacraments, then, the worshipers must have reverence and respect for the other members of the Church, as well as the willingness to have their own experience of salvation mediated through the common expression of the faith of Christ and the Church.

Kilmartin's *Sacraments, Signs of Christ* introduces central themes that are found throughout his later work. He mentions the role of the Holy Spirit in the bestowal of grace on the humanity of Christ, on the Blessed Virgin, and on Christians.[17] He points out that since the sacraments continue Christ's worship of the Father, they express the faith not only of the Church but of Christ himself. Kilmartin de-

[13] Ibid., 18.
[14] Ibid., 22.
[15] Ibid., 23–24.
[16] Ibid., 24.
[17] Ibid., 13.

scribes the practice of the sacraments as a profession of faith[18] that calls forth a response of more conscious faith from the individual participants in the celebration. He insists that the sacraments, signs of the relationship between Christ, the Church, and the Father, are events whose salvific effect is accomplished precisely in their interpersonal character.[19] He emphasizes that the encounter between worshiping Christians and the divine Persons is signified by the interpersonal relationships among the members of the liturgical assembly. Since the sacraments are constituted precisely in the interpersonal relationships of the members of the Church at prayer, the active participation of the members of the liturgical assembly in the event of worship is not merely desirable but is essential for the communication of the sacramental grace.

"Patristic Views of Sacramental Sanctity"

Writing for other teachers of theology,[20] Kilmartin used second-, third- and fourth-century teaching about baptism to trace the Church Fathers' developing understanding of the relationship of Christ, the Holy Spirit, and the Church. According to the patristic vision, he reported, the liturgy is the means by which Christians are consciously incorporated into the representation of the mystery of Christ. Christians, then, come to participate in the mystery of Christ through their participation in the visible acts of the Church.[21]

As the Church Fathers developed the language of Trinitarian theology, they came more and more clearly to describe the Christian's union with Christ, dying and rising, as the gift of the Holy Spirit.[22] By the end of the fourth century, Kilmartin reported, both filial adoption and conformation to Christ were described as the action of the economic Trinity; in baptism the Spirit anoints the Christian, configuring the Christian's life to Christ's. This life in Christ is further strengthened in the other sacraments, especially in the Eucharist.[23]

The patristic view of sacramental sanctification, Kilmartin noted, is quite different from that of scholasticism. Scholastic theology treated

[18] Ibid., 12.

[19] Ibid., 23.

[20] Kilmartin, "Patristic Views of Sacramental Sanctity," *Proceedings of the Catholic College Teachers of Sacred Doctrine* 8 (1962) 59–82.

[21] Ibid., 60, 62–63.

[22] As with Irenaeus: ibid., 68–69.

[23] Ibid., 80.

the work of redemption as completed on Calvary, with its effects applied in the present time through the sacraments. The Church Fathers, in contrast, considered the redemption as a continuing work of God accomplished through the operation of the Holy Spirit. By conforming the Christian's life to that of Christ, the Holy Spirit acts to save the world around the Christian. This salvation is accomplished through the entirety of the Christian life, but particularly through liturgical celebrations.[24] Here, for the first time, Kilmartin wrote about the limitations of scholasticism and noted the Greek Fathers' teaching that the Holy Spirit has a personal role in human sanctification. This article serves as the introduction to all his later writing, in which the activity of the Holy Spirit in the sacraments holds an increasingly central place.

THE CHALLENGE OF VATICAN II

Twentieth-century developments in scriptural, patristic, and liturgical scholarship, spurred by the *Mysteriengegenwart* controversy, led to the Second Vatican Council's description of the liturgy. The Council's treatment of sacramental sanctification, Kilmartin believed, challenged theologians to move beyond the scholastic teaching on the sacraments. Key passages for understanding this call are found in *Sacrosanctum Concilium*, which details the theology underpinning the liturgical reform and renewal, and in *Lumen Gentium*, which envisions the Church as a kind of sacrament, most truly visible in its liturgical celebrations.

That the liturgy was given first place on the Council's agenda was, "at least partially, the result of a new awareness in theological circles of the importance of liturgy in the life of the Church."[25] The *Mysteriengegenwart* controversy had emphasized that importance, and the liturgical movement had publicized the papal teaching that "the primary and indispensable source of the true Christian spirit is active and intelligent participation in the liturgy."[26]

[24] Ibid., 81.
[25] Kilmartin, "The Sacred Liturgy: Reform and Renewal," in *Remembering the Future: Vatican II and Tomorrow's Liturgical Agenda*, ed. Carl A. Last (New York: Paulist Press, 1983) 34.
[26] John Gurrieri, "Catholic Liturgical Sources of Social Commitment," in *Liturgical Foundations of Social Policy in the Catholic and Jewish Traditions*, ed. Daniel Polish and Eugene Fisher (Notre Dame, Ind.: Univ. of Notre Dame Press, 1983) 20, referring to Pius X, *Tra le Sollecitudine* (1903).

Sacrosanctum Concilium describes the liturgy in terms of the paschal mystery, which is the cause and goal of the world's salvation. The mystery of Jesus' dying and rising and the sending of the Holy Spirit, the Constitution on the Liturgy says, reveals God's intention to draw all persons into the divine life. This salvation is a Trinitarian work, in which the Holy Spirit unites human persons with Christ as they offer their lives to receive the Father's gratuitous self-communication. Christ's saving response to the Father's love is continued in the Church's life and is celebrated in the liturgy. The liturgy, then, both manifests the action of Christ and the Spirit in the Christian life and is the means by which the Church consciously accepts that action. This active acceptance of the divine gift is the source and summit of all the Church's life; it offers God acceptable worship and constitutes the Church as sacrament of salvation for the world. Christian worshipers, through their conscious, active participation in the liturgy, come to share in the paschal mystery. Strengthening this participation, therefore, is the fundamental principle of the liturgical reform mandated by the Council.[27]

The Paschal Mystery in the Church's Life: Vatican II and Paul VI

Vatican II's treatment of the paschal mystery stands in sharp contrast with Pius XII's use of the language of mystery in *Mystici Corporis* and *Mediator Dei*. "Characteristic and worthy of comment is the theological starting point from which the Council understands the liturgy. It is no longer the predominantly anthropological point of view, which sees the liturgy primarily as the human rendering of worship to God, and which is still predominant in Pius XII's encyclical *Mediator Dei,* but the theocentric concept of the divine saving action."[28] The Council emphasizes the primacy of the divine action, describing liturgical worship as part of the human response to God's initiative. This approach entails a significant change of focus from that of scholastic theology.

---

[27] Kilmartin, "Reform and Renewal," 35–37; Vatican II, *Sacrosanctum Concilium: Constitution on the Sacred Liturgy* (hereafter cited as *SC*) 2, 5–11, 14. English translation in Austin Flannery, O.P., ed., *Vatican II: The Conciliar and Post Conciliar Documents,* vol. 1 (Collegeville: The Liturgical Press, 1975).

[28] Johannes Betz, "Die Gegenwart der Heilstat Christi," in *Wahrheit und Verkündigung: Festschrift M. Schmaus,* ed. L Scheffczyk et al. (Munich: Schöningh, 1967) 1813.

Vatican II's Constitution on the Sacred Liturgy sets the general principles for the restoration of the liturgy in the context of a Trinitarian vision. "The Word made flesh, anointed by the Holy Spirit, [was sent by the Father] to preach the Gospel to the poor, to heal the contrite of heart, to be a bodily and spiritual medicine: the Mediator between God and man. For his humanity united with the Person of the Word was the instrument of our salvation. Therefore, 'in Christ the perfect achievement of our reconciliation came forth and the fullness of divine worship was given to us.'"[29] Christ's work of redemption, accomplished through the paschal mystery, results in the "sacrament of the whole Church" (SC 5), which carries on the work of salvation "through the sacrifice and sacraments" (SC 6).

The constitution teaches that Christ is present in order to associate believers with himself in the work of salvation (SC 7), repeating *Mediator Dei*'s list of modes of Christ's presence in the liturgy. The Council notes the importance of the symbolic communication that is at the heart of the sacrament. "The liturgy . . . involves the presentation of man's sanctification under the guise of signs perceptible by the senses and its accomplishment in ways appropriate to each of these signs" (SC 7).[30] For the celebration of the liturgy to have its proper effect, then, the members of the Christian assembly must be aware of what they are doing (SC 11) and give themselves to be configured to Christ's paschal mystery (SC 12). In this way they will come to full, conscious, and active participation both in the liturgy and in the mystery that it celebrates (SC 14).

The Council teaches that liturgical celebration is an event of faith: the sacraments are truly called "sacraments of faith" because they not only presuppose faith but nourish, strengthen, and express it. The liturgical expression of faith disposes the worshipers to receive sacramental grace, to worship God, and to live lives of holiness and love (SC 59).

The Council's teaching on the modes of Christ's presence in the life of the Church was developed more comprehensively in Paul VI's encyclical *Mysterium Fidei*, of September 5, 1965. This letter stresses the fundamental nature of Christ's presence in the Church's faith. "Since it is he who through faith dwells in our hearts, and through the Holy Spirit whom he gives us pours forth his love in the Church,"[31] Christ

[29] SC 5.

[30] SC 4–5.

[31] Paul VI, *Mysterium Fidei: Encyclical Letter on the Doctrine and Worship of the Eucharist*, September 3, 1965, *Acta Apostolicae Sedis* (hereafter cited as *AAS*) 57 (1965)

is present in the Church as it prays, performs works of mercy, and lives the life of faith. Christ is also present in the Church's preaching and in the work of the shepherds who guide the Church. The liturgical presence of Christ follows upon these other modes of presence in the Church's life. "In a manner even more sublime, Christ is present in his Church when it offers the sacrifice of the Mass in his name and administers the sacraments. . . . As for the sacraments, they are, as all know, the actions of Christ."[32] This treatment of the modes of Christ's presence in the Church expands on that found in *Mediator Dei* and *Sacrosanctum Concilium*, connecting the various modes of Christ's presence in the Church with each other. Here Christ's presence by faith, through the gift of the Holy Spirit, in the Church's life of prayer and works of mercy is explicitly connected to his presence in the celebration of the Church's liturgy.

The teachings of the Council and of Paul VI on the modes of Christ's presence in the liturgy were gathered together in the instruction *Eucharisticum Mysterium*, of May 25, 1967: "He is always present in a body of the faithful gathered in his name. He is present, too, in his Word, for it is he who speaks when the Scriptures are read in the Church. In the sacrifice of the Eucharist he is present in the person of the minister . . . and above all under the species of the Eucharist."[33] This listing of the modes of Christ's presence in the liturgy follows the order found in *Mysterium Fidei* rather than that of *Mediator Dei* and *Sacrosanctum Concilium*. The emphasis has shifted: Christ's presence by faith in the liturgical assembly is placed before any other liturgical mode of presence.[34]

In light of the development of magisterial teaching about the modes of Christ's presence in the liturgical celebration, it is striking that Casel's mystery theology has found such great acceptance. Christ is present in the Church's life in order to incorporate Christians into his Pasch, so that together with him they offer spiritual

---

753–774, nos. 35–39. Translation in *Documents on the Liturgy, 1963–1979* (Collegeville: The Liturgical Press, 1982) 384–385 (hereafter cited as *DOL*).

[32] Ibid.

[33] Sacred Congregation of Rites, *Eucharisticum Mysterium: Instruction on the Worship of the Eucharistic Mystery* (May 25, 1967), *AAS* 59 (1967) 539–573. Translation issued by Congregation. Austin Flannery, O.P., ed., *Vatican II: The Conciliar and Post Conciliar Documents*, vol. 1 (Collegeville: The Liturgical Press, 1975) 9.

[34] Kilmartin, *Christian Liturgy: Theology and Practice* (Kansas City: Sheed and Ward, 1988) 312–313.

sacrifice to the Father. This sacrifice, which embraces the entire Christian life of faith, prayer, and works of mercy, is represented in the liturgy. Indeed, liturgical celebration should teach Christians to offer their lives with Christ, that the mystery of his self-offering may be reproduced in their living. "The Church's intention is that the faithful not only offer this victim but also learn to offer themselves and so to surrender themselves, through Christ the Mediator, to an ever more complete union with the Father and each other, so that at last God may be all in all."[35]

Insofar as Christ incorporates Christians into his sacrifice, the conciliar and postconciliar documents indicate that both the glorified Christ and the temporal saving deeds through which he acts are present in the various modes that operate in the liturgy. Christians' incorporation into the paschal mystery is effected by participation in the liturgy; this participation itself provides the modes by which Christ becomes present. While the Church's magisterium clearly affirms the mystery presence, however, it has neither embraced nor rejected any particular position proposed during the *Mysteriengegenwart* controversy.

Theological Implications of Vatican II

The Council's description of the liturgy, Kilmartin wrote, carries several important theological changes. First, Catholic teaching, from the Reformation through *Mediator Dei*, considered Christian worship primarily as the exercise of the virtue of religion. *Sacrosanctum Concilium* emphasizes that Christian liturgy begins with God's action. God's gift of faith, "in which we are so grasped by Christ that we become one with him and he with us," underlies Christian worship; this worship "derives from Christ's present activity in the worshippers in the Spirit."[36] Worship, then, is dialogical; in the entire liturgical event God is acting and the community is responding in faith. The divine action in the liturgy continues the self-communication offered in Jesus' life; the Church's response continues Jesus' answer of self-sacrificing love of the Father.

Sacrosanctum Concilium treats Christian worship in light of the divine initiative, a descending motion of God's love, and the human re-

---

[35] Sacred Congregation of Divine Worship, "General Instruction of the Roman Missal," 4th ed. (March 27, 1975) no. 55, f. Translation by Vatican Polyglot Press, in *DOL*, 482.

[36] Kilmartin, "Reform and Renewal," 38.

sponse, an ascending offering of self, made perfect in Christ and continued in the Church. This presentation, Kilmartin believed, suggests that the mystery presence should be described in a way that involves a dynamic of dialogue between God and humankind.

Second, scholastic theology considered the ordained minister, officially deputed to represent the whole Church, as the active subject of the liturgy; the laity participated only indirectly, by their intention and devotion, in the work done by the ordained minister. According to *Sacrosanctum Concilium,* however, the entire liturgical assembly is the direct subject of the liturgical action: "Liturgical services 'are celebrations of the Church, namely the whole people of God united and ordered around their bishops' (*SC* 26.1)."[37] The hierarchy, then, do not stand as mediators between the laity and God, as some scholastic theologies might imply; rather, the divine self-communication is mediated through the active interrelationship of the entire assembly that celebrates the liturgy.

Mysterium Fidei links the liturgical presence of Christ to the entire life of faith of the Church. Christ's liturgical presence is a special manifestation of Christ's saving presence in the entire life of the Church. *Eucharisticum Mysterium* indicates that the primary mode of Christ's liturgical presence is that in the liturgical assembly, by faith. The other modes of liturgical presence may then be ordered to that in the assembly.

Third, the Council reunited liturgy and sacraments. Scholastic theologies separated the sacrament, the action of Christ to give grace, from the liturgy, the Church's action aimed at eliciting the appropriate dispositions from the recipient of the sacrament. The Council taught that in the entire liturgical action God communicates sanctification, and the community of faith responds in praise.

The interrelated modes of Christ's presence point to the importance of the entire liturgical event by locating Christ's presence in the assembly and in the ministers, in prayer, song, and sacramental act. The all-inclusive nature of Christ's liturgical presence indicates that the whole celebration is meant "to serve as a transparency for the active presence of Christ and so to draw the community into personal union with him and his Paschal Mystery and into worship of the Father."[38]

[37] Ibid., 39.
[38] Ibid.

The teaching of *Sacrosanctum Concilium* about the modes of Christ's presence in the liturgy, Kilmartin insisted, can be understood only in light of these theological changes, which set the Council's teaching apart from that of scholasticism. Again and again in teaching and writing he would return to the dialogical nature of worship, to the assembly's role as active subject of the liturgical event, and to the recovery of sacrament as liturgy, as the prayer of the Church in the Holy Spirit.

METHODOLOGICAL SEARCH FOR REINTEGRATION OF *LEX ORANDI* AND *LEX CREDENDI*

The Council's emphasis on the Church's self-realization in its celebration of the liturgy, and on the liturgical assembly as the subject of the liturgical action, Kilmartin believed, presented Catholic theologians with a new task. The rule of belief articulated in doctrinal formulas of the Church's magisterium *(lex credendi)* must be reintegrated with the rule of prayer contained in the Church's liturgical celebrations *(lex orandi)*. The relation between the two rules, both of which express the Church's faith, had been raised during the *Mysteriengegenwart* controversy. Casel had argued that the *lex orandi* should predominate, since in the liturgy Christ is present with his saving acts; the liturgy, then, contains what must be believed. Pius XII, in answer, had stated that the *lex credendi* must determine the way of prayer. Vatican II highlighted the interrelationship of the two rules without giving precedence to either.

Contemporary scholarship has continued to investigate the nature of this relationship. It appears that during the first Christian millennium, although official teaching was often described in terms of the celebration of the liturgy, both the formulations of prayer and the shape of liturgical celebration were responsive to questions of doctrine. The interplay between liturgy and belief, however, lessened as time went on. It is generally agreed that during the second millennium the *lex credendi* has predominated, even to the point where the connection between belief and worship became less than clear.[39]

Kilmartin believed that Vatican II, by drawing attention to the liturgical celebration as the event in which the Church is constituted

---

[39] Kevin W. Irwin, *Context and Text: Method in Liturgical Theology* (Collegeville: The Liturgical Press, 1994) 3–32, summarizes recent scholarly discussion on the relation of *lex orandi* and *lex credendi*.

and manifested, made it necessary to rediscover the authentic faith contained in the Church's worship. Agreeing with many other theologians that the two rules should complement each other, being held in creative tension, he suggested the formulation "The law of prayer is the law of belief and vice-versa."[40]

Methodological Problem: Determining the Lex Orandi

The goal of reintegration of the *lex orandi* and the *lex credendi*, however, poses a methodological question. The law of belief has predominated for the last thousand years, and both the Church's official prayer and Christian piety reflect that imbalance. The Council, recognizing this, called not just for reform of official prayer but also for harmonization between liturgical and individual piety and spirituality (*SC* 11–13). Thus the liturgical reform envisaged by the Council included the education of clergy and people (*SC* 14–19), a return to the simplicity of the original Roman liturgy (*SC* 34), and the clear use of symbols in rites that evoke full, conscious, and active participation of the liturgical assembly (*SC* 50, 59).

This call for pervasive reform, however, leaves unanswered the question of how to determine the content of the Church's law of prayer. Kilmartin approached that question using the classical statement about the relationship between prayer and belief given by Prosper of Aquitaine. Prosper argued that the liturgy shows what has been believed always, everywhere, and by all Christian people. The ancient prayers for the conversion of evildoers, for example, demonstrate the Church's belief that conversion comes only through grace; thus, Prosper argued, the rule of prayer shows that grace is necessary for conversion. Kilmartin, following Prosper's lead, looked for evidence of the faith that has been held always, everywhere, and by all Christians. That evidence, he argued, is contained above all in the official prayers of the ancient, undivided Church and in indications of how the prayers were interpreted by the ritual action of the liturgical community.

"It is recognized that every human experience reaches its full expression by way of symbolic action and word and that this is true of the life of faith. The liturgy, being a celebration of the life of faith, is understood to express the faith in a way which surpasses any particular formulations of the teaching office of the Church or theologians. . . .

[40] Kilmartin, *Christian Liturgy*, 97.

51

However, we cannot arbitrarily choose our liturgical sources. Rather we should employ those which reach back to the times of liturgical origins in the East and the West. . . . From these origins we can trace the genuine stream of the liturgical tradition of East and West. Hence we are better able to judge to what extent later local verbal and gestural additions and the theology reflected in them are in agreement with the authentic ecclesial tradition."[41]

Kilmartin, then, would attempt to investigate the faith of the Church through analysis of the structure and content of classical official prayers, in the light of what is known about their interpretation in the liturgical action. His writing, however, shifted back and forth from consideration of ancient texts and liturgical performance to systematic reflection on the faith celebrated in these rites. As a result, his method for determining the *lex orandi* from the interplay of official text and ritual interpretation was not always clear.[42]

Methodological Example: The Eucharistic Prayer
as Witness to the Church's Faith

Kilmartin's approach to discovering the *lex orandi* is demonstrated in his many writings on the Eucharist.[43] Considering the evidence of Scripture, patristic teaching, and the texts of the classical Eucharistic Prayers, he concluded that the entire eucharistic liturgy consecrates the praying Church to living the sacrifice by which Christ established the New Covenant. He argued that the post-Tridentine *lex credendi*, with its emphasis on the moment of consecration of the bread and wine, diminished the eucharistic faith of the ancient Church. The "moment of consecration" theology, he insisted, should be understood in its proper context: it was shaped by the late scholastic reflection on the Eucharist, by theological controversy over the real

[41] Kilmartin, "Pastoral Office and the Eucharist," in *Bread from Heaven*, ed. Paul Bernier (New York: Paulist Press, 1977) 138, 139.

[42] Kevin W. Irwin, *Liturgical Theology* (Collegeville: The Liturgical Press, 1990) 52, makes this observation.

[43] Kilmartin, *The Eucharist in the Primitive Church* (Englewood Cliffs, N.J.: Prentice-Hall, 1965), begins his examination of Eucharistic Prayers. Although his thought on the subject continued to develop throughout his career, his thinking at the time of his death was remarkably consistent with his earlier positions. Accordingly, this section does not trace a chronological development. Instead, under various thematic headings, it refers to articles and books written over a period of almost thirty years.

presence of Christ in the eucharistic species, and by a liturgical practice that did not include the sacramental communion of the worshiping assembly. The *lex credendi*, then, addresses dogmatic concerns of the times in which it arose, but it does not hand on the richness of eucharistic faith contained in the *lex orandi*.[44]

Earlier scholasticism had preserved the ecclesiological dimension of the Eucharist through its use of the concept of "consecration of the body and blood." This *consecratio* embraced "(1) the transitus of the elements into the eucharistic flesh and blood, (2) the transitus of the consecrated flesh and blood into the heavenly body of Christ, and (3) the purpose of the twofold transitus, namely, the integration of the liturgical community into this single transitus of Christ from suffering to glory in virtue of its self-offering made in union with Christ in the power of the Holy Spirit."[45] This concept makes clear that the aim of the eucharistic liturgy is the consecration of the liturgical assembly to the sacrifice of Christ and emphasizes the transformation of the assembly through its union with Christ in the Holy Spirit.

By the end of the twelfth century, however, responding to theological disputes about the somatic real presence of Christ in the Eucharist, the term "consecration" had come to be used only in relation to the eucharistic elements. The ecclesiological dimension of the eucharistic sacrifice gradually came to be explained through its Christological dimension. The Eucharist is the sacrifice of Christ, who is the Head of the Church, so the Eucharist may be called the sacrifice of the Church insofar as it is the sacrifice of Christ, the Head of the Church. The priest reciting the narrative of the institution of the eucharistic sacrament, now considered as "words of consecration," acts *in persona Christi*, not *in persona Ecclesiae*. At the "moment of consecration" the priest directly represents Christ the Head and only indirectly represents the Body of which Christ is the Head. According to this late scholastic interpretation, the essence of the sacrament is contained in

[44] The shift from the patristic to the scholastic approach to eucharistic theology, and the weakened emphasis on ecclesiological aspects of the sacrament found in the scholastic tradition, is detailed in Mary M. Schaefer, *Twelfth Century Latin Commentaries on the Mass: Christological and Ecclesiological Dimensions* (Ann Arbor: University Microfilms, 1983), and is more generally described in Henri de Lubac, *Corpus Mysticum* (Paris: Aubier, 1949). Kilmartin, *The Eucharist in the West* (Collegeville: The Liturgical Press, 1999) 127–143.

[45] Kilmartin, "The Catholic Tradition of Eucharistic Theology: Towards the Third Millennium," *Theological Studies* 55 (1994) 417.

the moment of consecration, and the sacramental sign is the separate consecrations of bread and wine. While the integrity of the rite demands that the priest receive sacramental communion, the communion of the liturgical assembly is neither assumed nor given theological significance.[46] This "moment of consecration" approach to the eucharistic sacrifice is found in *Mediator Dei* and was presumed by Casel and his interlocutors in the *Mysteriengegenwart* controversy.[47]

Kilmartin argued that the eucharistic faith of the Church is far richer than the "moment of consecration" theology handed down in the *lex credendi*. To recover the fullness of that faith, he began with scriptural evidence, moved through testimony from the primitive Church, and ended with the classical Eucharistic Prayers, whose texts were fixed in the late fourth century. The post-Tridentine *lex credendi*, he believed, could be properly understood and appreciated when integrated into the ancient faith of the undivided Church taught in the *lex orandi*.

SCRIPTURAL TESTIMONY TO EUCHARISTIC FAITH[48]

Privileged witness to the Church's eucharistic faith is found in the Scriptures. In his early investigations, Kilmartin paid special heed to the New Testament texts that touch on the Eucharist. Several aspects of his treatment of the Pauline doctrine in the First Letter to the Corinthians and of the narratives of eucharistic institution in the Synoptic Gospels are particularly important for his understanding of the mystery presence.

Primacy of the ecclesiological dimension of the Eucharist
The earliest New Testament witness to the Church's eucharistic faith, in the Pauline letters, emphasizes the relationship of the Eucharist to the Church. It is because of that relationship that Paul criticizes the behavior of the Corinthians at their sacramental meal (1 Cor 11:17-34).

Kilmartin reported a scholarly consensus that when Paul wrote to the Corinthians, the ritual celebration of the Lord's Supper was apparently found at the end of a common meal. The blessing of the bread, which marks the beginning of a Jewish festival meal, had been

[46] Ibid., 418–420.

[47] Ibid., 420–427.

[48] Johannes Betz, *Die Eucharistie in der Zeit der Griechischen Väter* II/1 (Freiburg: Herder, 1961), is Kilmartin's basic source for the interpretation of scriptural passages referring to the Eucharist.

moved to the end of the meal, when the final cup was blessed and shared. Since the meal had no formal start, those who arrived early could begin eating and drinking without waiting for the other members of the community. Paul rebuked the Corinthians for this behavior, which destroyed the common meal, the symbol and celebration of their membership in the one Body of Christ.

"The self-seeking at the agape meal is a sin against the community (vv. 17-22); it is also a sin against the eucharistic Christ (vv. 27-29), for whoever does not receive the Eucharist in a way consistent with its character as the body-given-for-many is guilty of a sin against the sacramentally present Christ. . . . One must, so says verse 29, 'distinguish the body,' that is, recognize the body in its specific claim to fraternal love.

"This passage is a profound revelation of the intimate relationship between love of one's neighbor and love of Christ. One cannot offend against brotherly love without offending against Christ Himself and rendering the reception of the Eucharist, which is the efficacious sign of the presence of the glorified Lord, a mockery and an occasion for the judgment of God."[49]

In Kilmartin's later work he would put great emphasis on the unity of the love of God and the love of neighbor. He found the teaching of that unity at the heart of Paul's understanding of the Church as the Body of Christ, and of the Eucharist as sacrament of Christ's Body.[50]

An essential role of the Eucharist in the life of the Church, Kilmartin held, is that of "effecting and increasing not only the union of God with [people] but the union of [human persons] among themselves."[51] The Pauline doctrine on the Eucharist, he wrote, is preeminently a teaching on the life of the Church, on the unity of the members of the Church, and on the demands of love of God and of love of neighbor. "In the measure that the community lives in union with one another in love, it is a concrete proclamation of the redemptive death of Jesus."[52] The eucharistic celebration, in this understanding, proclaims the death of the Lord as truly saving insofar as it manifests the communion that

---

[49] Kilmartin, *Primitive Church*, 89–90.
[50] Kilmartin, "Eucharist and Community," in Bernier, ed., *Bread from Heaven*, 34–44.
[51] Kilmartin, *Primitive Church*, 91.
[52] Kilmartin, "Eucharist and Community," 39.

Christians, freed from sin and bound in a unity that overcomes the divisions of social class or wealth, have with each other. Because the Corinthians' ritual meal did not express equality in the Body of Christ but rather the disdain of the rich for the poor, Paul judged that it was not truly the Lord's supper that they ate.[53]

The Pauline narrative of the institution of the Eucharist thus has a clear ecclesiological emphasis. Kilmartin found that emphasis in the other accounts of institution as well.

Institution narratives: Participation in the sacrifice that established the New Covenant

The post-Tridentine *lex orandi* focused on the transformation of the bread and wine, ascribing theological significance to the separate consecrations without referring to the sacramental communion of the members of the liturgical assembly. In contrast, the four New Testament accounts of the institution of the Eucharist highlight the relationship between eating the blessed bread and drinking the blessed cup and participating in the New Covenant. These narratives connect Jesus' self-sacrificing response to the Father's love and the Christian's sacramental communion in the covenant sacrifice of Christ. "In using the concept of covenant Jesus reveals that by his death God will erect a new order of salvation in which [people] will share in the final *berith* (covenant) surpassing all others."[54] The covenant people share in the covenant sacrifice not only spiritually, by their intention, but also sacramentally, by eating and drinking the sacrificial food and drink.

Though the scriptural institution accounts differ from one another, Kilmartin wrote that they exhibit "a uniform relational system which must be found in all celebrations claiming to be conformed to the tradition of the night of betrayal."[55] In that system both the prayer of thanksgiving and the sharing of food and drink are essential. "The sharing of bread and cup symbolizes the community of life among the participants; the prayer of praise confesses the foundation of this relationship."[56]

[53] Ibid., 38.

[54] "The Last Supper and Earliest Eucharists of the Church," in *The Breaking of Bread,* Concilium 40, ed. Pierre Benoit, Roland Murphy, and Bastiaan van Iersel (New York: Paulist Press, 1969) 38–39.

[55] "Sacrificium Laudis: Content and Function of Early Eucharistic Prayers," *Theological Studies* 35 (1974) 268.

[56] Ibid., 269.

In traditional Jewish meal blessings, Kilmartin observed, table fellowship is based on a common relation to God. Jesus' blessing of the bread and the cup, however, reveals that while Jesus and the disciples share a common union with the Father, the disciples' union with the Father is based on their personal attachment to Jesus.[57] The sharing of the bread and the cup establishes an identity between the life of Jesus and the lives of the disciples, grounded on the quality of his life "given for you." "Ultimately the union between Jesus and the disciples is based on their participation in his new relation to the Father, sealed by his obedience 'unto death, even death on a cross' (Phil 2:8)."[58] In this light, Jesus' words of blessing over the bread and the cup proclaim the faith in which he offers his life to the Father for the life of the world. The disciples express their participation in Jesus' sacrificial faith, the faith of the New Covenant, by their eating and drinking.[59]

The four New Testament institution narratives, considered in the context of Jewish table prayers, reveal that the transformation of the eucharistic elements is directly related to their consumption by the disciples. Jesus' words of blessing over the bread and the cup reveal how the food and drink are ordered to Jesus' saving act; the blessings of the salvation accomplished through Jesus are appropriated through their consumption.[60] "By this bread and wine, now identified with his body and blood, Jesus mediates to the disciples not merely a share in the table blessing but more properly a share in the blessings derived from his 'given body' and 'shed blood': freedom from the power of sin and a new covenant union with God."[61]

It is through the faith expressed in their eating and drinking, then, that the disciples would have a share in the fruits of Jesus' sacrificial death. According to the relational system found in the texts, the blessing of the bread and the cup must not be considered apart from the consecration of the disciples to Jesus' sacrifice through their consumption of the blessed food and drink.

---

[57] Ibid., 269.

[58] Ibid., 269–270.

[59] Ibid., 271.

[60] Kilmartin, "The Eucharistic Prayer: Content and Function of Some Early Eucharistic Prayers," in *The Word in the World*, ed. Richard J. Clifford and George MacRae (Cambridge: Weston, 1973) 118.

[61] Kilmartin, "Last Supper," 40, 41.

Table blessing and participation in the New Covenant

The interpretation of the scriptural evidence of the Church's eucharistic faith is rooted in the relationship between the table blessing and the consumption of the food and drink. This relationship is found in the Jewish tradition of festival meals: the blessing of the bread and cup invokes God's presence for the entire meal, and the participants' eating and drinking the blessed food and drink express their active acceptance of God's covenant blessing. For the community of Jesus' disciples, faith-filled participation in the blessings of the New Covenant, for which God is thanked in the table prayer, is sealed by the act of eating and drinking in the memory of Jesus.[62]

The meaning of the eucharistic celebration of Christ's sacrifice is fixed in the Church's memory by the words of blessing over the bread, "my body which is given for you" (1 Cor 11:24), and over the cup, "the new covenant in my blood" (1 Cor 11:25). Christians participate in the New Covenant by their sharing in Christ's covenant sacrifice; sharing in Christ's faith, they offer their lives in love for "the many." This offering, as well as the consequent reception of covenant blessings, is symbolized in the proclamation of the Eucharistic Prayer and in sacramental communion in the sacrificial food and drink.[63]

PATRISTIC EVIDENCE OF EUCHARISTIC FAITH

Kilmartin reported as a common opinion among scholars in the early 1970s that when the blessing and sharing of the bread and the cup were joined together at the end of the meal, the Jewish grace after meals, the *birkat ha-mazon*, became the model for the Church's thanksgiving prayer. The Jewish grace "contained a brief blessing of God who nourishes [people], a thanksgiving for the promised land, and a petition for Israel, Jerusalem, and the Temple. The early Christian version probably contained a brief benediction, followed by a thanksgiving prayer referring to Christ, and a petition for the coming of the Kingdom."[64] The traditional form of the prayer shows the connection between thanksgiving and petition: God is praised by remembering God's mighty deeds; the memory of God's past actions,

---

[62] Kilmartin, "Catholic Tradition," 445–448.

[63] Kilmartin, "Eucharist and Community," 37–39, 44.

[64] Kilmartin, "Eucharistic Prayer," 118. See "Sacrificium Laudis," 275. High points of scholarly discussion on the descent of the Eucharistic Prayer from the thanksgiving after the meal are given by Enrico Mazza, *The Eucharistic Prayers of the Roman Rite* (New York: Pueblo, 1986) 12–21.

whose effects continue in the present time, grounds the petition for blessings in the future.[65] The prayer, spoken by the one presiding over the meal, is the prayer of all those who share table-fellowship, proclaiming a common faith, a common memory of God's saving deeds, and a common commitment to God's covenant. All those at the table give their assent both verbally, with their "Amen," and gesturally, with their drinking the blessed cup.

In the early Church, Kilmartin wrote, this form of prayer, moving from thanksgiving to petition, was used as a blessing over both the bread and the cup at the end of the community's meal, and so provided the pattern for eucharistic praying. As the traditions of eucharistic prayer developed, a narrative of the institution of the Eucharist, in which Jesus' life was revealed as sacrificial response to God's self-communication, was included in the prayer text. This narrative was either part of (as in the Roman Canon) or immediately followed by (as in the Anaphora of John Chrysostom) a sacrificial prayer of anamnesis and offering, connecting the self-offering of Christ with that of the Church.

The introduction of the narrative of institution of the Eucharist into the pattern of eucharistic praying, Kilmartin noted, followed a common practice in Jewish euchology. On feasts or sabbaths, table blessings are expanded by the insertion of particular mention of God's action in founding the feast and calling for its observance. These inserts or "embolisms" might be found in either the thanksgiving or the petition section of the *birkat ha-mazon*. In whichever section of the prayer the embolism occurs, it reminds those at the meal that their celebration is done in obedience to God's command, reminds God of the divine promise to bless the people, and thereby grounds the petition for God's continued blessings.[66] "The recalling of the patrimony of the Lord's Supper bequeathed by Jesus served to evoke thanksgiving from the community and to instruct it concerning the origin, meaning, and procedure of the rite. Moreover, it highlighted the

[65] This pattern of prayer, as later scholarship has emphasized, is not limited to table prayers but is "found in the narrative context in the Old Testament, as well as in traditional Jewish private and public prayer." Kilmartin, "Epiclesis," *New Catholic Encyclopedia* 18: Supplement (New York: McGraw-Hill, 1988) 77.

[66] Kilmartin, "Ecclesiological Implications of Classical Eucharistic Prayers," *Wort und Wahrheit*, Supplementary Issue No. 5: Fifth Ecumenical Consultation Between Theologians of the Oriental Orthodox Churches and the Roman Catholic Church, Vienna-Lainz, September 18–25, 1988 (Vienna: Herder, 1989) 85.

ultimate goal of the whole prayer of praise and thanksgiving: to petition God to realize again the saving event of the Lord's Supper in the
assembly."[67] Thus the movement of the Jewish blessings that served
as models for the Eucharistic Prayer reveals that the institution narrative must be understood in light of this relation of thanksgiving, or
memory, and petition. The combination of thankful memory and confident petition for continued graces expresses "the dynamics of the
covenant relation initiated by God, and continually actualized in the
liturgy of the Church."[68]

From patristic preaching and from other texts describing early Eucharistic Prayers, Kilmartin traced the developing stages of Christology and pneumatology and noted changes in the way the sacrifice of
Christ and the Church is described. He made special note of the different descriptions of Christ's priesthood in classical Western and
Eastern prayers.

In the third and fourth centuries the activity of Christ in the eucharistic liturgy was frequently described in a fourfold sense: Christ
is the priest offering the sacrifice, which is both his and the Church's;
he is the victim being offered; he is the host of the sacrificial banquet;
and he is the sacrificial food eaten by the participants in the sacrifice.
In these early prayers Christ is not only described as high priest
through whom the Church comes before God in the power of the
Holy Spirit but is also seen as consecrator of the bread and wine. This
understanding of the eucharistic sacrifice, once emphasized in
prayers and homilies from Egypt, Alexandria, Syria, Asia Minor, and
Rome, was gradually replaced by newer theologies among the
Churches of the East. Of the classical Eucharistic Prayers, he noted,
only the Roman Canon preserves this conception of sacrifice.[69]

The classical prayers of the Eastern Church speak of Christ's sacrificial activity in the Eucharist in a way quite different from that of the
Roman Canon.[70] In the Trinitarian controversies of the fourth century,
the Arians argued that Christ, whom the Church's prayers described
as priest interceding with the Father, must be inferior or subordinate to
the Father, for a mediator is inferior to the one with whom he inter-
cedes. In response, the Eastern Church Fathers emphasized that

[67] Kilmartin, "Eucharistic Prayer," 120.
[68] Kilmartin, "Epiclesis," 77.
[69] Kilmartin, *Primitive Church*, 153.
[70] Kilmartin, "The Active Role of Christ and the Spirit in the Divine Liturgy,"
Diakonia 17 (1982) 96–97.

Christ's high priestly position and function belong to his humanity, not to the Person of the Logos: in his humanity Christ acted as priest, but in his divinity he is equal to the Father. As a result, they came to describe the Eucharist less as action of the glorified Christ than as representation of Christ's past saving acts.[71] John Chrysostom, for example, in the *Homilies on Hebrews* (ca. 402), taught that Christ's priestly offering is completed; he has sat down at the Father's right hand and reigns in equality with the Father. Yet Christ is active as the Church performs the memorial of his sacrifice, for he makes the Church participate in that sacrifice. "The anamnesis in faith serves as the clasp that binds the cross and the eucharistic sacrifice in such a way that the Christian shares in the mystery of the historical sacrifice."[72]

Theodore of Mopsuestia ascribed Christ's priesthood to the activity of the Holy Spirit, who gave Christ's humanity the gift of mediating life and immortality. Because of his offering of himself, Christ was raised from the dead by the glory of the Spirit, and his humanity was thoroughly divinized, making it the cause of immortality for the Church. The Holy Spirit continues to operate in the Church, Christ's Body, uniting the Church with Christ.[73] For Theodore, the transformation of the eucharistic elements signifies not Christ's death but his resurrection:

". . . the transformation can only be explained by the descent of the Holy Spirit whom the priest invokes over the elements; it is like the transformation that the Spirit effects on the body of Christ without life in the tomb by elevating it to immortal life, and making it the source of immortal life for us. . . . We are now present in spirit to Christ's resurrection each time that the Spirit descends on the bread without life to make it the body of Christ given for life. . . . Filled by the Spirit, it nourishes and fortifies the new life that we receive from baptism, and it is pledge of immortal life."[74]

As Theodore's teaching illustrates, the fourth-century Eastern shift in the Church's understanding of Christ's activity in the eucharistic sacrifice was accompanied by an increased emphasis on the action of

[71] Ibid., 98–100.

[72] Kilmartin, "Spirit and Liturgy: Notes for Lectures at Creighton University, June, 1992," (Kilmartin Archives, Jesuit Community at Boston College) 30; "Active Role," 102.

[73] Kilmartin, "Active Role," 102. "Catholic Tradition," 428, n. 65, refers to various interpretations of Jesus' self-offering "through the eternal Spirit" (Heb 9:14).

[74] Kilmartin, "Spirit and Liturgy," 33–34.

the Holy Spirit. In response to the "Pneumatomachi," who denied that the Holy Spirit was a divine Person, the Church Fathers emphasized the Spirit's divinity by adding to the Eucharistic Prayers an explicit invocation of the Holy Spirit to sanctify the assembly through sanctification of the gifts of bread and wine.[75] The Eucharistic Prayer of the Roman Church, in contrast, understood the sanctification of gifts and assembly as the work of the divine power, described as the angel who brings the offering of the earthly Church into union with the eternal offering of Christ in heaven.

Together with the Eastern developments in the language of priesthood and sanctification came a change in the imagery used to speak of the transformation of the bread and wine. In the second century, Justin and Irenaeus, teaching of "the appropriation of the elements by the Logos who makes them his body and blood,"[76] used an analogy of "eucharistic incarnation";[77] just as the Word took flesh and blood for himself in the incarnation, so the Word takes flesh in the eucharistic food and drink. This concept continued to be found in the West until it was replaced by that of transubstantiation, which was also considered as an action of the Word.

By the late fourth century in the East, however, both the historical and the eucharistic incarnations were described as actions of Word and Spirit together; the Spirit, who united the humanity of Christ with the Word in the historical incarnation, unites the eucharistic elements with the Word. The Greek Fathers considered the Spirit's sanctification of the humanity of Christ, of the eucharistic elements, and of the liturgical assembly as a personal action. The Spirit-epicleses of the Eastern anaphoras reflect this development of pneumatology and give rise to an understanding that it is the Spirit's action that brings Christ to the Church and brings the Church to Christ.

Whether conceived of in the Western or in the Eastern fashion, however, the image of eucharistic incarnation clarified the purpose of the eucharistic liturgy: the incarnation of the Word in those who eat and drink and their resulting communion with the Father in the Holy Spirit.

The classical Eucharistic Prayers themselves, then, give evidence of changes in theological descriptions of the eucharistic celebration. Nevertheless, Kilmartin observed, "the relational structure of the ac-

[75] Kilmartin, "Active Role," 98.
[76] Kilmartin, "Eucharistic Prayer," 125.
[77] Kilmartin, "Sacrificium Laudis," 277.

counts of institution remains: thanksgiving to God for His mighty works in Christ is the *sacrificium laudis* of the Church undertaken with a view to obtaining deeper communion with the Father, especially through the sacrament of the humanity of Christ."[78] The texts of the classical Eucharistic Prayers testify to the Church's belief that communion in the sacramental food and drink has the effect of establishing the Christian in communion with the Persons of the Trinity.[79]

LITERARY-THEOLOGICAL ANALYSIS OF EUCHARISTIC PRAYERS

Kilmartin's analysis of the classical Eucharistic Prayers led him to three conclusions. First, all the prayers ask for the renewal of the covenant made in Jesus Christ. Second, the proclamation of God's actions in the past and the petition for renewed blessings are not only interrelated, but the very memory of God's actions has an epicletic or petitionary character. Third, the high point of the prayer is the epiclesis for sanctification of the liturgical assembly.[80]

Kilmartin never presented his understanding of the literary-theological structure of the Eucharistic Prayer in a fashion that is conspicuously accessible to the reader. Only in his first book, *The Eucharist in the Primitive Church*, did he provide extensive quotations from translations of the classical prayer texts. This allowed him to address a broader audience than the scholarly community familiar with the prayers in their original languages.

In the years following the publication of that book, translations of the classical texts became more easily accessible to the interested reader, and Kilmartin's quotations from the texts became much less

---

[78] Ibid., 287.

[79] Kilmartin, *Primitive Church*, 126.

[80] Kilmartin, "Ecclesiological Implications of Classical Eucharistic Prayers," gives the most concise presentation of his thought on the content and structure of the Eucharistic Prayer. The most complete study of the Eucharistic Prayer is that of Cesare Giraudo, *La struttura letteraria della preghiera eucaristica. Saggio sulla genesi letteraria di'una forma. Tôdâ veterotestamentaria, berakâ giudaica, anafora cristiana,* Analecta Biblica 92 (Rome: Biblical Institute, 1981). Giraudo holds that the Eucharistic Prayer has had a more complicated history than Kilmartin thought in the 1970s. The two scholars agree on the structure and dynamic of the prayer. Kilmartin refers to Giraudo in "Catholic Tradition," 443, n. 105, and *The Eucharist in the West,* 322–337. Cf. Kilmartin, "The Jewish Thank-offering Meal as Background for the Lord's Supper: State of the Question," in *The Papin Gedenkschrift: Dimensions in the Human Religious Quest II. Scriptural Dimensions,* ed. Joseph Armenti (Ann Arbor: University Microfilms, 1986) 410–428; Mazza, *Eucharistic Prayers,* 12–29.

frequent. In 1975, in a newsletter for religious educators, he re-marked: "The sacrament most with us, the Eucharist, is being fruit-fully approached from a study of the content and function of the eucharistic prayer itself, i.e., from the communal expression of eu-charistic faith used in the liturgies of the various church traditions for the East and West."[81] He recommended that religious educators be-come familiar both with the classical texts treated in Louis Bouyer's *Eucharist*[82] and with the study of new Eucharistic Prayers by John Barry Ryan.[83]

When writing for scholarly journals, Kilmartin apparently assumed that readers would have the prayer texts close at hand and would follow his analysis with one eye on the text to which he was refer-ring.[84] His 1992 course "Spirit and Liturgy," however, was offered for students who might not be familiar with liturgical sources. Accord-ingly, the notes that he prepared for distribution to the class included a translation of the Anaphora of John Chrysostom and the approved English text of the third Eucharistic Prayer of the Roman Sacramen-tary. This section will make reference to these two texts in order to il-lustrate Kilmartin's argument.

Covenant renewal

All the classical Eucharistic Prayers mirror the same basic under-standing of the dynamic covenant relationship between God and God's chosen people[85] and express the Church's desire "for fellow-ship with Christ, the sharing in his saving work, and his glory medi-ated through the 'food of immortality.'"[86] Like the Jewish table blessings, the Eucharistic Prayers are spoken by one person, whose

[81] Kilmartin, "Recent Literature: the Human Dimension of Religion," *PACE* 5 (May 1975).

[82] Louis Bouyer, *Eucharist: Theology and Spirituality of the Eucharistic Prayer* (Notre Dame, Ind.: Univ. of Notre Dame Press, 1968).

[83] John Barry Ryan, *The Eucharistic Prayer: A Study in Contemporary Liturgy* (New York: Paulist Press, 1974).

[84] The standard collection of Eucharistic Prayer texts is A. Hänggi and I. Pahl, eds., *Prex eucharistica: Textus e variis liturgiis antiquioribus selecti*, Spicilegium Friburgense 12 (Fribourg: Éditions Universitaires, 1968). English translations of the classical texts are most easily found in Ronald C. Jasper and Geoffrey J. Cuming, *Prayers of the Eucharist, Early and Reformed* (New York: Pueblo, 1992).

[85] Kilmartin, "Ecclesiological Implications," 85; "Epiclesis," *New Catholic Ency-clopedia* 18: Supplement (New York: McGraw-Hill, 1988) 77–78.

[86] Kilmartin, "Epiclesis," 77.

words express the entire assembly's intention to enter more deeply into the covenant relationship through the prayer of thanks and praise. Both this intent and the fact that the one proclaiming the prayer text speaks in the name of the whole liturgical assembly are made clear by the dialogue that begins the Eucharistic Prayer.[87]

In the course of the prayer the liturgical assembly speaks to God both in thankful memory and in petition that God renew and strengthen it in the covenant relationship.[88] God is praised first of all for God's own self, then for the two great works of creation and salvation. This movement is clearer in the Eastern prayers, whose texts are fixed.[89] In the Roman tradition the opening section of praise and thanksgiving is variable, emphasizing different moments of the divine action according to the cycle of feasts and seasons.[90] In both Eastern and Western prayers God is explicitly praised for creating the Church, the people of the new covenant who offer thanks by remembering what God has done for them.[91] It is because the liturgical assembly is aware that God has called it together to offer thanks and to ask for covenant renewal that it dares to claim that its worship has communion with the heavenly liturgy, with the saints and angels who cry, "Holy, Holy, Holy!"

[87] The Roman prayer, however, begins with the simple greeting "The Lord be with you." Chrysostom's makes the Trinitarian covenant relationship more explicit: "The grace of our Lord Jesus Christ, and the love of the God and Father, and the fellowship of the Holy Spirit be with you all." In both prayers the presider invites ("Let us give thanks . . .") and receives ("It is fitting and right . . .") the assembly's assent to the praise and thanksgiving that follow.

[88] Kilmartin, *The Eucharist in the West*, 339.

[89] Chrysostom: "It is fitting and right . . . . For you are God, ineffable, inconceivable, existing always and in the same way, you and your only-begotten Son and your Holy Spirit. You brought us out of not-being to being, and when we had fallen, you raised us up . . . . For all these things we give thanks . . . , for all that we know and do not know, your seen and unseen benefits that have come upon us."

[90] In the standard beginning of the Roman prayers, the assembly both names God as almighty and immortal and claims a personal relationship with God: "Father, All-Powerful and Ever-Living God, we do well always and everywhere to give you thanks." Praise and thanks are then offered for specific reasons, often including both creation and the history of salvation, "through Jesus Christ our Lord."

[91] In the Roman prayer, "From age to age you gather a people to yourself so that from east to west a perfect offering may be made to the glory of your name." In Chrysostom's, "You brought us out of not-being to being, and when we had fallen, you raised us up again; and did not cease to do everything until you had brought us up to heaven, and granted us the kingdom which is to come."

In confidence that arises from the thankful remembrance of God's saving action, the prayer moves to the petition that God act to renew the assembly in faithfulness to the covenant. Praising God for the covenant sacrifice of Jesus Christ, the assembly asks for the gift of offering itself in union with Christ's sacrifice,[92] and so participating in the covenant relationship.[93] The prayer indicates the assembly's expectation that God's action of covenant renewal will be signified, sealed, and celebrated in its sacramental communion.[94]

This consideration of the content of the Eucharistic Prayers has implications for the way in which the mystery presence should be described. "From the analysis of the christological dimension of the Eucharistic Prayer the eucharist emerges as a symbolic reality that enables the liturgical assembly to participate in the once-for-all death and resurrection of Christ through the renewal of the ritual of the bread and cup, which Jesus gave at the Last Supper for that purpose. The idea that the eucharistic celebration is the liturgical medium of participation in the single *transitus* of Jesus from suffering to glory is gleaned from the Eucharistic Prayer itself, from the *lex orandi*."[95] The Eucharistic Prayer, then, indicates that the liturgical assembly, by sharing in the sacrifice of Christ, passes into the covenant relationship of communion with the Persons of the Trinity. The mystery presence of Christ and his saving deeds should be treated in the light of the Eucharistic Prayer's emphasis on covenant renewal that is granted through the memory of faith and the sacrificial meal.

[92] Roman: "We offer you in thanksgiving this holy and living sacrifice. Look with favor on your Church's offering and see the Victim whose death has reconciled us to yourself." Chrysostom: "We offer you also this reasonable and bloodless service, and we beseech and pray and entreat you, send down your Holy Spirit upon us and on these gifts set forth . . . ."

[93] Roman: "We hope to enjoy for ever the vision of your glory, through Christ our Lord, through whom all good things come. Through him . . ." Chrysostom: "And send out your mercies upon us all, and grant us with one mouth and one heart to glorify and hymn your all-honourable and magnificent name, the Father, the Son and the Holy Spirit, now and always and to the ages of ages."

[94] Roman: "Grant that we who are nourished by his body and blood may be filled with his Holy Spirit and become one body, one spirit in Christ. May he make us an everlasting gift to you and enable us to share in the inheritance of your saints . . ." Chrysostom: "so that (these gifts) may become to those who partake for vigilance of soul, for forgiveness of sins, for fellowship with the Holy Spirit, for the fullness of the kingdom of heaven, for boldness toward you, not for judgment or for condemnation."

[95] Kilmartin, *The Eucharist in the West*, 355.

ever a valuable clue to the correct interpretation is supplied by the law of prayer. For it is evident that the orientation of the Eucharistic Prayer is from the ecclesial assembly to the Father of Jesus Christ. From this point of view it appears that the eucharistic assembly is presented sacramentally to the once-for-all saving event accomplished in Jesus Christ for the sake of all humanity."[110]

The dynamic of the Eucharistic Prayer, then, points to the liturgical assembly's being represented to the Father in the Holy Spirit through its memorial of the foundational event of the New Covenant.[111]

In word and action the Church remembers Jesus' prophetic use of bread and wine to symbolize the disciples' participation both in his self-offering and in God's acceptance of his sacrifice. Jesus' blessing of God over bread and wine at the Last Supper expressed his faith that God would establish the New Covenant in his blood; eating and drinking the sacraments of his body and blood signify participation in that faith in which the New Covenant was established. The epiclesis for sanctification of the communicants at least implicitly asks for participation in the faith and the sacrificial attitudes of Christ so that through their eating and drinking the worshipers may share in his communion with the Father.

There is no indication in the dynamic of the prayer that the foundational event is perennialized and made present to the worshipers. If such a movement is postulated, it must be based on some other ground than the movement of the text of the prayer.

5. In the light of the *lex orandi* revealed in the Eucharistic Prayers, it is possible to develop a truly systematic theology, that is, one that demonstrates the interrelationship of the various aspects of the life of faith. The *lex credendi* codified by theologians from the decrees of the Council of Trent does not relate the various aspects of the Christian mystery to one another; it is not truly systematic.

Kilmartin observed that the construction of such a theology was not the aim of the Council of Trent, nor was it a task that the theologians

---

[110] Kilmartin, *The Eucharist in the West*, 355–356.

[111] Kilmartin, "Catholic Tradition," 450, points out that Giraudo and he agree on the dynamic of the Eucharistic Prayer: through the prayer the assembly is represented to Christ's temporal deeds. Casel held that the dynamic moved in the opposite direction: the deeds of Christ are represented to the assembly. Giraudo, however, holds with Casel that Christ's deeds have been perennialized, a position that Kilmartin rejects.

at Trent were prepared to undertake. Indeed, theological treatises on the Eucharist written between the ninth century and the Council of Trent, especially those treatises that concentrated on the consecration of the gifts, show no awareness of the literary structure or theological movement of the Eucharistic Prayer. Without such awareness, "they reduced the whole problematic to an imaginary 'central space' within the Eucharistic Prayer with the result that the Words of Institution were poised in the air without access to the other elements of the structure."[112] With the recovery of the Eucharistic Prayer as a unit in which the words of institution are embedded, with a new understanding of the literary-theological movement of the Eucharistic Prayer, it becomes possible to construct a theology of the Eucharist that is truly systematic. Such a theology, Kilmartin believed, should be able to address the question of the mystery presence of the temporal deeds of Christ in a more satisfactory manner than the theology of the schools did.

OUTLINING A SYSTEMATIC THEOLOGY FROM THE *LEX ORANDI*

Kilmartin taught that liturgy is primarily prayer to the Father for covenant renewal, made through Christ and in the Holy Spirit. The Church's prayer, expressing the faith of which Christ and the Holy Spirit together are the source, witnesses to the divine initiative of self-communication that reaches out to all the world. Both the prayer and the sacramental action manifest the dialogue between God and human persons; that dialogue is further represented in the various parts that make up the liturgical celebration.

In order to support and clarify the content of the *lex orandi* revealed through the study of liturgy's form of meaning and celebration, Kilmartin believed that a systematic theology of the liturgy should be developed. The relationship between Christ's deeds and the liturgical celebration should be described within the framework of such a theology. Among the major aspects of a truly systematic theology of liturgy are those listed below.

Trinitarian theology

Liturgy is a revelation and realization of the Church as the work of the economic Trinity. That work of God is carried out through the inter-

---

[112] Kilmartin, *The Eucharist in the West*, 351–352. The concept of a "central space" is treated in Giraudo, *Eucaristia per la Chiesa. Prospettive teologiche sull'eucaristia a partire dalla "lex orandi"* (Rome: Gregorian, 1989) 520–556.

related missions of Word and Holy Spirit, sent by the Father into the world to effect the self-communication that is the divine plan. All Christian theology is based on the revelation of the economic Trinity, and its formulation should make this Trinitarian foundation evident.

Christology

The liturgy celebrates that Christ is the New Covenant between God and the world, embodying both God's offer and the appropriate human response. Human persons enter into this covenant on the side of Christ's humanity, through participation in the response of faith that he expressed in the blessing and sharing of bread and wine at the Last Supper. The liturgy also proclaims that Jesus' love of the Father was realized through acts of love for his disciples and for all the world.

The traditional image of eucharistic incarnation achieved through the descent of the Holy Spirit points to the development of a Spirit-Christology that can address the temporal development of the humanity of Christ. If Jesus Christ is seen to have a history of faith and holiness, the growth of his humanity in such a history can be related to the growth in faith and holiness of fully constituted human persons.

Theological anthropology should proceed from this Spirit-Christology, which emphasizes that human nature is fulfilled in personal union with the divine Persons. Fully constituted human persons reach this union through developing a history of faith and of love of God and neighbor.

Pneumatology

As the liturgy demonstrates the shape of the economy of grace, it manifests the relationship of the Holy Spirit to Christ and to the Father. The anamnetic section of the Eucharistic Prayer has an epicletic character; the memory of God's saving deeds, especially the memorial of Christ's sacrifice, depends on the activity of the Holy Spirit. Christ is present only in the Spirit.

The Spirit is invoked to transform and sanctify both the sacramental gifts and the liturgical assembly. The prayer texts imply that the Spirit brings Christ to the Church, and the Church to Christ. The mutual presence of Christ and Church to each other results from the personal action of the Spirit. The petitions for sanctification of all the Church, and for the gathering of all people and the entire world into God's Kingdom, indicate the Spirit's activity in fulfilling the promise of salvation. This action of the Spirit is one of creating unity, or communion of persons. The invocation of the Holy Spirit, then, indicates that the Spirit is the mutual love uniting Father and Son. The structure of the epicletic section of the classical Eucharistic Prayers indicates that all the graces for which the Church prays are the gift of the Holy Spirit; the outlines of a theology of grace, then, are indicated by pneumatology as well as by Christology.

Ecclesiology

The *lex orandi* describes the Church as the context for personal encounter with Christ in the Spirit and as the sacrament of Christ's presence for the salvation of the world. The Church is a covenant people that the Triune God re-creates, through memory and faith, in the liturgical celebration. The liturgy claims that the Church lives the same life of faith as Christ did. The Church prays for the gifts of worship, witness, and service that characterized Christ's life. The Church asks that its living of the one life of faith might be the sacrifice of praise that brings salvation, and that in cultic celebration it might realize its true self as sacrament of the action of God in Christ. The liturgy claims that the Church, by the activity of the Holy Spirit, is a communion of persons united in faith with the saints in heaven and with one another on earth.

The classical prayer texts speak of the particular liturgical assembly as the Church, united in prayer with the Church in heaven. The interpersonal character of the celebration, and the invocation of the Holy Spirit to unite the members of the assembly in the communion of the Trinity through the sacrifice of Christ, has its own implications for an eschatology which stresses that individual salvation involves participation in a community of persons.

These classical prayer texts, asking for covenant renewal in forms determined by historical and cultural particularities, also express a belief that Christ and the Spirit have been active in the local Church's history of sin, conversion, and transformation. The liturgical assembly's sanctification is reached through that history, through which the community and its members are conformed to Christ.

The third chapter of this work lays out in greater detail the elements that Kilmartin united into a systematic theology of liturgy, organizing these elements in a synthetic fashion and indicating the theologians on whom he relied as he constructed an explicitly Trinitarian approach to the question of the *Mysteriengegenwart der Heilstat Christi*.

Chapter Three

The Mystery of Christ in Us:
Trinity and Sanctification

The classical Eucharistic Prayers, in Kilmartin's analysis, describe
the mystery of Christian worship as a participation in Jesus Christ's
covenant relationship with the Father in the Holy Spirit. The prayer
texts, he found, describe the liturgy as the verbal and gestural prayer
that expresses the faith of the New Covenant. In this faith the Church
proclaims that the greatest of God's saving deeds is the offer and acceptance of Trinitarian self-communication in Jesus Christ. Confident
of the divine purpose revealed in Jesus Christ, the liturgical assembly,
acting as the covenant people, petitions the Father to send the Holy
Spirit to unite it with Christ, bringing the Church and its members
into the communion of the Trinity.

From the perspective of the *lex orandi*, according to Kilmartin, all
Christian theology should be done in the light of this Trinitarian self-
revelation.[1] The liturgy proclaims and celebrates the economy of divine self-communication, indicating that participation in the paschal
mystery involves personal relationships between Christian worshipers and the divine Persons. These relationships are described in
the liturgical greeting that invokes "the grace of our Lord Jesus Christ,
the love of God and the communion of the Holy Spirit" (2 Cor 10:13-
14). They are also indicated by the dynamic of the Eucharistic Prayers,
through which the liturgical assembly is made present to the Father in
the Holy Spirit by its memorial of the saving deeds of Christ.

God has chosen to reveal and communicate self through the economy in which Christians come to the Father through the Son in
the Holy Spirit; Trinitarian theology, then, should begin with the

---

[1] The following paragraphs summarize the argument made in Edward J.
Kilmartin, *Christian Liturgy: Theology and Practice* (Kansas City: Sheed and Ward,
1988) 100–111, and passim.

relationships that God establishes with human persons. In this economy God is encountered as one who is open to receiving love.[2] Indeed, the classical prayers of the Church claim that God desires to receive the covenantal love of the members of the liturgical assembly, united with the sacrificial offering of love of Jesus Christ through the action of the Holy Spirit.

This is an image of God that seems to contradict the classical metaphysics that describes the Creator as the impassible and immutable One who has no need to create or to relate to creatures. Kilmartin, however, insisted that the understanding gained by classical metaphysics should not be rejected but should rather be integrated into the Christian revelation using the distinction between nature and grace. In the order of nature, God is perceived as Creator, transcending the created world and in no way affected by it. In the order of grace, however, God freely and lovingly determines the divine self to a relationship with creatures in time and space. This revelation is received only in the order of grace, by participation in the covenant faith of Jesus Christ. This distinction between nature and grace, Kilmartin remarked, is made by Eucharistic Prayers that both praise God as Creator and ask for deepening of the interpersonal relationship that the liturgy celebrates.

In the faith of the New Covenant, Christians know that the transcendent God has established a personal relationship with them, revealing self as triune by those relationships. In the eucharistic liturgy they celebrate that the Holy Spirit sanctifies them, unites them in the Body of Christ, and gives them communion with the Father. A theology rooted in the liturgy, Kilmartin insisted, should incorporate this revelation of the economic Trinity into its speculation on the inner life of God, as well as into all facets of its description of the life of faith.

In light of the *lex orandi*, then, Kilmartin worked to develop a theology that would be sufficiently Trinitarian to respect the implications of the Church's liturgical celebrations of the divine mystery. His reading of journals and reviewing of books, especially those in German, exposed him to the conversations of systematic theologians who were addressing the theology of the Trinity using categories that he found to be congenial with the outlook of the classical Eucharistic Prayers. He incorporated many of those writers' insights into his own theology.

[2] Ibid., 146.

Kilmartin ultimately concluded that the model of Trinitarian life that has dominated Christian theological history, one based on the fact of the missions of Son and Spirit, does not sufficiently reflect the interpersonal dynamic of the economy celebrated in the liturgy. That model, he argued, should be complemented by one that stresses the relationship between the divine Persons, into which Christians are brought through their participation in the covenant sacrifice of Christ.

While developing his Trinitarian theology of the liturgy, Kilmartin remained in the transcendental Thomist tradition represented by Karl Rahner. Rahner developed the doctrine of the Trinity from the revelation of the divine self-communication in Jesus Christ and the continuation of that divine action in the Church. As was seen in Chapter 2, Kilmartin had adopted Rahner's approach to liturgical celebration as an event of Trinitarian communion before the Second Vatican Council.

After the Council Kilmartin attempted to enrich Rahner's doctrine by giving greater stress to the personal action of the Holy Spirit in the economy of sanctification. He adopted the personalist approach of the Australian Jesuit John Cowburn, who stressed the revelation of interpersonal love in the economy of grace. He responded to theological discussion of relationship and divine Being by embracing the relational ontology articulated by the German theologian Ludger Oeing-Hanhoff. His consideration of the life of faith celebrated in the liturgy brought him to Hans Urs von Balthasar's work on the faith of Christ, the covenant faith that gives Christians access to Trinitarian communion. Kilmartin insisted that according to the *lex orandi*, the Holy Spirit has a proper personal mission, in which the qualities of the Spirit's Person are revealed. Even with these adjustments, however, he came to the conclusion that the traditional model of the Trinity, moving from the missions of Word and Spirit to their procession from the Father as Source, does not adequately describe the sanctification of Christians that the liturgy celebrates. The "procession model," he wrote, must be complemented by a model of "return" or "bestowal," based on the divinizing work of God through which the creature returns self to the Father in union with the sacrifice of Christ.

Kilmartin articulated his ascending theology of the Trinity from 1979, when he first described an ascending Spirit-Christology, until his death in 1994.[3] To understand his own position, it is helpful to

---

[3] Kilmartin, "A Modern Approach to the Word of God and the Sacraments of Christ: Perspectives and Principles," in *The Sacraments: God's Love and Mercy*

describe briefly the way in which the theologians on whom he most relied articulated some facets of their understanding of the Trinitarian self-revelation in the economies of incarnation and grace. These writers relate Trinitarian theology, Christology, pneumatology, and ecclesiology with one another, as Kilmartin did in his pamphlet on the sacraments and in his analysis of the Eucharistic Prayer. The bulk of this chapter uses Kilmartin's complementary models for Trinitarian theology as its organizing principle. A concluding section addresses the subject of liturgical anamnesis, noting some systematic and ascetical sources to which Kilmartin referred in his treatment of the Holy Spirit's action in the Church's liturgy.

PROCESSION MODEL OF THE TRINITY:
DESCENDING CHRISTOLOGY,
PNEUMATOLOGY, ECCLESIOLOGY

The "procession model" of the Trinity, which moves from the fact of the missions of the Word and the Holy Spirit in the economy of salvation to conclusions about the inner life of God,[4] has its scriptural roots in the Gospel of John. John describes Jesus, the Incarnate Word, as acting in relation to the Father in the realm of the Holy Spirit, just as he did in his pre-incarnate state.[5] When Jesus hands over the Spirit in his death on the cross (John 19:30), the Spirit continues Jesus' work in the Church which is formed by the water of baptism and the blood of the Eucharist.[6] In the sending of the Word by the Father and the sending of the Spirit from the Father through the Word, the divine Persons are revealed.

This approach to speaking about the Trinity emphasizes the unity of God and the equality of Persons, since both Son and Spirit are sent, or proceed, from the Father as from their source. This model, too, says something about the relationship of the Persons, for the

---

Actualized, Proceedings of the Theological Institute 11, ed. F. A. Eigo (Villanova, Pa.: Villanova University Press, 1979) 64–88, is his first outline of a Spirit-Christology. He first describes an ascending model of the Trinity in "The Active Role of Christ and the Holy Spirit in the Sanctification of the Eucharistic Elements," *Theological Studies* (hereafter *TS*) 45 (1984) 244–253.

[4] Kilmartin, *Christian Liturgy,* 120.

[5] David Coffey, "The Holy Spirit as the Mutual Love of the Father and the Son," *TS* 51 (1990) 207.

[6] Ibid., 208.

Spirit is given not only by the Father but also by Jesus, both in his dying and in his resurrection appearances. This fashion of speaking about the Trinity from the missions of Word and Spirit has dominated theological reflection in both Western and Eastern Churches. It is also found in Karl Rahner's transcendental Thomist recovery of Trinitarian theology, which set the basic categories within which Kilmartin worked.

Karl Rahner: Divine Self-Communication, Incarnation and Grace, and Trinitarian Procession

At the heart of Rahner's theological system is the Greek insight of the divine self-communication that results in the divinization of human persons through the work of the Trinity.[7] God reveals the divine self by personal self-communication in the economies of incarnation and grace.

Christian faith experiences God's self-communication in Jesus, whose life is the perfect revelation of God's self and in whom God's self-communication is perfectly accepted in a human life. From the claim of faith that God is truly revealed in Jesus, Rahner considered the inner life of God who reveals self, speaking of the Word as God's self-expression and the Holy Spirit as God's acceptance of that Word as truly God's own.[8] According to this understanding, God communicates self to the world through the modalities of Word and Spirit. The Word Incarnate is the perfect expression of the *Theos*, the unoriginate One of the Old Testament—truly divine, yet distinct from the One whose Image he is. The Word Incarnate is accepted by the *Theos* not just as Image but as Son; the Word accepts self as the Son of the Father. The personal acceptance by which the Father claims the Incarnate Word as his own Image, and by which the Incarnate Word accepts himself as the Father's beloved Son, is the Holy Spirit. The relational structure of God's self-expression in the incarnation, Rahner held, expresses a structure of relation found in God's own being: God's inner self-communication takes place through the generation

---

[7] Rahner's reliance on the Greek patristic writers is developed by David Coffey, "The Palamite Doctrine of God: A New Perspective," *St. Vladimir's Theological Quarterly* 32 (1988) 334–342.

[8] Karl Rahner, "Remarks on the Dogmatic Treatise *De Trinitate*," *Theological Investigations* (hereafter cited as *TI*) 4 (Baltimore: Helicon, 1966) 98; "The Theology of the Symbol," *TI* 4, 224–234.

of the Word and its acceptance in the Spirit. Thus Rahner came to the axiom that the "economic Trinity" is the "immanent Trinity" and vice versa.[9]

The divine self-revelation in Jesus, Rahner wrote, also reveals the relationship between matter and spirit. In Jesus Christ, according to the ancient faith of the Church, a human nature is hypostatically united with divinity. This hypostatic union demonstrates that matter is intrinsically oriented toward spirit and that the material world is capable of communicating spiritual reality, since it has borne the weight of communicating ultimate spiritual reality in the Incarnate Word.[10]

The incarnation further reveals that humanity's ultimate fulfillment is personal union with God;[11] God intends the striving toward transcendence that is basic to human knowledge and self-awareness to culminate in the personal experience of Transcendence itself. Rahner taught that Jesus' final act of self-transcendence as he died on the cross, giving himself entirely back to the Father, is the perfect statement of what is possible for humankind. Jesus is not just an exemplar, however, but the Absolute Bringer of Salvation, who fulfills God's purpose of personal self-communication with the created world by his total giving of self to the transcendent God.[12]

Jesus Christ, then, is the perfect actualization both of God's loving offer of self-communication and of the human potential for accepting God's offer. By Jesus' free and definitive self-transcending gift of self to God, the divine plan for human destiny is fulfilled. Jesus' choice of self-transcendence is fully realized at the moment of his death, the ultimate point of self-definition for the human person. The absurdity and injustice of the cross, then, are the context in which Jesus fully and finally realized the choice of God as the goal of his human life.[13]

---

[9] Rahner, *The Trinity* (New York: Crossroad, 1977) 22. Cf. Gary Russo, "Rahner and Palamas: A Unity of Grace," *St. Vladimir's Theological Quarterly* 32 (1988) 158, 165.

[10] Rahner, *Trinity,* 89.

[11] Rahner, "*De Trinitate,*" 93; Gerald A. McCool, S.J., *A Rahner Reader* (New York: Crossroad, 1981) 44.

[12] Rahner, "Experience of the Holy Spirit," *TI* 18 (New York: Crossroad, 1983) 206; *Foundations of Christian Faith* (New York: Crossroad, 1989) 424.

[13] Rahner, "The Eucharist and Suffering," *TI* 3 (London: Darton, Longman and Todd, 1967) 162; Rahner and Angelus Häussling, *The Celebration of the Eucharist* (New York: Herder and Herder, 1968) 15.

Rahner points out that according to Christian faith, Jesus' dying and rising reveals him as the sacrament, "both a symbol and therefore distinct from the reality it symbolizes, and the real presence of the reality it symbolizes,"[14] operating in space and time, of God's salvation.[15] His presence as sacrament of the offer and acceptance of salvation, of personal relationship to God, is made continuously accessible for the world by the sending of the Spirit, who makes the Church the sacrament of Christ.[16] With the glorification of Christ, then, the Holy Spirit enters on a personal mission as the mediation between Christ and the members of the Church.[17] It is through the gift of the Holy Spirit, Rahner wrote, that human persons accept the divine self-communication.[18]

The Church, sacrament of God's offer of personal relationship with humankind and of Christ's acceptance of that offer, actualizes itself in every liturgical celebration, especially in the celebration of the Eucharist.[19] Every eucharistic celebration, Rahner wrote, makes the mystery of Christ and the Church really present[20] and expresses the unity of the love of God and the love of neighbor, leading its celebrants to live a fuller life of self-transcendent service.[21]

For Rahner, then, Christ's humanity is God's ultimate self-disclosure, the symbol through which God makes self uniquely present in the world. The Church is sacrament of Christ's humanity, making the personal presence of God accessible for human beings' experience, acceptance, and response. The Church is given this role through the glorification of Christ and the sending of the Holy Spirit,

[14] Michael Skelley, *The Liturgy of the World: Karl Rahner's Theology of Worship* (Collegeville: The Liturgical Press, 1991) 37.

[15] Rahner, *Theology of Pastoral Action* (New York: Herder and Herder, 1968) 45.

[16] Rahner, "The Word and the Eucharist," *TI* 4, 274; *Pastoral Action*, 83; *Foundations*, 428.

[17] Rahner, "The Presence of the Lord in the Christian Community at Worship," *TI* 10 (New York: Herder and Herder, 1973) 75.

[18] Rahner, "The Oneness and Threefoldness of God in Discussions with Islam," *TI* 18 (London: Darton, Longman and Todd, 1984) 118; "Some Implications of the Scholastic Concept of Uncreated Grace," *TI* 1, 324–326; McCool, *Rahner Reader*, 139.

[19] Rahner, *The Church and the Sacraments* (New York: Herder and Herder, 1963) 79; "Presence of the Lord," 75.

[20] Rahner, "Presence of the Lord," 76.

[21] Rahner, "Eucharist and Suffering," 164; "The New Image of the Church," *TI* 10 (New York: Crossroad, 1977) 19.

who makes the Church the presence of Christ, the primary sign of God's offer of self-communication to the world. The Church, in turn, expresses and constitutes itself in the sacraments, celebrations of faith that make the symbolic reality of the Church present in concrete fashion for the salvation of human persons.[22] One commentator on Rahner's work writes, "In worship, we experience our orientation to God and, more importantly, God's orientation to us. There is a dialogical quality to worship."[23]

In his reflection on the self-communication of the Trinity, Rahner adjusted an axiom canonized in Western scholastic theology: *Indivisa opera Trinitatis, sicut et indivisa est Trinitatis essentia.*[24] According to the common understanding of this axiom, God's dealings with creatures are considered to be works of the Godhead as a whole, involving efficient causality. Since in these works *ad extra* the Trinity acts in unified fashion (or "as one principle"), the divine action does not reveal characteristics that belong to one or other of the divine Persons. Only the incarnation, in which the Word took flesh by a personal action, is considered an exception to this axiom (though the incarnation is at the same time understood as the work of all three Persons acting as one principle). The sanctification of human persons, while attributed to the Holy Spirit by the language of prayer, is not considered to involve a personal action of the Holy Spirit but is rather seen as a work of the Godhead acting as one principle.

In order to stress the divine self-communication, Rahner distinguished between the divine efficient causality with which the Trinity works *ad extra* and the "quasi-formal" causality with which God brings created beings into the divine life. Rahner described the efficient causality through which God creates as a deficient mode of the divine self-communication, necessary but not sufficient for that bringing of the creature into the Trinitarian life that God intends. It is by a "quasi-formal" causality, like (but more successful than) the formal causality with which human persons communicate ideas or self, that human persons come to share in the divine life. Created by divine efficient causality with the goal of union with God, the human person is imprinted with the divine life by quasi-formal causality

[22] Skelley, *Liturgy of the World,* 41.

[23] Ibid., 43.

[24] "The actions of the Trinity are undivided, just as the essence of the Trinity is undivided."—Augustine, *De Trinitate* (DS 3326). See Rahner, *Trinity,* 76–77.

through the indwelling of the Holy Spirit. The result of that imprinting by the Spirit, given to the person as Uncreated Grace, is the establishment of the person as "a new creation," filled with created grace.

In Rahner's view, then, personal self-communication between Creator and creature is achieved by God's acting as the mediation between created persons and God. This mediation, which establishes real relations between human persons and God, is accomplished by the gift of the Holy Spirit;[25] created persons are related to the Father through the action of Christ in the Holy Spirit. Their new life in Christ is one of "mediated immediacy" to the Father; that mediation is a proper mission of the Holy Spirit, acting in a way characterized by the Spirit's own personal qualities.[26]

According to Rahner, then, the *opera omnia* axiom must admit not just of the one exception of the incarnation but of a second, of grace. Both the incarnation and the gift of the Holy Spirit, in this view, are modes of the one divine work of self-communication. The theology of grace must then be developed as a theology of the Holy Spirit. Yet, since all grace comes through Christ, the relationship between Christ and the Spirit has to be explored if we are to understand our faith.

The terms in which Rahner framed the question, however, did not allow him to pursue this explanation in what Kilmartin considered a fully satisfactory way. Stressing the unity of divine consciousness, Rahner taught that there is no inner-Trinitarian dialogue: the Father speaks; the Word is spoken. The Spirit is breathed forth as self-acceptance by Father and Word acting as one principle, but should not, Rahner argued, be spoken of as the mutual love of Father and Son; such a mutual act would involve a speaking by the Word and a reception by the Father and perhaps even imply some sort of change in God, none of which is explained by the personal relation of speaking and being spoken. At the same time as he developed the Holy Spirit's place in the economy of grace, then, Rahner was unable to bring the activity of the Spirit as Uncreated Grace back into the life of the Trinity, and so satisfactorily complete the application of the economic- immanent axiom of the Trinity.

It seems to this author that it may be complained against Rahner that his theology is insufficiently Trinitarian, that he does not follow the implications of the Spirit's activity in the economy of grace as

---

[25] Rahner, "Oneness and Threefoldness," 118; "Uncreated Grace," 139.
[26] Skelley, *Liturgy of the World*, 132.

mediated immediacy between the Christian and Christ and between the Christian and the Father.[27] In the economy of grace, the Spirit acts as the mediation between divine and human persons; the Spirit does not stand between them but constitutes the relationship between them. If this mediation is a personal action, it would imply that in the immanent Trinity the Spirit acts in analogous fashion, that the Person of the Spirit is expressed in the relationship of Father and Word, into which the Christian is brought by the economic Trinity. In this way it would be seen that the Spirit is not Person in the same way as Father and Word are Persons, that the Spirit is, indeed, the mutual love of Father and Word.[28]

John Cowburn: "Person" and "Love" in Trinitarian Self-Communication

The Australian Jesuit John Cowburn, a student of Rahner, attempted to develop the understanding of the Holy Spirit as the mutual love of Father and Son by exploring the nature of personal relationship, applying a phenomenology of love to the communitarian life of the Trinity. From consideration of the Trinity as an interpersonal relationship of love, he developed a view of liturgical celebration as an expression of the divine love. Kilmartin found that Cowburn's personalist approach to the missions of Son and Spirit helps deepen an understanding of the Spirit's action in Jesus' life and in the life of the Church.[29]

Following Rahner's principle that the relationships that Christians experience with the Persons of the Trinity give them knowledge of

---

[27] Kilmartin, *Christian Liturgy*, 155, concludes a presentation of the procession model that is heavily dependent on Rahner's thought by noting its shortcomings in relating the action of sanctification in the liturgy to the immanent Trinity. Rahner is mildly criticized for his treatment of the prayer of Jesus, ibid., 171–174. Kilmartin had great personal and professional respect for Rahner, and few criticisms of Rahner's work can be found in Kilmartin's published writings.

[28] Kilmartin, *Christian Liturgy*, 106–108, makes this point against a "typical modern Catholic approach" to the action of the Trinity in the liturgy. Cf. 126–129, where the difference between the "procession by knowledge" and the "procession by love" are discussed. Cf. David Coffey, *Grace: The Gift of the Holy Spirit* (Manley, N.S.W., Australia: Catholic Institute of Sydney, 1979) 33–87.

[29] John Cowburn, *Love and the Person* (London: Chapman, 1966) 36–39. In the introductory lecture of the 1992 course "The Holy Spirit and the Liturgy," treating the various books listed as bibliography for the course, Kilmartin claimed that Cowburn used the term "person" in the same way as he did.

God's own self,[30] Cowburn reflected on the life of love that is grace. He trusted that the dynamics of human love would disclose the dynamics of the procession of the Spirit as the mutual love of Father and Son.[31]

Cowburn suggests that there are two types of love: "cosmic love," which is generative of like nature, and "ecstatic love," which relates persons to each other in their uniqueness.[32] Cosmic love is expressed in the first procession in the Trinity: the self-possession in which God expresses self by generating the divine Word. The Word shares perfectly in the divine nature, and so is the perfect Son, begotten by God. As a human person expresses self and comes to know self in a son or daughter,[33] so the Father knows the divine nature in the willed self-communication of begetting the Son.[34]

The second procession in God rises immediately upon the first and is the meeting of Father and Son precisely as Persons. Between Father and Son there is not only unity of nature and consciousness but a personal willing of the other as other. Cowburn calls this "ecstatic union." In such a union the difference of the Persons is not obliterated but is enhanced even as the two Persons become one in a subjective entity called "We," which is objectified in some work of love.[35]

In breathing forth the Holy Spirit, Cowburn writes, Father and Son become one as distinct Persons expressing their mutual love in action. The ecstatic unity of Father and Son is the active principle of the Holy Spirit. The love involved is personal, arising from the mutual recognition of unity of nature and distinction of Persons, but it may be called free only in a qualified sense, for the Holy Spirit is not contingent but is truly God.[36]

Cowburn then considered the economy of grace from the point of view of God's loving self-communication.[37] While agreeing with

[30] Ibid., 48, with a footnote to Rahner, "Uncreated Grace," 345.

[31] Cowburn, *Love and the Person,* 38–39.

[32] These different types of love are acts of one spiritual faculty rather than of two. They are not as clearly distinct from each other as are the acts of knowing and willing. This weakness is pointed out in an otherwise positive review by Colin Garvey in *Philosophical Studies* 17 (1968) 338–342.

[33] Cowburn, *Love and the Person,* 82.

[34] Ibid., 244.

[35] Ibid., 249.

[36] Ibid., 252. Cowburn does not address the question of how an interpersonal love cannot be free. L. Oeing-Hanhoff's relational ontology, described below, is more precise in describing divine relationships than Cowburn's analogy of love.

[37] Ibid., 400.

Rahner on the implicit acceptance of God contained in loving acts, Cowburn claimed that the distinctively Christian act of faith is assent to the personal self-communication of the Persons of the Trinity accomplished in Jesus Christ.[38] The believer's acceptance of that self-communication puts him or her in a new relationship, in which "the divine persons love us as persons, or with an ecstatic love; this is by nature reciprocal in the sense that it needs to be returned in kind."[39]

The incarnation, Cowburn wrote, expresses both the cosmic love that generates the Son and the ecstatic love that breathes forth the Spirit. God's perfect self-expression in the created realm lifts a particular humanity, that of Jesus of Nazareth, at the moment of its creation, to personal union with the Word. This personal union is accomplished with Mary's cooperation, which God requested and she freely gave. Jesus, then, "is the 'work of love' produced by divine and human persons together as the symbol of their ecstatic oneness, which he objectivizes."[40] He redeems humanity by a free, definitive acceptance of God's plan of personal self-communication with creatures capable of ecstatic love.[41]

The activity of Word and Spirit begun in the incarnation, Cowburn argues, continues in the Church, as the ecstatic, personal love of God raises the Christian to a supernatural level, a level of intimacy with the Trinity that will find its fulfillment in the interpersonal communication of heaven.[42] The ecstatic love that lifts the Christian to the life of grace must also be expressed in action. Because the human life is lived in time, not in the immediacy of God, that love must be objectivized in a life that affirms the personal relationship that God has established with the individual believer. The Christian's life of faith, therefore, must include acts that express not only the cosmic love of other human beings because of their shared human nature but also ecstatic love, which affirms the other in personal uniqueness.[43]

The life of grace binds Christians together with special intimacy as they objectivize their union with the divine Persons by carrying on the work of Christ.[44] This union is especially the work of the Holy

[38] Ibid., 331.
[39] Ibid., 373.
[40] Ibid., 406.
[41] Ibid., 408.
[42] Ibid., 377–382.
[43] Ibid., 390–391.
[44] Ibid., 405–406.

Spirit, bond of love between the Father and the Son, between Christ and the Christian, and between one Christian and another. The union that Christians have with one another in the Holy Spirit is objectivized with special force and clarity in the public self-expression that is the Church's liturgy.[45] The Church's liturgy, then, especially the Eucharist, should be understood as the conscious articulation of Christians' acceptance of the divine love, involving both personal self-fulfillment in ecstatic love and loving service of other worshipers.

Cowburn's development of a theory of Trinitarian life using the analogy of love, his description of the economy of incarnation and grace as resting on interpersonal acts of love, uniting God and human persons, and his treatment of the Church's liturgy as event of interpersonal love would be picked up in Kilmartin's treatment of the Trinitarian self-communication celebrated in Christian liturgy.

Ludger Oeing-Hanhoff's Relational Ontology

The *opera omnia* axiom of classical Trinitarian theology attempts to guard the concept of the immutable, impassible One against the implications of relations with created reality that would introduce change into the Divine. Ludger Oeing-Hanhoff, rather than attempting to adjust that axiom as Rahner did, argues that the Trinitarian revelation shows that the category of relation belongs to being as such. God has revealed self as essentially relational and has established relations through the incarnation and grace that transcend the infinite distance between Creator and creature. The existence of these divinely established relations makes it possible and desirable to think of mutual self-communication in the economies of incarnation and grace.[46]

Kilmartin praised Oeing-Hanhoff's formulation of an ontology that recognizes that "the proper being of a person is the coming together of being and relation, of being and meaning for others."[47] For human persons experience their own being as relatedness, a relatedness that they have perceived as long as they have been conscious. They distinguish personal relatedness with other conscious persons from

---

[45] Ibid., 408–409.

[46] Ludger Oeing-Hanhoff, "Trinitarische Ontologie und Metaphysik der Person," *Trinität*, Quaestiones Disputatae 101, ed. W. Breuning (Freiburg: Herder, 1984) 163.

[47] Kilmartin, *Christian Liturgy*, 147. The following paragraphs trace Kilmartin's paraphrase, on pp. 146–152, of Oeing-Hanhoff, "Trinitarische Ontologie," 158–163.

objective relatedness to things, but in both cases they consider that when a being is "for someone," it realizes its essence. Thus relationality is experienced, not as an accidental characteristic, but as transcendental, a property common to being as such.

This approach, Kilmartin wrote, is helpful because it illustrates how all the aspects of life are related to the realization of personhood; it is not a static ontology, but one that describes being as both continuous and changing, as it is experienced by human persons. This approach also connects the person's basic relatedness to the Trinity, giver and sustainer of the individual's being, with the person's relations with other creatures, especially with other persons; the person responds to the divine gift of life through relationships in time and space. These relationships are constitutive of the person and realize the person's relationship to the Persons of the Trinity.

In the economy of salvation, through the missions of Word and Spirit, God has opened self to personal relatedness with human persons. Human persons realize their personal relatedness with Father, Word, and Spirit through interpersonal actions in space and time. In the interpersonal context of the sacramental event, the performance of the sacramental sign realizes the relationship between Christ and the liturgical assembly in a way that transforms and gives deeper meaning to the lives of the human persons involved.

In Oeing-Hanhoff's approach, the stress of classical Western theology on the essential simplicity of the divine Being is reconciled with the changes implied by interpersonal relationship by introducing the concept of personal modification into the consideration of the one divine knowing and willing. God, as spiritual being with full knowledge of self, forms the perfect image of self, the eternal Word. Both Source and Word are identically the divine life, so they inhere in each other and have identity of knowing and willing. Since the one divine Being is differentiated through the expressed Word, however, the divine knowing and willing may be said to be accomplished by two subjects, Source and Word, in such a way that the divine willing is modified in the Word's self-affirmation and self-love. The divine knowing and willing is also modified to personal love between the Source and the Word through the Spirit's self-expression. This personal love, Oeing-Hanhoff suggests, is the bestowal of self on the other, a mutual love, modifying the divine will to a second way of self-mediation of the divine Persons to each other. Through this mutual love the one divine Being, without losing or changing its identity, is brought forth in the mode of being gift. The way of existence of God that now obtains in the mode of gift is the Holy Spirit breathed forth in love. Thus is constituted the third divine Person.[48]

In Oeing-Hanhoff's understanding, "Person is a mode of existence of divine being that is communicable."[49] The divine Persons are not mere modes of a divine being but are the divine being itself in three determined modes of existence. As modes of existence of the common divine essence, the Persons live in one another, but their common knowing and willing is modified by their personal modes of existing. The Father, for example, has the divine knowledge and will as the source of all; the Son, in the way of the Word expressed by the Father. Thus the one divine being, and the one divine knowledge and will, is also modified in the divine "production" of the Word and Spirit. Similarly, in the economy of divine self-communication to created beings, it can be said that the will of the Father to send the Son is modified to the will of the Son to send himself and to empty himself.[50]

Considering the relationality of the divine modes of existence, Oeing-Hanhoff suggests that person is "a mode of existence of a rational essence to the other and in the other."[51] The divine Persons, he writes, are by nature being-for-others and being-in-others. Finite persons, by comparison, are persons *in themselves* and come to be persons for others in a linguistic community. They can also choose not to be for others.[52]

Human persons, in this viewpoint, celebrate the graceful choice of being-for-others in the liturgy of the Church. In communion with the Father through the Son in the Holy Spirit, they are able consciously to constitute themselves as a linguistic community of persons-for-others. Their relationship with one another and with God is able to reflect and realize the relationship that is at the heart of being. In this understanding, then, not only is Rahner's concept of the Trinity corrected to allow for mutual dialog within the Trinity and for treating the Spirit as mutual love, but the divine activity in the economy of grace is more clearly manifested as the divinization of human persons.[53]

---

[48] Oeing-Hanhoff, "Trinitarische Ontologie," 160.

[49] Ibid., 160, quoted in Kilmartin, *Christian Liturgy,* 151.

[50] Oeing-Hanhoff, "Trinitarische Ontologie," 162.

[51] Ibid., 162, quoted in Kilmartin, *Christian Liturgy,* 152.

[52] Oeing-Hanhoff, "Trinitarische Ontologie," 162–163.

[53] Kilmartin, *Christian Liturgy,* 152, 154–155.

Kilmartin remarked that had Thomas Aquinas worked with a relational rather than a static ontology, he might have addressed the *Mysteriengegenwart* question in a different fashion. The choices that Jesus made, his history as person-for-others, are, according to a relational ontology, the means by which he realized himself in time and space. Wherever the glorified Christ is personally present, the temporal actions that make up his personal self-realization would, in Oeing-Hanhoff's viewpoint, be said to be present as well. Aquinas, however, operated within a static ontology that distinguished between the substance of the person and the accidental events of the person's life. That static ontology was accepted by both Protestants and Catholics in the Reformation debates over the presence and action of Christ in the sacraments, and by Casel and the other participants in the *Mysteriengegenwart* controversy.[54]

Hans Urs von Balthasar on the Faith of Christ

Kilmartin's insistence that liturgical celebration must be considered in the context of faith, a theme stressed in Söhngen's[55] and Rahner's sacramental theology and in *Sacrosanctum Concilium*, raises the question of the relationship between the faith of individual Christians and the faith of the Church. By participating in the liturgical celebration, whose formal structure and official prayers express the faith of the Church, the individual Christian appropriates that faith as his or her own. Is there, however, a sense in which it may be said that Christians actually participate in the faith of Christ? Kilmartin found Hans Urs von Balthasar's investigation into the faith of Christ to be helpful in addressing this question.[56]

Scholastic theology, defining faith as belief in something that is not seen, concluded that Christ, partaking in the beatific vision because of the constant mutual presence of Father and Son, could not be said

[54] Kilmartin, "The Catholic Tradition of Eucharistic Theology: Towards the Third Millennium," *TS* 55 (1994) 409, n. 7, attributes this insight to Alexander Gerken, "Kann sich die Eucharistie ändern?" *Zeitschrift für katholische Theologie* 97 (1975) 427, n. 17. See Kilmartin, *Christian Liturgy*, 156, n. 16.

[55] Cf. Gottlieb Söhngen, "Christi Gegenwart in uns durch den Glauben (Eph. 3.17). Ein vergessener Gegenstand unserer Verkündigung von der Messe," *Christi Gegenwart in Glaube und Sakrament*, ed. F. X. Arnold (Munich: Pustet, 1967). Paper presented to the Abt-Herwegens-Institut at Maria Laach in 1949.

[56] Hans Urs von Balthasar, "*Fides Christi*, An Essay on the Consciousness of Christ," *Explorations in Theology II: Spouse of the Word* (San Francisco: Ignatius, 1991; German original 1961).

to have faith.[57] Tracing the development of the concept of faith in the Bible, von Balthasar commented that the biblical concept of faith indicates not just the proper way for the covenant people and individual members of God's chosen people to relate to God, but even more basically God's manner of behaving toward the people. The Bible, von Balthasar points out, portrays God as the faithful one, and the people's faith in God as response to God's faithfulness. According to this understanding, Jesus surely must be said to have lived that human disposition of faith that God's covenant demands.[58]

That Jesus' faith is the perfection of the covenantal relationship between the Father and the chosen people, von Balthasar wrote, is explained by Jesus' nature as the Incarnate Word. In Jesus' faith is found both perfect trust in God's faithfulness and the free choice of God as the fulfillment of Jesus' life. The Incarnate Word embodies "the fidelity of the Son of Man toward the Father, a trust that is placed in God once and for all and yet is realized anew in each moment of time. In the Son of Man we find the unconditional preference for the Father, for his essence, his love, his will and command in relation to all of (Christ's) own wishes and inclinations. We see the unflinching perseverance in this will, come what may."[59]

Not only does Jesus live by faith with the unconditional devotion to the Father that sets him apart from every human person who has come before or since, but he also shares that faith with his disciples. The disciples' faith is a participation in Jesus' own faith, enabling them to receive the love of God flowing through Jesus and to return that love with Jesus' own love of the Father.[60] In the resurrection, the faith that the disciples had received in Christ's personal presence is made accessible in the Church. It is in this way, von Balthasar argued, that we can understand the description of Jesus as the author and perfecter of our faith in the Letter to the Hebrews (12:2). He gives God's love its concrete, unique realization in human history by his self-offering in faith and love on the cross,[61] and in his glorification he makes his followers participate in his own faith. Christian faith, von Balthasar holds, is lived in Christ, within whom the Christian perceives

[57] Ibid., 65, 68.
[58] Ibid., 43.
[59] Ibid., 52–53.
[60] Ibid., 54, 55.
[61] Ibid., 56.

and experiences the Father's faithfulness and responds with the trust that characterized the life of Jesus Christ.[62]

According to von Balthasar, then, Christ is, in himself, the meeting of the faithfulness of God and the human response to God's loving faithfulness. He incarnates God's fidelity, making it present and accessible in his humanity; he is sacrament of God's faithfulness and continuing offer of self-communication to humankind. His response to God's fidelity is the fulfillment and elevation of all human response to God, since, as the Incarnate Son, he experiences and responds to God's loving faithfulness to the highest possible degree; he is sacrament of the perfect human response to God's love. In himself, Jesus Christ is the substantial covenant between God and humankind, binding the two together in an irrevocable fashion precisely because of the hypostatic union that constitutes him as Incarnate Son.[63]

Furthermore, von Balthasar argued, the Christian attitude of faith does not pass away in heaven. Since the finite creature can never comprehend the infinity of God, Christ even in his glorified humanity cannot comprehend the totality of God. Even as his humanity is fixed in the beatific vision, then, he, like all the saints, exercises faith in the sense of belief in what is not seen.[64] In its scriptural and liturgical sense, more importantly, faith is the eternal attitude of Christ and the saints as they receive and respond to God's self-communication. The faith of Christ, both God's faithfulness and human response, is celebrated in both the earthly and the heavenly liturgies.[65]

The faith found in Christ, according to von Balthasar, embodies the covenant made in his self. "Most important is the insight that Christian faith cannot be understood except as enfolding oneself in Jesus' most interior attitude."[66] In his resurrection Christ sends the Holy Spirit to draw Christians into his faith, which has become the faith of the Church.[67]

The Church, then, cannot exist apart from the faith of Christ; it lives in the faith of Christ and must celebrate that faith in order to exist. Because faith is its life, it is a praying Church; its prayer, espe-

[62] Ibid., 58.
[63] Ibid., 59–60.
[64] Ibid., 69.
[65] Ibid., 74.
[66] Ibid., 63.
[67] Ibid., 78, 79.

cially its Eucharistic Prayer, is the performative form in which its faith is found. Following out von Balthasar's insight, Angelus Häussling writes that the faith expressed in the Church's liturgy is not a first step in a process of arriving before the divine mystery; rather, it is "the indispensable and enduring way to participate in the mystery; and the mystery is not something that those who have attained to the fullness of faith arrive at, but the way, abiding in the Church, to testify to faith before God."[68] In the liturgy, Häussling says, Christians participate in and express the "ontic" faith of Christ: "not a concept, not a subjective remembrance, but a reality of being."[69] As the performative form of the act of faith, the celebration of the liturgy is the way Christians enter into the covenant that Christ embodies.

As we have seen, Kilmartin spoke of the liturgy in terms of covenant renewal and entering by faith into the New Covenant. Jesus Christ, by his saving death, enters into a covenant relationship with the Father. This covenant, "just as that which existed between Yahweh and the Israelites, is initiated by God, not by [people]. . . . As the Son of God sent by the Father, Jesus initiates the covenant which will be definitive."[70] Jesus, however, not only initiates and establishes that covenant but is the substantial covenant between the triune God and humankind. It is Jesus' faith that is saving; participation in that faith brings Christians into the covenant that is Christ's own self.[71]

Kilmartin added to von Balthasar's treatment of Christ's faith by developing the relationship between the Holy Spirit and the faith of Christ. Kilmartin would also insist on distinguishing between the personal, incommunicable faith of Jesus and the Spirit of that faith, which can be shared. Jesus' personal faith was based in his experience of the hypostatic union, as his humanity developed through particular historical events; that faith is unique to his Person.[72] The Spirit of Christ's faith, however, is given to the Church as mediation of the presence of Christ in the Church's life of faith. The Church actualizes the Spirit of Christ's faith in the liturgy and so enters into communion with the Father through the faith of Christ. Kilmartin

[68] Angelus Häussling, "Odo Casel—noch von Aktualität?" *Jahrbuch für Liturgiewissenschaft* 28 (1986) 384.

[69] Ibid., 383.

[70] Kilmartin, "Bread from Heaven," *Bread from Heaven*, ed. Paul J. Bernier (New York: Paulist, 1977) 63.

[71] Ibid., 64.

[72] Kilmartin, *Christian Liturgy*, 154, 167–170.

would develop these insights in an ascending Spirit-Christology that highlights the action of the Holy Spirit in the incarnation and the life of faith of Jesus of Nazareth. In this perspective, von Balthasar's description of the relationship between the faithfulness of God, the faith of Christ, and the Church's faith, of which the liturgy is the performative form, appears even more significant.

Proper Personal Mission of the Holy Spirit

The traditional theologies of both the Eastern and Western Churches employ the procession model of the Trinity, based on the missions of Word and Spirit in the incarnation and grace. The Eastern Churches consider that the mission of the Holy Spirit is a proper one, belonging personally to the Spirit, in a manner analogous to the personal mission of the Incarnate Word. The Western Church has traditionally held that only the mission of the Word is properly personal, and that the divine action in the economy of grace is an undivided work of the Godhead acting as one principle. In the Western view, sanctification is described as an activity of the Holy Spirit only "by appropriation"; the economy of grace is not considered to reveal properly personal qualities of the Spirit analogous to those of the Word revealed in the incarnation.[73]

This lack of pneumatology is, no doubt, related to the lack of a Spirit-epiclesis in the Roman Canon. The Eastern Church has traditionally interpreted the Spirit-epicleses in its anaphoras as ascribing properly personal activity to the Spirit. The new Eucharistic Prayers of the Roman Rite have Spirit-epicleses, but these can be interpreted either as ascribing a personal mission to the Spirit[74] or as merely attributing the Godhead's common activity of sanctification to the Spirit.

Kilmartin claimed that the Western denial of a proper mission of the Spirit was due to a misapplication of the two axioms: *Omnia opera Trinitatis (in mundo) sunt indivisa; In Deo omnia sunt unum, ubi non obviat relationis oppositio.* The first axiom was commented on by Rahner, who held that it refers to creation and efficient causality, not to the economy of divine self-communication in incarnation and grace. In

---

[73] Ibid., 108, 162.

[74] This is the teaching of Pope John Paul II, *Dominum et Vivificantem: On the Holy Spirit in the Life of the Church and the World,* May 30, 1986 (Washington, D.C.: USCC, 1986) no. 62, p. 124. See n. 270, referring to the first epiclesis of the second Eucharistic Prayer. The Pope, however, states that it is not his intention to answer any questions still open among theologians: no. 2, p. 8.

the economies of incarnation and grace, the Three Persons act to-gether, undividedly, but not necessarily in a manner that confuses their personal characteristics. The second axiom also relates to crea-tion, affirming the unity of divine operation in the world. Kilmartin warned that for it to be properly understood, it should be balanced against another axiom: *In Deo omnia sunt tria, ubi non obviat unitas es-sentiae.* "This axiom affirms that the only grounds for distinguishing divine Persons is strictly inner-Trinitarian, but also that real relations between the divine Persons and works of God in the world are pos-sible, provided that creatures are capable of being drawn into the Trinitarian life."[75]

Kilmartin reported that many Roman Catholic theologians today agree with the traditional Eastern position that the Holy Spirit has a proper personal mission in the economy of salvation. "They award a personal mission to the Spirit on the ground that the Holy Spirit is the power of assimilation of created spirits into the Trinity. This al-lows us to see that there is a 'grace of Christ' in which ordinary human beings participate: the same Spirit who draws human persons into union with the Son."[76] This development of pneumatology in the West has been especially encouraged by Pope Paul VI and Pope John Paul II, who have followed the Vatican Council's call for the Western Church to treasure the riches of the Eastern liturgy, especially its pneumatology and emphasis on Trinitarian communion.[77] Paul VI spoke of the Spirit's working in and through the Vatican Council and, indeed, through all the Church's history. The Spirit brings the Church to greater awareness of its true nature as it lives the faith of Christ from one generation to the next. In the process, the Spirit transforms the Church's features so that it may be recognized by people of vari-ous ages and cultures as sacrament of salvation for the world.[78] Paul VI's description of the activity of the Spirit, who, over time, conforms the Church to Christ and to the true nature of humankind, supports a theology that ascribes a properly personal role to the Spirit. Pope John Paul II, in his encyclical on the work of the Spirit in the life of

[75] Kilmartin, "Spirit and Liturgy: Notes for lectures at Creighton University, June, 1992" (Kilmartin Archives, Jesuit Community at Boston College) 20.

[76] Kilmartin, *Christian Liturgy,* 20.

[77] Kilmartin, "Catholic Tradition," 434, n. 90.

[78] Kilmartin, "Paul VI's References to the Holy Spirit in Discourses and Writ-ings on the Second Vatican Council, 1963–1965," in *Paolo VI e i problemi ecclesio-logici al Concilio* (Brescia: Istituto Paolo VI, 1989) 404.

the Church, traces the calls of his predecessors for development of pneumatology and, for his part, teaches that the transformation of the eucharistic gifts is properly the action of the Spirit.[79]

Kilmartin followed the direction indicated by the Council and the Popes, teaching that the personal activity of the Spirit, as principle of unity between Christ and the Church, grounds a proper understanding of the Christ/Church relationship.

"The unity between Christ and the Church is a unity in plurality of persons. . . . The bond of unity is the Holy Spirit. In this optic three false understandings of the Church are to be avoided: a monophysitic, or overdrawn identification of Church with Christ; the Nestorian tendency, or overdrawn separation of Church from Christ; and an overdrawn identification of Church with the Holy Spirit. This danger is avoided by introducing the concept of 'mediated immediacy.'"[80]

The Holy Spirit, according to Kilmartin's concept, is the mediation of the personal and immediate unity between Christ and the Church.[81] Christ shares the Spirit with the members of the Church; they experience the Spirit as Spirit of Christ, and, in that Spirit, they have com-

[79] Kilmartin, "Catholic Tradition," 434, referring to John Paul II, *Dominum et Vivificantem*, no. 62, p. 88.

[80] Kilmartin, "Catholic Tradition," 435.

[81] Kilmartin offers these comments on "mediated immediacy" in a diskette file "Summary of Bibliography" (Kilmartin Archives, Jesuit Community at Boston College):

"N.B. Mühlen's distinction which goes beyond 'mediated immediacy.' To clarify the notions of mediation and immediacy it is suggested that the term immediate be substituted by that of direct.

"Direct: The inspiration of Scripture is direct but mediate. A direct action with mediation (word and sacrament); direct action without mediation (vertical intervention of God received and exercised in a direct and actual dependence).

"By the mediation of Jesus he does not accord to us an encounter with himself, but with God directly. The Spirit is not a mediator between Christ and us. He is the mediation of the mediator, and in this sense it is he who permits a direct encounter with Jesus himself. The experience a priori of the Spirit categorializes itself in the mediations a posteriori of the word, sacraments and ministry. The direct character of the relation with God does not exclude mediation by the experience that man makes of himself, community and by the historical autotransmission of the Spirit in Jesus Christ. (Bernard Sesboüé, "Bulletin de théologie dogmatique: Pneumatologie," *Recherches de Science Religieuse* 76 [1988] 123–124)" Kilmartin, *The Eucharist in the West*, ed. Robert J. Daly (Collegeville: The Liturgical Press, 1999) 357.

munion with the Father. Establishing this communion of persons is a work that belongs to the Holy Spirit, who, uniting the Word with the humanity of Christ, mediated Christ's offering of self to the Father on the cross, and who is thereby revealed as acting within the Trinity as mediation or mutual love between Father and Son.[82]

Kilmartin's Use of These Insights: Yield of the Procession Model

In the time immediately following the Second Vatican Council, Kilmartin's writing about sacramental celebration continued to center around issues of faith, covenant renewal, and sacramental significa-tion. In each of these areas his personalist appropriation of transcen-dental theology is clear. The role of the Holy Spirit, understood not just as the transcendent force of Rahnerian Trinitarian theology but as ecstatic love, the ground of interpersonal affirmation and acceptance, became more explicit in his developing system. Although he wrote more and more clearly about the work of Christ and the Spirit, how-ever, he had not yet worked out a theology of the Trinity that re-flected the liturgy's affirmations about the Persons at work in human sanctification.

During this time Kilmartin continued to ground his work on Rahner's description of the liturgy as the Church's self-realization, achieved in the Spirit and through Christ. He saw the need for a more developed pneumatology to explain how the assembly is actu-ally constituted as Church, able to receive the gift of Christ. He spoke of the sacraments as acts of Christ and of the Church, arguing that the ordained minister represents Christ because he represents the faith of the Church.[83] He described the texts and structure of the liturgy as the Church's explicit assent to Trinitarian self-communication and insisted that the members of the liturgical as-sembly should be aware, above all, that their sacramental commun-ion is a proclamation and a sharing of faith.[84] In his reflection and teaching during this time, he came to appreciate both the benefits and the insufficiency of the procession model of the Trinity.

---

[82] Kilmartin, "Catholic Tradition," 435–436.

[83] Kilmartin, "Apostolic Office: Sacrament of Christ," *TS* 35 (1975) 243–264. For Kilmartin's treatment of the need for faith in the ministers of the sacrament of matrimony, see "When Is Marriage a Sacrament?" *TS* 34 (1973) 275–286.

[84] Kilmartin, "The Basis of the Sunday Mass Obligation," *Emmanuel* 81 (1975) 298–303; "Christ's Presence in the Liturgy," *Emmanuel* 82 (1976) 237–243.

The procession model, Kilmartin wrote, casts no light on the breathing-forth of the Holy Spirit as a distinct Person, on the relationship of Son and Spirit, or on the working of the Holy Spirit in the economy of grace.[85] According to the usual Western use of the procession model, the humanity of Christ is created by the Trinity acting undividedly; the Word assumes and sanctifies the humanity of Christ in the hypostatic union and anoints the humanity with the grace of the Spirit. Fully constituted human persons, in contrast, are sanctified by the work of the Spirit sent by Christ. The Spirit takes Christians to Christ, who takes them back to the Father.

The economic Trinity, then, is described as acting in a different order in the sanctification of Christ's humanity than it does in that of fully constituted human persons.[86] This is problematic if the incarnation reveals the self-communication of God by which Christians are saved. If Jesus' own living was graced in a different fashion from that of Christians, what relation has the "grace of Christ" by which they are saved to Jesus' human experience of the Father? How are Christians to participate in the grace of Christ's faith, since Christ's faith is based in the hypostatic union, in which fully constituted human persons have no share?[87]

A theology grounded in the Trinitarian revelation that the liturgy celebrates, Kilmartin argued, must relate its conception of the inner-Trinitarian life to the return of Son and Spirit, together with the saints and with a transformed creation, to the Father. It is this return of Son and Spirit to the Father, after all, that he found expressed in the epicletic movement of the classical Eucharistic Prayers. The *lex orandi*, he wrote, celebrates a relationship between Father, Son, Spirit, and Church that is not clarified by the fact of the processions.[88] Kilmartin rejected the impulse to explain the return of creation to the Father by an inversion of the procession model. Such an attempt, he argued, is not grounded in the fact of the Trinitarian processions that is the basis for the model:

"When the process of sanctification of human realities is explained in a way that corresponds to an inversion of the procession model the

[85] Kilmartin, *Christian Liturgy*, 155, 170. Coffey, *Grace*, 31.
[86] Kilmartin, *Christian Liturgy*, 111–112.
[87] Ibid., 154.
[88] Coffey, "The 'Incarnation' of the Holy Spirit in Christ," *TS* 45 (1984) 480. Kilmartin, *Christian Liturgy*, 135–157.

question is posed: What accounts for this inversion? The statement of the fact (that) the salvation history manifestation of the immanent Trinity is an inversion of the inner-Trinitarian processions does not represent a solution but rather is the formulation of a problem."[89]

Kilmartin concluded that the procession model of the Trinity must be complemented by another model that explains the return of sanctified persons to the Trinity. This model relates the activity of the Holy Spirit in the economy of grace to the life of the immanent Trinity.

BESTOWAL MODEL OF THE TRINITY:
INTERRELATION OF CHRIST AND THE HOLY SPIRIT
IN ASCENDING SPIRIT-CHRISTOLOGY

Reintegration of the *lex orandi* and the *lex credendi*, Kilmartin insisted, must respect the teaching of the classical Eucharistic Prayers about the Trinitarian self-communication. These prayers proclaim that the Holy Spirit unites human persons to Christ, making them the sacraments of Christ's humanity for the salvation of the world and bringing them into communion with the Father through their union with Christ. Trinitarian theology, he said, should attend to this basic element of the Church's faith.

In Kilmartin's understanding, the ascending movement that lifts the Church to communion with the Father reveals the personal action of the Holy Spirit in the life of Christ and in the Church. Rather than focusing on the fact of the missions of Word and Spirit, he emphasized the process by which the Word became flesh and acquired a human history. In his view, "the becoming of the Word incarnate, as an activity of the Trinity, is a revelation of the inner-Trinitarian life."[90]

Kilmartin's attempt to reintegrate the *lex orandi* and the *lex credendi*, then, as seen in the second chapter, stresses the interrelationship of Christ and the Spirit in the economy of sanctification. He came to consider the Spirit-Christology of the Synoptics, recovered for the West by Matthias Scheeben and Heribert Mühlen, as essential for a proper understanding of the relationship between Christ and the Church.[91] Neither Scheeben nor Mühlen, however, moved beyond

[89] Kilmartin, "Spirit and Liturgy," 21.

[90] Ibid., 121.

[91] Kilmartin, "Modern Approach," 64–67. *Christian Liturgy*, 161, briefly assesses their contributions.

the procession model of the Trinity, as Kilmartin came to believe it was necessary to do. In this area there was no great systematic thinker like Rahner who had developed a model for thinking about the Trinity from the viewpoint of the ascent of human persons through the activity of the Holy Spirit.

In constructing his ascending approach to speaking about the Trinity, Kilmartin returned to scriptural testimony, as he had in his study of the Eucharistic Prayers. In company with some other theologians in the Catholic tradition, he began to sketch an ascending theology based in the action of the Spirit in the life of Jesus. After Kilmartin had articulated the basic structure of an ascending model of the Trinity, he met the Australian theologian David Coffey, whose "bestowal model" he came to embrace.[92]

Scriptural Foundations: The Role of the Holy Spirit in the Life of Jesus

The Synoptic Gospels, especially the Gospel of Luke, ground an ascending Christology that emphasizes the work of the Holy Spirit throughout Jesus' life and work.[93] The Spirit of God overshadows Mary at the moment of conception; thus Jesus is born through the action of God's Spirit. Indeed, Jesus' divine Sonship is constituted at his conception by the bestowal of the Spirit on him (Luke 1:35).[94] Jesus, who grows through his childhood in wisdom, age, and grace, is again anointed with the Spirit at his baptism. From that point he takes on a public role as one who embodies a unique relationship to other people because of his unique relationship with the Father. Jesus' life of faith comes to its highest realization when, in the power of the Spirit, he dies believing in the Father's love.[95] In Jesus' dying he hands the

[92] David Coffey, *Deus Trinitas: The Doctrine of the Triune God* (New York: Oxford, 1999), uses the term "model of return" for what he had earlier termed the "bestowal model." In *Christian Liturgy*, however, Kilmartin used "bestowal"; that usage is followed here.

[93] For a typical development of the Spirit's action in the life of Christ, cf. John O'Donnell, "In Him and Over Him: The Holy Spirit in the Life of Jesus," *Gregorianum* 70 (1989) 25–45. A summary of neo-scholastic developments of Spirit-Christology is given in Ralph Del Colle, *Christ and the Spirit: Spirit-Christology in Trinitarian Perspective* (New York: Oxford, 1994) 34–63.

[94] O'Donnell, "In Him and Over Him," 202.

[95] Ibid., 27–37. David Coffey, "The Resurrection of Jesus and Catholic Orthodoxy," *Faith and Culture* 3 (1980) 109, summarizes the relation of the Spirit to Jesus' life of grace. Cf. John H. McKenna, "Eucharistic Epiclesis: Myopia or Microcosm?" *TS* 36 (1975) 276.

Spirit back to the Father; in his resurrection the Spirit is experienced by the apostles as both the Spirit of Christ and the Spirit of God, the Spirit who binds the apostles together in a new common life.

Addressing the Theological Tradition:
David Coffey's Bestowal Model of the Trinity

Kilmartin believed that the liturgical celebration of the economic Trinity reveals the interrelation of the divine Persons and the personal characteristics of the Holy Spirit as mutual love of Father and Son. The personal activity of the Spirit is revealed in the sanctification of human persons as they are united with the Word in an ascending history of faith. This ascending movement, Kilmartin believed, must be reconciled with the theological traditions that have emphasized a descending Christology and the procession model of the Trinity. Kilmartin's study of the *lex orandi* had convinced him of the need to work with an ascending Christology even before he met David Coffey.[96] Coffey's development of an ascending theology of the Trinity won Kilmartin's respect, shown in footnotes liberally sprinkled throughout books and articles.

Although the procession model of the Trinity has dominated the history of theology, Coffey wrote, another view of the immanent Trinity can be found in Catholic theological tradition, even in scholasticism.[97] Coffey's early work attempts to incorporate Augustine's teaching that the Spirit is the mutual love of Father and Son into the scholastic legacy of reflection on the Trinity. Following the direction indicated by Thomas Aquinas in the *Commentary on the Sentences*, he argues that while knowledge is constituted in the generation of an intellectual image of the thing known, love does not produce something distinct from the act itself. The procession by knowledge, for the early Thomas, is a different sort of procession than that by love; that which proceeds according to knowledge or love will be Person according to the manner of its procession.[98]

---

[96] Kilmartin, "Modern Approach," 65–68.

[97] Coffey, *Grace*, 12–15.

[98] Understood in this way, that which proceeds according to knowledge, the Word, may become incarnate in the person of Christ. That which proceeds according to love is incapable of incarnation except insofar as love may be said to be incarnate in a person's life. To say "One of the Trinity has become man" is to say too little; it is precisely the Word who is capable of incarnation.

Coffey claims that Thomas's early position gives some understanding not just of the processions of the Son and the Spirit but of the relationship between the processions.[99] Since the relationship between the processions indicates the relationship between the source and those who proceed, the *oppositio relationis* axiom may be used to heighten the importance of the "notional" acts, those that are not "essential" or common to all three Persons, within the Trinity.[100] Being breathed forth by Father and Son, Coffey says, indicates the personal quality of the Spirit as mutual love; it is the active spiration, the common notional act, of the Unoriginate Father and the Only-Begotten Son that distinguishes the Spirit as Person.[101] Coffey then interprets the *opera Trinitatis ad extra* in Rahnerian fashion as involving both efficient and formal causality. In this view the work of creation, done merely by efficient causality, prepares for and is ordered toward the works by formal causality, which establish a real relationship between Son or Spirit and personal creatures.

Having made this preparation, from the viewpoint of scholastic theology, to speak of the Spirit as mutual love, Coffey considers the incarnation, which traditional Western theology views as a personal action of the Son as well as an action of the Trinity acting as one principle. Coffey points out that the Son is incarnated as the Beloved of the Father, so the incarnation must involve the Spirit, the personal love by which the Father loves the Son. The Holy Spirit, Uncreated Grace, must be considered the grace given to Christ in his conception and personally operative in his entire life. The same Spirit graces Christians from their adoption as children of the Father and throughout their lives of faith.

Coffey thus arrives at a unity of grace: the grace of Christ is the grace of the Christian. The Spirit, whose personal quality is that of mutual love of Father and Son, binds the Church together as the

---

[99] Coffey, *Grace*, 12.

[100] There are four "notional" acts within the Trinity: generation (of the Son by the Father), filiation (the Son's being begotten by the Father), active spiration (the breathing forth of the Spirit), and passive spiration (the Spirit's being breathed forth). According to traditional Western theology, active spiration is the work of Father and Son, who together breathe forth the Spirit, acting as one principle. Eastern theology emphasizes that the Father alone is the source of the Spirit as well as of the Son, but that the Father's active spiration is done in relation to, or through, the Son. These differences in describing the procession of the Holy Spirit are among the most serious obstacles to reestablishing communion between East and West.

[101] Coffey, *Grace*, 22–25; Del Colle, *Christ and the Spirit*, 107.

102

Body of the Beloved Son, giving the community and its members the grace of Christ in which to live lives of love. Coffey claims that his recovery of the mutual-love tradition found in the early works of Thomas Aquinas, but not in the *Summa Theologiae*, shows that Trinitarian theology belongs not at the margins but at the center of the Christian life.[102]

Coffey's inward-moving view considers the manner of the Trinitarian processions, shows how with the procession of the Spirit God is sufficient unto self, and so emphasizes the freedom of God's self-communication.[103] Considering the Holy Spirit as the mutual love of Father and Son, Coffey developed a model of the Trinity that considers both the incarnation of the Word, "the ground given in the world for penetrating to the distinction of the Father and the Son," and the sending of the Spirit upon the Church, "the ground given in the world for attaining to knowledge of the Holy Spirit as a distinct divine Person."[104] The sacramental economy, he holds, corresponds to an ascending Christology that emphasizes the Spirit's role in the incarnation itself, as well as in the life of Christ. At the moment of its creation the Spirit is bestowed on the humanity of Christ as the love of the Father for the Son.[105] The Spirit elevates the humanity of Christ, sanctifying it and uniting it hypostatically with the Person of the Word.[106] As a result, the Spirit in which the Word loves the Father in the immanent Trinity is Jesus' own spirit, and the eternal transcendental love of the Word for the Father is at the root of Jesus' human personality.[107] Jesus expressed this transcendental love, his unique relationship with the Father, through discrete acts of love for his brothers and sisters. He returned the Spirit of his transcendental love to the Father through the categorical acts by which he invited his brothers and sisters into his loving relationship with the Father.

While Jesus developed in a human fashion through his memory, understanding, and will, both his experience of the Spirit as the

[102] Coffey, *Grace*, passim, especially 1–42, 261.

[103] Coffey, "Incarnation of the Holy Spirit," 470.

[104] Coffey, *Grace,* 184.

[105] Ibid., 148.

[106] Coffey, "A Proper Mission of the Holy Spirit," *TS* 47 (1986) 238.

[107] Ibid. The love of the divine Persons for one another is "transcendental"; it is constituted and expressed in their eternal interpersonal relationship. Human love, in contrast, is expressed in discrete "categorical" actions tied to space and time.

Father's love for him and his return of love to the Father kept grow-
ing. In his death on the cross, Jesus fully actualized his gift of self to
the Father even as he fully accepted the gift of the Holy Spirit as the
gift of the Father's love. In his death, then, was the final and fullest
expression of that giving and receiving of the Spirit that characterized Jesus' entire life.[108]

Coffey describes Jesus' sending of the Spirit upon his disciples to
unite them in the love of the Father as his final act of love of neighbor.[109] This act brings salvation, because it puts the disciples in direct
relationship with the Father.[110] With this sending of the Holy Spirit
by Christ in the moment of his death and glorification, the Holy
Spirit entered upon a personal, proper mission.[111]

Jesus' own lived relationship with the Father in the Holy Spirit,
Coffey writes, reveals the relationship of the divine Persons to each
other. The Father, begetting the Son, breathes forth and bestows the
Spirit on the Son as his love for the Son. The Son, in response, bestows the Spirit on the Father as his love for the Father. The generation of the Son and the breathing forth of the Spirit are thus seen to
be related to each other in a way that expresses the unity and distinction of Persons required in traditional Trinitarian theology.[112]

This "bestowal" model of the Trinity allows Coffey to relate the
sanctification of the humanity of Christ to that of human persons.
Its use connects the economy of grace more directly to that of the
incarnation.[113]

"Within the Trinity the Father's love, which is the Holy Spirit, rests
upon the Son as its proper object. When in execution of the divine
plan of salvation this love is directed beyond the Godhead into the
world, to bring about the Incarnation, the central component of this
plan, it will exhibit, in its most radical form, the following two characteristics of personal love. It will be *creative* and it will be *unitive*,
with the former characteristic subordinated to the latter, as with all
love."[114]

[108] Coffey, *Grace*, 74, 153.
[109] Coffey, *Grace*, 150; "Incarnation of the Holy Spirit," 478.
[110] Coffey, *Grace*, 154, 166–167.
[111] Coffey, "Proper Mission," 239; *Grace*, 156–160.
[112] Coffey, "Proper Mission," 234.
[113] Ibid., 237.
[114] Coffey, "Incarnation of the Holy Spirit," 472.

As the unitive love of God draws the humanity of Christ into that union with the Father that belongs only to the Son in the immanent Trinity, Coffey writes, the hypostatic union of that humanity and the Word is brought about by the Father through the Spirit, not by the Word alone.[115] The same unitive love of God is manifested when the Spirit, the soul of the Church, unites Christians with the Person of Christ, the object of the Father's love.[116] As the Spirit was the medium through which Jesus gave self to the Father, Coffey says, so the Spirit enables members of the Church to return self to the Father in love.[117]

In the economy of salvation, then, the Spirit unites human natures with the Person of the Word, giving them the same relation to the Father as is enjoyed by the Word. In the case of Christ, the union is hypostatic: the humanity of Christ is united with the Person of the Word. In the case of other human persons, the union is sacramental: fully constituted human persons are united with the Word in a real union of grace, a personal union, but not a unity of person.[118]

In the returning gift of the Spirit, Coffey writes, Christ bestows the Spirit on the Father as the love of the Incarnate Word for the Father. United with Christ in the Holy Spirit, Christians participate in that bestowal of the Spirit of love that is the response of Christ to the Father's self-communication.

"We have received, ultimately from the Father, a bestowal of the Holy Spirit which makes us sons and daughters of the Father and draws from us a response of love for the Father. The innate unitiveness of the Father's love, which is the Holy Spirit, is actualized fully only in our response, which is a human love enabled, elicited and sustained by the Holy Spirit active within us."[119]

Human persons, Coffey writes, bestow their human love in the Spirit on the Father, as a created participation in Christ's loving bestowal of the Spirit of his love on the Father.[120] Their bestowal of love on the

---

[115] Ibid.

[116] Coffey, *Grace,* 142.

[117] Ibid., 148.

[118] Ibid., 112. This distinction is commonly made by the Orthodox in their teaching on the divinization of human persons; see Dumitru Staniloae, *Theology and the Church,* trans. Robert Barringer (Crestwood, N.Y.: St. Vladimir's, 1980) 28.

[119] Coffey, "Incarnation of the Holy Spirit," 475.

[120] Coffey, *Grace,* 176.

Father changes and grows during their lives, according to their human ability and with the intensity of their own personalities. As they grow in holiness, actualizing their sonship and daughtership through deeds that incarnate the love of God in this world, human persons develop personal histories of faith that are meant to culminate in the commitment of their whole selves to God and the saints in the beatific vision.[121]

The bestowal model of the Trinity, then, reflects the divine action in bringing human persons into Trinitarian communion through the great basic events of incarnation and grace. Coffey argued that because it responds to the basic revelation of the Trinity in human sanctification, it is a model that should undergird any treatment of the divine work of self-communication.[122] Kilmartin used Coffey's model to describe the activity of the Holy Spirit in the faith of Christ and that of the Church.

Kilmartin: The Holy Spirit and the Faith of Christ

"When the relationship of Christian faith to the mystery of Christ is discussed, the question of the faith of Christ himself should be introduced."[123] The mystery of Christ, Kilmartin wrote, includes both the incarnation as the mystery of the Father's fidelity and the response of the Incarnate Son to the Father's fidelity.[124] In Jesus' life of faith, he actualized his acceptance of his relationship with the Father, developing a personal history in which he accepted and responded to the divine self-communication. It is in that history of faith, not just in the hypostatic union of divinity and humanity, that he is the substantial covenant between God and humanity. "Christian participation in this substantial covenant takes place through the response of faith that is, in a certain sense, participation in the faith of Christ."[125]

In Kilmartin's understanding, Jesus' human faith, by whose exercise human persons were saved, was itself a freely received gift of the Holy Spirit whom Jesus experienced as the Father's unique love for him. The acts of worship, witness, and service which the Gospels attribute to Jesus were constitutive of his life of faith.[126] Through these

---

[121] Ibid., 151.
[122] Coffey, "Proper Mission," 233.
[123] Kilmartin, "Sacraments as Liturgy of the Church," *TS* 50 (1989) 541.
[124] Kilmartin, *Culture and the Praying Church* (Ottawa: CCCB, 1990) 85.
[125] Kilmartin, "Sacraments as Liturgy," 542.
[126] Kilmartin, *Christian Liturgy,* 167–169.

discrete acts Jesus accepted his relationship of intimacy with the Father, his identity as Beloved Son, as the meaning of his life.[127]

Jesus' preaching and action, then, arose from his own experience of relationship with the Father, which he invited the disciples to accept.[128] According to Luke's Gospel, Jesus' reception of the Holy Spirit at the time of his baptism made his mission clear: he was sent as Servant, to give his life for the people.[129] From that time he proclaimed the Father's love, and the Spirit gave his word power and efficacy to open that relationship to others. In his public ministry Jesus thus became the sacrament of God's offer of personal relationship to all human persons.[130]

Jesus persisted in faith, accepting his relationship as Son of the Father by a life lived in the power of the Holy Spirit. Even when faced with failure, he trusted in God, believing that what he had experienced in the Holy Spirit about the Father's personal love for him was indeed true. His words of blessing of bread and cup at his last meal with his disciples expressed that faith and his love for his friends. The cross on which Jesus refused to stop loving was the means of his fully actualizing his faith.[131]

At the moment of his death, Jesus' gift of self to the Father was humanly complete; his embodiment of the gift of the Holy Spirit was fully actualized, perfectly expressing his human love for the Father and for the Father's children.[132] Throughout his life Jesus had expressed his love for the Father by discrete acts of love for other human persons; in the moment of his death his final act of love for the Father was to pray for the Spirit of his Sonship to descend on his brothers and sisters so that they would love the Father as he did.[133] At the moment of his death Jesus, "incarnating" the Holy Spirit as the Son's love of the Father, was glorified. By his final human act, then, at the moment of his death and glorification, Christ sends the Holy Spirit to be the mediation between the disciples and the Father, thereby establishing the Church as the people who live in the New

---

[127] Ibid., 167.
[128] Ibid., 31.
[129] Ibid., 32.
[130] Kilmartin, *Christian Liturgy*, 184; "Spirit and Liturgy," 25.
[131] Kilmartin, *Christian Liturgy*, 185; O'Donnell "In Him and Over Him," 34–36.
[132] Kilmartin, *Christian Liturgy*, 185.
[133] Kilmartin, "Active Role," 421; *Christian Liturgy*, 188–189.

Covenant of love.[134] Kilmartin identified Jesus' sending of the Spirit as his high priestly work: "Through his eternal intercession (Heb. 7.25), the life-giving Spirit is sent in the final divine *kenosis*. . . . Now the Spirit binds believers to the dead and risen Lord."[135]

The Yield of the Bestowal Model

Kilmartin argued that the bestowal model establishes that there is a unity of grace: grace is the gift of the Holy Spirit. Since the Spirit is manifested in Jesus' life as Spirit of Sonship, and sent upon the world through Christ's humanity, all grace can also be described as the grace of Christ. That grace effects the sanctification of humanity and unites it, hypostatically in the case of Christ and sacramentally in the case of fully constituted human persons, with the Person of the Word. Grace appears as the active orientation of human persons to God, their openness to receive the divine self-communication.[136] Through grace humanity comes into communion with the Father.

The bestowal model, Kilmartin held, makes it possible to speak of the personal history of Jesus Christ and of Christians as the "incarnation" of the Holy Spirit. As those personal histories develop in cooperation with the love of the Spirit, the actions and decisions that make up a person's life appear as the means by which God's self-communication and the human response take flesh in history.

Such a developmental approach also lets Kilmartin assert that there is only one life of faith, which is the life lived by Jesus Christ in the Holy Spirit. Christians live that life of faith in a more or less conscious fashion; those whom Rahner called "anonymous Christians" live that life of faith in an unthematized way. Three aspects of its expression characterize the life of faith: worship, witness, and service. "However, any Christian activity has the aspects of preaching, service and worship. For the life of faith is a totality, embracing the whole of human existence, expressing itself fully in all the ways it is actualized."[137] Even when one characteristic is dominant, every manifestation of the one life of faith includes all three characteristics. Liturgical celebration, for example, is primarily worship, but in this worship the celebrants bear witness to their faith and serve one another by their personal presence and shared participation.

[134] Kilmartin, *Christian Liturgy*, 188–189; "Modern Approach," 74.

[135] Kilmartin, *Christian Liturgy*, 190.

[136] Kilmartin, "Modern Approach," 76.

[137] Kilmartin, *Christian Liturgy*, 73.

The bestowal model, Kilmartin held, also respects the dialogical movement revealed in liturgical celebration. In its description of the inner-Trinitarian life, initiative belongs to the Father; the Son's bestowal of the Spirit on the Father is response to the Father's love for the Son. In the economy of grace, human persons respond to the Father's bestowal of the Spirit upon them through sacramental participation in the Son's bestowal of the Spirit on the Father. The source of life, love, and action is the Father; the human response is created, graceful, and the divinely intended means of the accomplishment of the history of the world's sanctification.[138]

LITURGY, MEMORY, AND THE HOLY SPIRIT

Liturgy: The Life of Faith Under the Mode of Celebration

Celebration, Kilmartin held, is a primordial category of human life. Celebrations are social events in which people turn from the ordinary routines of daily existence and enact their relationship with one another and with reality as a whole in a stylized fashion that raises their consciousness and reveals the deeper meanings of everyday life. Celebrations provide persons with a way of embracing and understanding their lives in all their complexity, especially the "boundary situations" of death, suffering, or other experiences whose ambiguity calls out for powerful interpretative response. "They keep before the minds of the celebrants the pattern of life that is worthy of them."[139]

Part of the expansion of consciousness that occurs in celebration is the sense of belonging to a larger whole than is apparent to people in their daily routine. Celebration, Kilmartin pointed out, is inherently communal; it affirms that the value of daily life is found not in solitary, individual experience but in interpersonal relationship. Gathering as a community of persons, the celebrants find themselves representing, as well as interacting with, a larger reality. Thus, for example, those around the Thanksgiving table represent an entire family, even if family members are absent; at the same time they represent the nation and humanity as a whole.[140]

Kilmartin employed these understandings in describing Christian liturgy in terms of celebration of the memory of Jesus: "Liturgy is

---

[138] Kilmartin, "Spirit and Liturgy," 21.
[139] Kilmartin, *Christian Liturgy,* 76.
[140] Kilmartin, "Modern Approach," 91–92.

primarily the exercise of the life of faith under the aspect of being together 'in the name of Jesus' for the realization of communion, the
sharing and receiving, between God, community, and individual, in a
coordinated system of ministerial services."[141] Liturgical celebration,
he wrote, helps the worshipers discover themselves as members of a
community who receive the meaning of their lives from the Father's
love. The celebrants support one another in a faithfulness that can be
lived through the whole of their lives.

In the liturgy the Church celebrates the life of faith that it receives
in the Holy Spirit. By representing its own faith as the faith of Christ's
Church, the liturgical assembly represents all the earthly Church as
well as the heavenly Church and Christ himself. By representing its
faith, the Church also represents the saving deeds of Christ, which it
remembers as the foundational expression of its own faith. This is one
sense in which the Church, through the liturgy, manifests itself as
sacrament of Christ in the Spirit for the salvation of the world.

The French Contribution:
The Holy Spirit and the Church's Memory of Jesus

At the end of his life Kilmartin was still struggling to describe the
activity of the Holy Spirit in the life of the Church. He read the work
of other theologians who addressed the relationship between memory, the Holy Spirit, and the presence of Christ's redemptive work in
the lives of Christians and of the Church. In much recent theological
literature, he remarked,

"the concept of *anamnesis* is used to underscore the fact that more is
involved in the liturgy than the subjective recall of the community of
faith that takes place through symbolic language, verbal and gestural. . . . However, [this notion of 'objective memorial'] does not
adequately express the intimate relation between the activity of the
believing community and the mystery presence of Christ and his saving work."[142]

In his last book Kilmartin attempted to develop the relationship between the action of the liturgical assembly and the memory of
Christ's temporal deeds. This effort involved a return to articles that
he had first cited in 1971 as helpful in clarifying "the role of memory

[141] Kilmartin, *Christian Liturgy*, 77.
[142] Kilmartin, *The Eucharist in the West*, 303–304.

in relation to the problem of the presence of the historical redemptive act of Christ in the Eucharist."[143] The works of B. Faivre, Maurice Giuliani, Maurice Bellet, and Jean-Claude Sagne, all of whom were French Jesuits, considered the dynamics of memory and applied them to private and liturgical prayer. Kilmartin attempted to incorporate these theologians' insights into the understanding of liturgical *anamnesis* that he had gained from study of the Eucharistic Prayer.[144]

The memory of Christ as Savior, Bellet pointed out, arises from his action in the life of the believer and in the community of faith. Liturgical anamnesis is an activity of the life of faith by which Christ's past action is recalled in order to give meaning to the present:

"The anamnesis is a work, an act of faith: impossible outside it. It is faith in the 'dimension' of memory. This is why the passed is there as surmounted in the present, and in a present that is the unfolding of the 'Eternal' in our time; and by this, likewise, the passed is recognized without difficulty . . . Christ as act (as Word: acting word) realizes himself in us, in the heart of real history . . . in order that we might live."[145]

In its official prayer and sacramental action, the Church remembers the establishment of the New Covenant in Jesus Christ. But what guarantees the accuracy of the Church's memory? Paul, after all, told the Corinthians that their memory of Jesus was an incorrect one: "It is not the Lord's Supper that you eat" (1 Cor 11:20). Even when the participants in the liturgy are careful to recognize the Body, when they try to hold their lives open to being judged by the prayer and the ritual, their liturgical memorial of Christ's saving deeds might be sincerely but wrongly celebrated. The accuracy of liturgical memory, Kilmartin held, is the work of the Holy Spirit. In support of this claim, he cited a series of articles on the Spirit's activity in Ignatian contemplation. Both in contemplation of the mysteries of Christ's life and in liturgical *anamnesis*, he argued, the Spirit of Christ's faith given to the Church is actualized by the believers.

[143] Kilmartin, "Sacramental Theology: The Eucharist in Recent Literature," *TS* 32 (1971) 245. See "Modern Approach," 88; "Apostolic Office: Sacrament of Christ," *TS* 35 (1975) 255. Notes on the French articles discussed in this section were kept by Kilmartin in a file marked "Actual Presence of Redemptive Work—French Contribution."

[144] Kilmartin, *The Eucharist in the West*, 303–307.

[145] Maurice Bellet, "Anamnèse I: La mémoire du Christ," *Christus* 76 (1972) 531, quoted by Kilmartin, *The Eucharist in the West*, 304.

In 1954 an article on trends in spirituality noticed by chaplains of the Young Christian Workers in France began a discussion of the role of memory in human life and of the importance of the contemplation of events in the life of Jesus. The chaplains reported that their directees were reluctant to contemplate the details of the life of Christ; the Workers said, ". . . in the Person of Christ, we are more drawn toward the divinity of the Word than attracted by the humanity of Jesus."[146] These young people, committed Christians who took their spiritual lives quite seriously, were described as having a "theological piety."[147] Rather than considering Jesus' nativity or passion, they preferred to contemplate the incarnation or the resurrection. Their chaplains asked for help in persuading their directees of the importance of encountering Jesus, with all the particularities of time and culture, in their prayer.[148]

Among the responses to the initial article was a letter from Jean Guitton suggesting contemplation on the life of Christ in the manner urged in Ignatius Loyola's *Spiritual Exercises*. Guitton warned that for a strong commitment to the Person of Christ, "one must overcome temporal distance through concrete and human meditation on Christ, and rediscover Jesus separate from [the glorified] Christ."[149] Guitton prescribed Ignatian contemplation as an antidote to the spiritualizing tendency of the age.[150]

In the *Spiritual Exercises*, Ignatius insists that the exercitant return frequently in prayer to various scenes from the life of Christ in order to become truly a companion of Jesus. In the Ignatian understanding of contemplation, the Holy Spirit puts the retreatant into contact with the original event, where the Person of Jesus can be met and engaged. The dynamic of the prayer is most important: the retreatant is taken to the event by the Holy Spirit, who thereby guarantees that the retreatant's personal interaction with Jesus and with the other persons in the scene contemplated will further God's intention of making the retreatant truly a companion of Jesus. The retreatant is instructed to pay attention to the particular details of the biblical scene, details that are supplied largely by the person's imagination, as are the conversations and interactions among the persons in the scene.

---

[146] Maurice Giuliani, "Présence actuelle du Christ," *Christus* 1.1 (1954) 103.
[147] Ibid., 105. Kilmartin, *The Eucharist in the West,* 304.
[148] Giuliani, "Présence actuelle," 109.
[149] Ibid., 99.
[150] Ibid., 99–100.

Yet Ignatius insists that the retreatant go repeatedly to the event in prayer, take a role in the event, and derive spiritual fruit from participation in the scene. Ignatius trusts that the Holy Spirit will ensure that the retreatant's experience is a true one, that Jesus will be truly encountered in the contemplation, and that the movements of the retreatant's soul will accomplish what the Father intends, so that the events of Christ's life become saving mysteries for the one who contemplates them. This type of prayer, then, shows the divine action in the human memory.[151]

The larger context of such contemplation, of course, and the guarantee of its communicating the personal attitudes of Christ, is the faith of the Church, which provides the Gospel stories and attests to their truth. Steeped in that faith, the retreat director is instructed to listen carefully and help the exercitant discern the movements of the Holy Spirit from those of "the enemy of our human nature." Guitton remarked, "It is in the Church that I behold Christ and I determine if I am, together with or in his attitudes, in his prayer."[152]

The Ignatian contemplation itself, like the Church within which it is practiced, is rooted in faith in the resurrection: the risen Christ sends his Spirit, so Christians live from the resurrection, in the Holy Spirit. "It is because Christ risen makes us live from his Resurrection by communicating to us without ceasing his Spirit that we are able 'to remember' the gestures of Jesus (Cf. Jn. 2.22; 12.16; 14.26; 15.26, etc.), and that this remembrance changes the history of Jesus according to the flesh into mysteries actually present and living for us."[153] At the end of his life Kilmartin argued that the Holy Spirit acts in the same way in the Ignatian contemplation of the mysteries of Christ's humanity and in liturgical anamnesis. This is a proper personal activity, he held, expressing the Spirit's qualities as mutual love.

B. Faivre addressed the dynamics of the prayer of memory in light of Augustine's treatment of time and memory, and of the metaphysical distinction between temporal succession and eternity. For God in eternity, all beings and events are totally present. For human persons in time, memory unifies past and present. Through memory, then,

---

[151] Ibid., 100.

[152] Ibid., 103.

[153] Ibid., 107, quoted by Kilmartin, *The Eucharist in the West*, 305. Kilmartin's handwritten notes translate this passage and note its quotation in a further article on this discussion: G. Martelet, "Présence actuelle du Christ," *Christus* 2.5 (1955) 56.

human persons participate, in a sense, in the divine eternity. Faivre employed this insight as he described human sanctification in terms of the memory's being lifted to participation in the divine eternity.[154] In the prayer of memory, Faivre said, Christians can recover God's past actions and find that they reveal God's goodness in the present. This sort of prayer should be repeated often, as Ignatius advised with contemplation of scenes from the Gospels, till the person develops an emotional resonance with the Person of Christ and enters into communion with him in the event. The contemplation, in Ignatius's understanding, shapes the retreatant's emotions, so the retreatant will naturally act according to the mind and heart of Christ. The dynamic of this prayer of memory is always the same: the person goes to the event; the event does not come to the person.[155]

Faivre, then, treats memory as presence: to remember is to make oneself present to self, to others, to God. Only God is totally present to self; human beings must overcome alienation through their use of memory. The person becomes present to self, takes possession of self, as in memory he or she gathers together the moments of past existence and makes of them a unified experience of being. The person cannot be present to others without memory; another personal being is not revealed and accepted in an instant, but over time, as an interpersonal history is created and shared. With a history in common, two persons may become present to each other, entering into personal communion by means of their memory.

Human persons, Faivre argued, enter into communion with God by discovering God's presence in memory. This is the lesson of the Scriptures: "Remember, O Israel," for God cannot be grasped in the present; one cannot see God and live, but by memory of God's past actions one recognizes that God is acting in the present. The Gospel witness is consistent with this: Jesus is frequently misunderstood by the disciples, who discover the truth only later, through memory. Faivre claims that the classical resurrection encounter on the road to Emmaus sets up a dynamic of absence, with presence achieved in memory. This story suggests that in the order of grace memory is ele-

[154] B. Faivre, "Eucharistie et mémoire," *Nouvelle Revue Théologique* 90 (1968) 278–290. See Kilmartin, "The Eucharist in Recent Literature," 245–246.

[155] Faivre, "Eucharistie et mémoire," 282. Unlike Giuliani, Faivre does not describe this movement in memory as the activity of the Holy Spirit. Since he speaks of the Spirit's activity in the Church's liturgical memory, as we shall see below, it is surprising that he omits to do so here.

vated, through reflection on the past and especially through the breaking of the bread, to perceive things as they are, united in the eternal divine knowledge and love.[156]

Christ's memory, Faivre suggests, participates in the divine "memory" to the highest possible extent and prefigures the divinely planned participation of all people in that memory.[157] At the Last Supper, Jesus is present to his coming passion, which he has already predicted, and symbolizes that presence through the blessing and sharing of bread and wine.[158] With Christ's glorification, his human memory is divinized, for he remembers not just the moment of his death but his resurrection and sending of the Spirit. With the gift of the Holy Spirit, Christ gives the Church the power of his memory, which structures its relations with the Father.

Faivre considers the sacraments, in which things and actions provoke the memory of Christ's Pasch through the Holy Spirit, as the means by which Christ lifts human persons to participate in his divinized memory. As an illustration, Faivre comments on the visible presence of a loved one, which spurs the memory of a history of relationship, makes the lover present to events of the past, and draws the person into active communion with the beloved. In the eucharistic celebration, the sacramental Body and Blood of Christ are the visible and gestural signs by which the Christian is made present in memory to Jesus' gift of himself on the cross. The sacramental gifts are ordered to the act of communion, for memory is fulfilled in communion. In the sacramental communion of the Church, Christians overcome alienation and become present to themselves, their fellow worshipers, the saints of past, present, and future by becoming present in memory to Christ's Pasch. This sacramental communion manifests the integration or recapitulation of all things in Christ.[159]

Jean-Claude Sagne, relating the prayer of memory to psychology, distinguished between memory as the presence of the personality-forming events of the past and the desires that awaken or suppress

[156] Ibid., 283–284.

[157] Jesus' human memory is elevated to the highest possible level because of the Hypostatic Union. As a result, he is more present to (and less alienated from) self, others, and God than any other person.

[158] Ibid., 285. Faivre considers the Last Supper the first Mass; the passion is present through Jesus' anticipatory "memory" and is signified in the blessed bread and wine, as in all other Masses.

[159] Ibid., 285–290.

memory. The deepest of those desires is the creaturely desire for God, grounded on the Spirit of God who configures human persons to Christ as God's children.[160] It is this desire, at the base of personal existence, that Sagne calls "the memory of the heart." He argued that the Holy Spirit is active above all in that deepest memory, drawing the human person to fulfillment in such a way that the memory of Christ becomes more and more expressed in the memory of the gradual transformation of the person's own choices and actions.[161]

Kilmartin applied Sagne's insights on the role of memory in personal prayer to the official prayer of the Church. He held that in the liturgical celebration of the memory of Jesus' life of faith the Holy Spirit actively integrates personal memory and arouses the desire for God in order to conform Christians to Christ.

Kilmartin held that the activity of the Holy Spirit in the prayer of memory is properly personal; the Spirit acts in the same way both in individual Christians' contemplation of the mysteries of Christ's life and in the liturgical assembly's celebration of those mysteries. In either case, the Spirit of Christ's faith makes Christian persons present by memory to the temporal actions of Jesus Christ in order that they might know him not as an idea but as the Person whose Spirit they share. In the prayer of faith, the Spirit unites Christians with the Person of Christ as they actively receive his attitudes of love for the Father and for the Father's children. In this way the Spirit of mutual love, who unites the humanity of Christ with the Object of the Father's love, moves Christians through desire and memory to accept the divine gift of communion with the Trinity.

Walter Kasper: Church as Sacrament of the Spirit

A more recent contribution to understanding the relation between the Spirit and the memory of the Church has been made by Walter Kasper. He writes that the Church is "the place of the Holy Spirit," where the Spirit is both memory of the past and creative desire pulling toward eschatological fulfillment.[162]

The Spirit has been called the soul of the Church, and its activity in the Church's memory has been described in that fashion from

---

[160] Jean-Claude Sagne, "La mémoire du coeur," *La Vie Spirituelle* 60 (1978) 189.

[161] Ibid., 197. This passage is translated in Kilmartin's handwritten notes.

[162] Walter Kasper, "Die Kirche als Sakrament des Geistes," in W. Kasper and G. Sauter, *Kirche—Ort des Geistes* (Freiburg: Herder, 1976) 14–55.

Augustine through *Mystici Corporis*.[163] Insofar as the Church is understood as a corporate person, created in Christ's resurrection, that image is valid and describes the Spirit's arousal of the corporate consciousness in memory.

The image of the Spirit as soul of the Church, however, also has its dangers, for it might be interpreted as implying that the Spirit operates only within the hierarchical structure of Roman Catholicism.[164] It is more accurate, Kasper says, to speak of the Church as sacrament of the Spirit. He draws three implications from this description: first, the Church is only sacrament, not the embodiment of the Spirit; second, the concrete visibility of the Church, with all its historical divisions and particularities, is part of the Spirit's sacramental signifying; third, the Church is improvisation of the Spirit, who leads Christians but provides no road map.[165]

While he valued Kasper's contribution, Kilmartin preferred to say, "The Church is Sacrament of Christ in the Holy Spirit." This formulation, he pointed out, unites the Christological and the pneumatological aspects of the Church. The Spirit is manifested by acting in the history of the lives of believers to make Christ present. "The Spirit hands on the tradition of Jesus Christ and, at the same time, hands on Jesus Christ himself. In this sense the Spirit can be called the living memory of the People of God."[166]

The activity of the Holy Spirit in making Christ present as sacrament of the sanctification of human persons, Kilmartin wrote, is clearly manifested in the Church's liturgy. In the liturgy the Holy Spirit continues the action, begun with the annunciation to Mary, of God's plan for self-communication to human persons through the incarnation of the Word. In the liturgy Christ in the Spirit makes present in humanly accessible fashion both God's offer of divinization through personal relationship and the appropriate human response of loving self-offering. The Spirit of Christ's faith, who is called the living memory of the People of God, rouses the memory of the attitudes of Christ's heart in the liturgical assembly so that the assembly may be consciously and actively united with Christ in the sacrifice of the New Covenant.

[163] Ibid., 43.
[164] Ibid., 44–45.
[165] Ibid., 44–52.
[166] Kilmartin, *The Eucharist in the West*, 306.

In sketching an ecclesiology, Kilmartin used the patristic theme of the Holy Spirit's anointing. The Spirit anointed Jesus at his incarnation as well as at his baptism and remained with him throughout his life. The same Spirit anoints members of the Church at their baptism and at its eucharistic renewal.[167] Kilmartin interpreted this anointing according to the personalist notion of encounter. The Spirit, sent by Christ, works in word and sacrament so that individual Christians might grasp and accept the gift of God's self-communication in Christ. As the agent of encounter, the Spirit relates Christians to Jesus; the Spirit is the mediation of personal intimacy between Christ and the Christian[168] and reveals Jesus as mediating God's movement toward human persons. Jesus, then, is indeed the mediator between God and human persons; his mediation, however, is done in the Holy Spirit. Only in the Spirit can human persons see Jesus as the real symbol of God's salvation, as God's offer of personal self-communication. Only in the Spirit do Jesus and human persons become personally present to each other.

This presence, Kilmartin insisted, is an immediate, personal presence. Nothing stands between Christ and the Christian, just as nothing stands between the Christian and the Father. The relationship between Christ and the Christian is a relationship in the Holy Spirit; the Spirit is the mediation of personal immediacy between Christ and the human person. In sacramental celebration the worshipers publicly recognize that offer of self-communication and praise God by accepting it.[169] Liturgical celebration, thus, is the forum for personal (that is, interrelated, not solely individual) recognition of, assent to, and cooperation with the work of the economic Trinity.

The Presence of Christ by Faith in Prayer

Kilmartin used the concept of the Spirit's mediation of the immediate presence of Christ to articulate how Christ is present and active in the Church at prayer.[170] Christ is present by faith in the individual

---

[167] Kilmartin, "Sacrificium Laudis: Content and Function of Early Eucharistic Prayers," *TS* 35 (1974) 279; "Theology of the Sacraments: Toward a New Understanding of the Chief Rites of the Church of Jesus Christ," in *Alternative Futures for Worship*, vol. 1: *General Introduction*, ed. Regis A. Duffy (Collegeville: The Liturgical Press, 1987) 155.

[168] Kilmartin, "Modern Approach," 68–74; "Sacraments as Liturgy," 536.

[169] Kilmartin, "Modern Approach," 74–79; "Theology of the Sacraments,"166.

[170] Kilmartin's earliest formulation of this question is in "Christ's Presence in the Liturgy," in *Bread from Heaven*, 104–111.

believers who actualize their faith by witness, service, and worship, but Christ is fully represented only in the action of the celebrating community. "Only through the celebrating community is Christ fully represented as the one who already unites the people of God and gives a share in the graces of the Kingdom."[171]

Liturgical celebration, Kilmartin insisted, is meant to be a transformative event of explicit faith: "Liturgy is the performative form of the act of faith."[172] The Church's liturgical self-actualization celebrates its relationship to God in the Holy Spirit; it is "an ecclesial symbolic act, animated by prayer, which expresses love of God and love of humanity."[173] The life that the liturgy celebrates, Kilmartin wrote, is the life that Jesus Christ receives from the Father, the divine life that is given to Christians through their union with Christ in the Spirit.[174]

Christ is present and saving in the liturgical celebration's expression of the prayer that arises from a lived faith.[175] This presence of Christ by faith in the life and prayer of the worshiping community, however, manifests the activity of the Holy Spirit.[176] The Spirit of Christ's faith unites believers with Christ, giving them communion with the Father.[177] Communal worship of the Father in the Spirit of Christ both forms and defines the Church.[178]

Liturgical celebration, Kilmartin insisted, can be understood only in terms of the relationship of Christ and the Church. This sacramental relationship, emphasized by Rahner and by the Vatican Council, depends on the personal activity of the Holy Spirit, through whom Christ becomes present in various modes in the celebration of the Church's life of faith.

Kilmartin was convinced that "the modes of presence of Christ in the Church must be related to one another within the scope of a theology of faith as form of life and act."[179] The interrelation of these

---

[171] Ibid., 110.

[172] Kilmartin, "Sacraments as Liturgy," 544; *Christian Liturgy,* 45–47.

[173] Kilmartin, "Sacraments as Liturgy," 545, 541.

[174] Kilmartin, "Bread from Heaven," in *Bread from Heaven,* 5.

[175] Kilmartin, *The Eucharist in the Primitive Church* (Englewood Cliffs, N.J.: Prentice-Hall, 1965) 80–82, 131.

[176] Kilmartin, "The Eucharist in Recent Literature," 260–261.

[177] Kilmartin, "Sacrificium Laudis," 269–271.

[178] Kilmartin, "The Basis of the Sunday Mass Obligation," 299.

[179] Kilmartin, "Office and Charism: Reflections on a New Study of Ministry," *TS* 38 (1977) 553, with a footnote to "Apostolic Office," 253–260.

modes of presence makes clear that Christian sanctification necessarily involves the interpersonal cooperation of worshipers, through which the Spirit makes Christ present. Liturgical presidency, for example, cannot be understood except in its dynamic relationship to the song and prayer of the assembly, to the proclamation of Scripture, and to the performance of the sacramental action. In the liturgy the modes of personal presence of Christ in the Holy Spirit form a dynamic whole.

In the celebration of liturgy, then, the nature of the Church is seen. The Church is a community of prayer, of thankful memory and petition for covenant faithfulness expressed in proclamation of God's word, songs of praise, and common action. The faith that its members share does not obliterate their personal uniqueness but is expressed through diverse and interdependent ministries. All the modes of Christ's presence in the liturgy point to essential characteristics of the Church instituted by Christ in the Holy Spirit, no one of which should be emphasized to the exclusion of another. Fundamental to all these presences, however, and underlying the distinctiveness of each, is the presence of Christ in the Spirit by faith in the liturgical assembly: the Church is above all an event of faith, praising God in the prayer of memory and in the epicletic petition for its transformation and the transformation of all the world.[180]

The Holy Spirit and Covenant Renewal in the Liturgy

Kilmartin wrote that the members of the Church proleptically experience the fullness of God's self-communication in the Spirit given to them as the Spirit of Christ's faith. By developing that faith in the action of their lives, they increase their understanding of and commitment to Christ's relationship with the Father.

The Holy Spirit makes Christians partakers in the New Covenant by giving them the faith that Christ actualized once for all in his death on the cross and his sending of the Spirit.[181] The Christian's participation in that covenant is actualized by the deeds of faith that make up the person's history and is celebrated in the liturgy.[182] "The communal acts of the faith of believers in the liturgical assembly are,

[180] Kilmartin, *Christian Liturgy,* 350–351.

[181] Kilmartin, "The Sacrifice of Thanksgiving and Social Justice," *Liturgy and Social Justice,* ed. Mark Searle (Collegeville: The Liturgical Press, 1980) 67; "Sacraments as Liturgy," 546.

[182] Kilmartin, "Theology of the Sacraments," 152, 171; "Modern Approach," 79.

as acts of the believing community, the actualization of their partici-pation in the mystery of Christ."[183] The texts of the liturgical prayers remind the worshipers that, united with Christ in the Holy Spirit by lives of faith, they are one with the blessed in heaven.[184]

Kilmartin's understanding of the mystery of Christ and the Church rests on the Holy Spirit's role as the mediation between the humanity and divinity of Christ, between Christ and the Father, between Christ and Christians (and therefore the mediation of Christians to one an-other), and between the Father and Christians.[185] In the economy of God's self-communication, then, the Spirit is the bond of love uniting the saints with the Persons of the Trinity. From that personal activity of the Holy Spirit, Kilmartin concludes that the Holy Spirit acts in the immanent Trinity according to the personal properties of mutual love demonstrated in the economic Trinity.[186]

The Spirit unites believers with the Person of Christ, who is him-self the covenant between the Trinity and humanity. Accepting the Spirit's gift of participation in Jesus' faith, believers enter that cove-nant from the side of Christ's humanity and stand in direct relation-ship with the Father, as sons and daughters with the Son.[187] It is this covenant relationship, the work of the economic Trinity, that celebra-tions of the liturgy, especially the Eucharist, ask God to renew.[188]

The life of the Church, then, comes from the Spirit as well as from Christ. The Son imparts the Spirit to individual Christians as they celebrate in particular assemblies so they might be conscious sons and daughters, sharing the faith of Christ.[189]

In prayer the believing assembly asks the Father to send the Spirit to unite it with Christ, the object of the Father's love, so that they might love the Father and one another as Christ loves the Father and all of them. Since the faith of Christ is handed on to the worshipers by one another, the full, conscious, active participation of the mem-bers of the liturgical assembly is the way in which the sacramental action is made effective. The various worshipers' expression of faith as they celebrate the liturgy is the means by which the gift of the

---

[183] Kilmartin, "Sacraments as Liturgy," 543; see 535.

[184] Kilmartin, *Christian Liturgy*, 189–192.

[185] Ibid., 170–171; "Modern Approach," 74; "Sacraments as Liturgy," 536.

[186] Kilmartin, *Christian Liturgy*, 132–133, 174–176.

[187] Ibid., 350–351.

[188] Ibid., 330.

[189] Kilmartin, "Theology of the Sacraments," 166, 172.

Holy Spirit, the faith of Christ, is actually given and received. The participation of each member of the worshiping assembly contributes to the sanctification of all, because the Spirit of Christ is mediated through signs of faith articulated and made attractive by the personal engagement of the various worshipers.[190]

The Holy Spirit offers the believer the gift of divine personal self-communication made historically, sacramentally accessible in Jesus' relationship to the Father. The offer of this grace is recognized and accepted by the believer, in the Holy Spirit, as the faith of Jesus in the Father. By actualizing that faith in a life that includes deeds of service and witness as well as public acts of worship, the Christian realizes self in deeds of love of God and of neighbor.[191] The life of the Christian who acts on Jesus' faith mediates the Spirit both to other Christians, in a life of faith that finds conscious expression in the communal celebration of the Eucharist, and to non-Christians, through the power of a visible life of love.

CONCLUSION

This chapter has traced the development of elements of Kilmartin's systematic understanding of the mystery of Trinitarian self-communication celebrated in Christian liturgy. The emphasis on the mystery of the economic Trinity may be found in his earliest works, as was observed in the previous chapter. As his career progressed, Kilmartin articulated more clearly the implications that he believed should be drawn from the Church's liturgical celebration of the Trinitarian self-communication.

His investigation into the *lex orandi* through analysis of the history and structure of the classical Eucharistic Prayers deepened Kilmartin's conviction that Christian theology must attend to the ascending dynamic of sanctification manifested in the liturgy. In order to respect that movement, which the liturgical texts describe as the activity of the divine Persons bringing human persons into the Trinitarian communion, he embraced an ascending Spirit-Christology and a bestowal model of Trinitarian life that emphasizes the truths about God's self that are revealed in the event of liturgical celebration. In

[190] Ibid., 148–149, 155, 163–173.
[191] Coffey, "The Pre-existent and the Incarnate Word," in *Faith and Culture* 5 (1983) 70.

the liturgy, he argued, the Holy Spirit is revealed as the mutual love uniting Father and Son, uniting the humanity of Christ with the divine Word, and uniting Christians with one another in the Body of Christ that is the Church.

It is within the systematic view sketched in this chapter, Kilmartin argued, that the theologian should investigate the mystery presence of Christ and his saving deeds in liturgical celebration. A proper approach to the mystery presence, he believed, is given in the dynamic of the prayer of memory, both private contemplation and liturgical *anamnesis*. Memory, he wrote, integrates the human person's discrete temporal experiences, allowing persons to understand who they are, to appropriate and interpret their experiences, and to perceive their own identity as persons moving through the dimension of time. The memory of the Church operates in somewhat the same way, insofar as the Church, sacrament of Christ in the Spirit, may be described as a corporate person, as Christ's personal presence to the world since his resurrection.

The Holy Spirit, whose activity in the life of faith of Jesus Christ is emphasized in Kilmartin's Spirit-Christology, continues to act in the life of Christians, who share in Christ's faith. In Jesus' life of faith, the Spirit acted as the Spirit of his faith, as Spirit of Sonship, of his experience of being loved by the Father and of offering himself in love for the Father. That Spirit is sent, ultimately by the Father, through Jesus' passion and death, to unite Jesus' disciples into his Body. The Spirit, then, comes to Christians as the Spirit of the faith of Jesus, the Spirit in which he sealed the New Covenant, the Spirit of his sacrificial self-offering.

Acting as the memory of the Church, Kilmartin argued, the Spirit is the architect of the Church's liturgy. The Holy Spirit ensures that as the Church's self-realization develops through time and across cultures, it still is a true memorial, not of the idea of Jesus' self-offering, but of Jesus Christ himself. Remembering Jesus, the Church makes memorial of the concrete temporal events in which Jesus Christ actualized his faith in response to the Father's love for him and for all the world.

In the light of Kilmartin's investigation into the prayer of memory, the invocation of the Holy Spirit, implied in the anamnetic section of the Eucharistic Prayer, is a petition for accurate and transforming memory of the events that have established the Church. Recognizing that the Spirit who gathers the Church into Christ's Body is the Spirit of Jesus' faith, the Spirit of Sonship, of mutual love, the Church asks that by remembering Jesus' acts of love through its verbal and gestural prayer the entire liturgical assembly may receive the covenant faith that brings Christians into the Trinitarian communion.

The dynamic of memory, Kilmartin believed, indicates that the Holy Spirit's action does not bring the perennialized essence of Christ's temporal actions from the past into the present of the liturgy. In private contemplation of the mysteries of the life of Christ, the Spirit takes the retreatant back to the biblical scene, gracing the retreatant with the encounter with Jesus Christ that is necessary in order for the retreatant to become a companion of Jesus. In the communal celebration of the liturgy, similarly, the Holy Spirit takes the liturgical assembly back to the cross in order to grace the assembly with the communion with the Trinity achieved by Jesus Christ in the Holy Spirit through his passion. As Spirit of Jesus' faith, the Spirit in the Church remembers his deeds and the attitudes of love they expressed. That memory integrates the Church's past history of grace, grounds hope for the eschatological future, and provides life and understanding in the present.

This chapter has indicated the elements that Kilmartin would gather together in his description of the mystery presence of Christ in the liturgy and has shown his dependence on particular theologians in developing his own understanding of the revelation of the Trinitarian self-communication. The fourth chapter will assemble those elements in a presentation of his proposed solution to the *Mysteriengegenwart* question.

Chapter Four

Synthesis of Kilmartin's Contribution:
The Activity of the Holy Spirit
in Liturgical Anamnesis

This chapter traces Kilmartin's understanding of the activity of the Holy Spirit in the Church's liturgical anamnesis of Jesus Christ and his saving deeds. This description involves three steps.

First, the temporal deeds of Christ are described as the realization of his life of faith and as the realization of his love of God in acts of love for his neighbor.

Next, three results or effects of Christ's temporal deeds are described. The Trinitarian plan of personal self-communication to created beings is fulfilled in his life of faith. The New Covenant between God and humankind is established in his personal history and sealed with his death. With his glorification the heavenly liturgy is established and is extended to time and space through the sending of the Holy Spirit upon the Church.

The third step is a consideration of liturgical anamnesis. The Church's liturgy celebrates the covenant faith in which Jesus Christ passed from this world to the Father. Through the liturgical memorial of the deeds in which the New Covenant was sealed, the Spirit of Christ's faith gives Christians the attitudes that Christ expressed in the covenant sacrifice. Actualizing the Spirit of Christ's faith in the liturgical celebration, Christian worshipers appropriate Christ's sacrificial attitudes in the particular situations of their own lives. They enter into the New Covenant on the side of Christ's humanity as they accept the gift of configuration to Christ in his self-offering response to the Father's love.

In the works written at the end of his career, Kilmartin outlined a systematic understanding of the liturgical celebration of the Church's faith. His own expression of this synthesis, however, was incomplete; he never gathered the elements of that synthesis, spread through the many writings of his long career, into a single extended presentation. As a result, even the summary of his theology in *Christian Liturgy* is incomplete.

Christian Liturgy deals with human celebration, insists on the importance of returning all theological reflection to the economic Trinity, and lays out the development of the Church's understanding of the liturgical presences of Christ from *Mediator Dei* through John Paul II's *Dominum et Vivificantem*. The book, however, offers no explicit treatment of liturgical anamnesis, a subject which, as has been seen, Kilmartin treats at some length in various articles.[1]

Similarly striking is that Kilmartin's "salvation history liturgical theology"[2] emphasizes historicity rather than history.[3] Kilmartin insists on the historicity of the divine self-communication in Jesus Christ. The fact that Jesus' humanity developed by acquiring a personal history of faith is central to Kilmartin's understanding of Christ and the Church. Salvation history, for Kilmartin, is "the history of the acceptance of God's love through the exercise of human freedom."[4] Kilmartin's ascending Spirit-Christology allows him to make the parallel between Jesus' life of faith, in which he experienced and responded to the divine self-communication, and the life of faith of ordinary human persons. The fact that Jesus had a history of faith in which the Holy Spirit was experienced and expressed is, for Kilmartin, an essential point.

Kilmartin was less concerned with the question of whether particular incidents reported in the Gopels actually occurred. The primitive Church's testimony to Jesus' character, to his loving relationship to the Father, to his life as "person for others," and to his prophetic use of bread and wine at the Last Supper was indeed central to Kilmartin's theology. This testimony, however, is witness to the faith of the Church, alive in the Holy Spirit of Christ's faith. Kilmartin treasured the scriptural accounts of Jesus' life precisely as testimony to the authentic faith of the Church.

---

[1] H. B. Meyer, "Eine Trinitarische Theologie der Liturgie," *Zeitschrift für Katholische Theologie* 113 (1991) 26, remarks on the lack of a specific treatment of anamnesis in *Christian Liturgy: Theology and Practice* (Kansas City: Sheed and Ward, 1988).

[2] Kilmartin used these terms to describe his theology of the Eucharist in "The Catholic Tradition of Eucharistic Theology: Towards the Third Millennium," *Theological Studies* (hereafter cited as *TS*) 55 (1994) 449, 456.

[3] Meyer, "Trinitarische Theologie," 26.

[4] Kilmartin, *Christian Liturgy*, 87.

Similarly, that the Church in the liturgy makes memorial of the Trinitarian self-communication in Jesus' life of faith is a point that Kilmartin addressed, in developing fashion and sometimes in passing, in articles spread over the years. Numerous articles detailing variations in liturgical practice testify to the importance he placed on understanding historical developments in order to discover the content of the *lex orandi*. He insisted that Christians should appreciate the historicity of the liturgical transmission of the Church's faith. For two millennia Christians have actualized the Spirit of Christ's faith, mediating the presence of Christ to each other, through concrete liturgical celebrations of communities with histories of sin and grace.[5] This understanding is more central to Kilmartin's theology than emphasis on one or other historical detail.

This chapter presents a synthesis of Kilmartin's work on the activity of the Holy Spirit in liturgical anamnesis. The various elements of this synthesis have been described in the second and third chapters of this book. Though Kilmartin developed all of these elements, however, he never assembled them into a single presentation, as is done here.

TEMPORAL DEEDS OF CHRIST

Kilmartin's discussion of the temporal deeds of Christ, like his entire theological system, is set in a Trinitarian context. The paschal mystery, which gives life to the Church, reveals the economic Trinity. The economy of Trinitarian self-communication, in turn, reveals the immanent Trinity. In other words, it is the transcendental love of the immanent Trinity that is expressed in the movement of the divine Persons toward a creation that is called into being in order to receive the interpersonal divine love in space and time. The action of the economic Trinity may in this sense be called sacrament of the immanent Trinity. Jesus Christ, then, is real symbol or sacrament of the economy of Trinitarian self-communication—both the movement of God toward created persons and the acceptance of the divine love by human persons who open themselves to God's grace. In Kilmartin's favored terminology, Christ is sacrament of the divine-human love of God and the divine-human love of humankind.[6] The Church, in turn,

[5] Ibid., 22, 60. The argument of *Culture and the Praying Church* (Ottawa: CCCB, 1990) is that inculturation of the liturgy is demanded by the fact that the Church's faith is mediated through liturgical celebration.

[6] Kilmartin, *Christian Liturgy*, 216–217.

is sacrament of Christ in the Holy Spirit. The Church's self-offering, united by the Holy Spirit with the self-offering of Christ, is sacrament of the transcendental love with which the Son responds to the Father's love in the immanent Trinity.

In considering the dialogical nature of the Trinitarian economy, it must be remembered that the divine self-communication is qualitatively different from communication among human persons. True self-communication, the gift of self that invites and establishes a lasting interpersonal communion, is possible only for God.[7] The communication of human persons with one another is always imperfect. There is a communication of facts or feelings, leading to moments of communion among persons with shared history and commitment. Human persons are unable to respond to the divine initiative by an answering communication of self; they can only open or offer themselves to receive the divine gift. In this self-offering the person accepts the meaning of life from God's hand rather than claiming to define the meaning of his or her own existence. This self-offering Kilmartin terms "sacrifice." A person's sacrificial offering is not achieved in an instant but is realized over time through a history of experiences and decisions that constitute a life of thankfulness, praise, and love.[8]

Acceptance of the divine self-communication results in the fulfillment and transformation of human nature, the divinization that is God's purpose. The highest possible realization of the graceful fulfillment and transformation of human nature has been achieved, by the divine action through Word and Holy Spirit, in the life of faith of Jesus Christ.[9] Through the history of actions by which he opened himself to receive the meaning of his life from God's hand, the divine self-communication has been accepted to the fullest extent possible to a human nature. His life of faith has become the one perfect response to the divine plan. The plan of Trinitarian self-communication is fulfilled in respect to other human persons through their participation in the faith of Christ.

Self-offering acceptance of the divine self-communication shapes the person's relationship not just with God but with other human persons. As persons develop a shared history of cooperating with the divine grace, they not only enter more deeply into communion with the

[7] Ibid., 82.
[8] Ibid., 55, 64–65.
[9] Ibid., 81–82.

Trinity but also are able to communicate more intimately with one another. Their communion with one another, based in common decisions and actions, is raised to new heights by virtue of their communion with God. One of the gifts celebrated in the liturgy is this graceful growth of communion. Liturgy, indeed, is the event of interpersonal communication in which Christians explicitly open themselves to receive the divine self-communication. The graceful communion among the worshipers who celebrate the Church's liturgy should be recognized as sacrament of the communion of Christ and the Church, as well as sacrament of the Holy Spirit, who is the transcendental love binding Father and Son in the immanent Trinity.

Realization of Jesus' Life of Faith in the Holy Spirit

Jesus' primary experience was the Father's loving self-communication;[10] as the Incarnate Son, his Person is the Word of the Father's self-communication, anointed with the Spirit of the Father's love. "The Holy Spirit is bestowed by the Father in the very act by which the created humanity of Jesus is sanctified and united in person to the Word . . . this sanctification by the Spirit is the fullest realization of the potential of a human being for unity with the divine."[11] Jesus accepted himself as beloved by developing a personal history of acts of self-offering to receive the Father's love.[12] The active, conscious acceptance of the divine offer of self-communication, which characterized both Jesus' action and his teaching, is the faith of Christ. "This response of faith by Jesus, carried on through the whole of his life, can be described as the progressive upward growth of his humanity toward the goal of the highest possible embodiment of the acceptable response to the covenant initiative of the Father in him."[13]

Jesus' history expressed his response to that self-communication of the Father which constituted him as Person. Although his divine Sonship was something given, in his humanity he had the task of realizing that Sonship in progressive, developing fashion through the exercise of human freedom, expressed in categorical acts of love. In this realization of his Sonship, Jesus developed his conscious knowledge of his relationship with the Father and experienced in his humanity the communion between Father and Son in the immanent

---

[10] Ibid., 167.

[11] Kilmartin, *Culture and the Praying Church*, 84–85.

[12] Kilmartin, *Christian Liturgy*, 169.

[13] Kilmartin, *The Eucharist in the West* (Collegeville: The Liturgical Press, 1999) 357.

Trinity. Considered in this light, Jesus' orientation in love toward the Father is the psychological dimension of the hypostatic union.[14]

The actions of Jesus' life, then, constitute a history of ascent in which the Incarnate Word developed and actualized a personality through choices and interactions with others.[15] Through these categorial acts the Word actualized self in human history. "By his human acts of faith the man Jesus responds to his own mystery, which is the mystery of the fidelity of the Father to his covenant with humanity."[16] The mystery of the Father's covenant fidelity also involves the action of the Holy Spirit, whose active presence must be considered central to the development of Jesus' historical personality. Not only was it by the Spirit's personal action that Christ's humanity was elevated to hypostatic union with the Word, but the Spirit rested upon Jesus, abiding in his consciousness as mediation of the Father's love for him and of his answering love of the Father. The Holy Spirit, then, may be called the content of Jesus' faith-relationship with the Father.

Jesus accepted the Father's loving self-communication in the Holy Spirit, whom he experienced as Spirit of the Father's love for him. He responded in the way proper to humanity: he expressed his self-offering love of the Father through acts of love for the Father's children. Through these actions the Spirit of the Son's answering love for the Father was expressed in categorical acts of love inspired by the Spirit.[17] Through his history of acts of self-offering response, his experience of the Father's loving self-communication deepened; his personal history, then, involved ever-deepening reception of the Father's gift as well as response to that gift.

Jesus' death sealed his personal history of responding to the Father's love through categorial acts of love for God and neighbor. His personal history of faith contains the fullest possible human acceptance of and response to God's offer of self-communication. "When his humanity was fully realized, in relation to the Father and to the whole of humankind, through the offering of his life for the world's salvation, the grace of the incarnation was fully realized in him."[18] In him, then, were fulfilled both the divine action of self-

---

[14] Kilmartin, *Culture and the Praying Church*, 85; *Christian Liturgy*, 154.

[15] Kilmartin, *Christian Liturgy*, 169.

[16] Kilmartin, "Sacraments as Liturgy of the Church" *TS* 50 (1989) 541.

[17] Kilmartin, *Christian Liturgy*, 169.

[18] Ibid., 154.

communication to a created humanity and the human response of loving self-offering to receive the divine gift. The Word had become as fully incarnated as possible in a human history of personal experience, choice, and self-acceptance. The Holy Spirit, as mutual love, was also "incarnated," that is, as fully expressed as possible in a personal history, in Jesus' history of experiencing the Father's love and responding by loving self-offering.[19]

Since the Word and the Spirit have developed this history, their personal activity has been modified through the actions that make up Jesus' life of faith. According to a relational ontology, "the proper being of a person is the coming together of being and relation, of being and meaning for others."[20] Jesus was totally fulfilled as a person of faith as he died; being and relation were united as he offered himself "once and for all to the Father in order to receive from the Father the meaning of his life." Being and meaning for others came together as he offered himself "as man for others to draw believers into personal communion with himself and so into communion with the Father."[21]

The categorial acts in which being and meaning came together to make up Jesus' life of faith have modified the presence of the Word in the world; the Word has become present in history as actualized in Jesus' personal development. Because of this history, the Incarnate Word in glory is always present as the Crucified One, now Risen. The Holy Spirit's action also has been modified through the personal history of Christ; the Spirit of mutual love is present as Spirit of the Father's love for Christ and as Spirit of Christ's loving response of self-offering to the Father. As the mutual love of Father and Son, the Spirit has a proper personal action of "divinization," of joining created humanities to the Person of the Word. This personal action has been modified through Christ's life; it communicates the attitudes of loving self-sacrifice that the Incarnate Word expressed throughout his life of faith and ultimately in his death on the cross.[22] The Holy Spirit, mediation of the Father's self-communication and of the Incarnate Word's sacrificial response, is sent upon Christians as the Spirit of Christ's faith, fully actualized in the death of the cross. The Spirit of mutual love, then, is received as Spirit of the faith of the New

[19] Kilmartin, "Sacraments as Liturgy," 541–542.
[20] Kilmartin, *Christian Liturgy,* 147.
[21] Kilmartin, "Catholic Tradition," 445.
[22] Kilmartin, *Christian Liturgy,* 172.

Covenant, through which human persons enter into the covenant sacrifice of Christ and so into the covenant relationship of communion with the Trinity.

Jesus as Beloved of the Father,
Loving the Father by Loving the Father's Children

Jesus actualized and developed his orientation to the Father through acts of love for his neighbor, manifesting the unity of the love of God and the love of neighbor: for human persons, the love of God is expressed preeminently in acts of love of neighbor. Through deeds of love for his neighbor, Jesus developed a history of categorical acts of love for the Father in the Holy Spirit. This history of human actions expressed the Word's transcendental love of the Father.

Jesus' actions communicated the belief that the Father's unique love for him expressed a divine offer of love to all persons. His mission was not just to be loved by the Father and to return that love through sacrificial self-offering but also to bring all people into that love. In his preaching, as well, he offered the gift of the Holy Spirit to those who believe.[23] As he announced the inbreaking of God's kingdom and the coming of a new dispensation of grace, he preached his Father's offering of self-communication in the Spirit to all people.[24] The appropriate response to this offer, he taught, is humble acceptance of God's gift through acts of love of God and of neighbor.

Jesus' prophetic blessing and sharing of bread and wine at the Last Supper proclaimed that the covenant sacrifice of his life was offered not for his own sake but for "the many." In his death, he believed, God's faithful love would be manifested, and a new covenantal relationship between God and human persons would be established through him. The table prayer and the sharing of food and drink revealed his faith that through his self-offering the Father would give "the many" a participation in the communion of the New Covenant.

RESULTS/EFFECTS OF CHRIST'S TEMPORAL DEEDS

Fulfillment of the Divine Plan of Self-Communication

Christ's history expressed an ever-deepening acceptance of his personal identity as the Beloved of the Father,[25] as his acts of love of

[23] Kilmartin, *Culture and the Praying Church*, 86.
[24] Kilmartin, *Christian Liturgy*, 215.
[25] Ibid., 167.

neighbor expressed his answering love for the Father. In this way the divine offer of self-communication was given perfect acceptance in human history, and in Christ God's purpose for creation was accomplished.[26] In this history the Trinitarian nature of this economy was also revealed, as the Holy Spirit mediated the Father's love for Christ and Christ's loving response to the Father; Christ's life of faith was lived "in the Holy Spirit."

Jesus' *transitus* to the Father at his death fulfilled the ultimate meaning of creation on the level of his own experience. The divine plan revealed in Christ, however, involves the free inclusion of all human persons in that *transitus*.[27] The fulfillment of that plan in the lives of "the many" is achieved through the action of the Holy Spirit, sent through the humanity of Christ. The Spirit of mutual love between Father and Son is sent "through Christ" to mediate the perfect human experience of the Father's love and the perfect human response of self-offering, which acquired its expression in human history through Christ. The Spirit comes to human persons through Christ, with a presence modified in human history by Christ's categorial acts of love.

The Spirit is sent from the Father in answer to the prayer of Christ that the Father's will be done, that human persons accept the divine offer of self-communication. At the moment of his death, Jesus expressed his trust and love by handing over his Spirit to the Father. Because he loved the Father in the way proper to human persons, he

---

[26] Kilmartin, following the teaching of Ignatius Loyola in the *Spiritual Exercises*, considered the whole of creation as the means God employs to bring human persons into the divine life of love. Kilmartin first expressed this understanding in a section of his doctoral dissertation that comments on the Reformation doctrine that created reality has been radically corrupted by human sin. Kilmartin described a Catholic view of the inherent goodness of creation and wrote that the renewal of creation in Christ is a transformation of human persons, so that they make proper use of a creation that itself is incapable of sin.

"This change of relation to God [i.e., sin] did, however, bring about the necessity of a new creation if God would again find a human resonance in the praise which the rest of creation, in its own way, continued to reflect. The work of the new creation, therefore, is directed immediately to man alone, though not to man as an individual. Its most basic characteristic, both in the state of the Messianic promise and in the state of its eschatological fulfillment is that of bringing together a *People of God*."—Kilmartin, "Eschatology and the Evanston Congress," S.T.D. dissertation (Rome: Pontifical Gregorian University, 1958) 220–221.

[27] Kilmartin, *Catholic Tradition*, 452.

asked the Father to send the Spirit of his own faith and love upon the disciples and upon all the world. In the Spirit, persons would know themselves as the Father's beloved children and would respond by loving the Father and one another as he did. But the love with which Jesus Christ loved the Father and was loved by the Father is the Holy Spirit, who rested upon him as the Father's love of the Incarnate Son. If human persons are to love the Father as Jesus does, they must also have the experience of being uniquely loved by that love with which the Father loves the Word Incarnate. That is possible only through a participation in the life of faith of Jesus, the Beloved, through the out-pouring of the Spirit of the Father's love for the Son.

Jesus' prayer for the sending of the Spirit, granted by the Father as the fulfillment of the divine plan for the world, is his high priestly mediation. It is also his highest expression of his love for the Father; his prayer expresses the obedience of the Incarnate Son to the divine plan for the world.[28] Through the sending of the Spirit the fulfillment of humankind is also realized. Human persons, created with an ori-entation toward the Transcendent, yearn for the perfect happiness of personal union with God; this yearning is fulfilled in the gift of com-munion with the Trinity. Jesus' greatest act of love of neighbor, there-fore, is his invocation of the Holy Spirit.[29]

Establishment of the New Covenant

The New Covenant between God and the world is made at the di-vine initiative and entered into freely by human persons. It is a cove-nant of divine self-communication, embodied in the hypostatic union of humanity and divinity in Christ. The embodiment of the covenant —both the divine offer and the human response—was completed in time and space through the history of choices and actions through which Jesus accepted and responded to the Father's love.

Christ himself, fully human and fully divine, is the substantial covenant between God and humanity. Human persons can enter this covenant on the side of Christ's humanity, by sharing in his covenant faith. Jesus' faith was the gift of the Holy Spirit, who is the mutual love of Father and Son; in the Spirit, Jesus realized the Father's love for him and his answering love of the Father. The Holy Spirit, given

---

[28] Kilmartin, *Christian Liturgy*, 169–171.
[29] Kilmartin, *Culture and the Praying Church*, 90.

to the disciples as Spirit of Christ's faith, is the mediation through which human persons participate in the covenant.[30]

The gift of the Spirit of Christ's faith, actualized throughout his personal history and given definitive shape in his death on the cross, creates the Church, the covenant people. This Spirit gives to the disciples their participation by faith in the New Covenant.[31] The Spirit, the content of Christ's faith, gives the disciples a share of both his experience of being uniquely loved by the Father and his sacrificial attitudes of response to the Father's love.[32] In this way the Spirit brings human persons into the covenantal relationship of divine self-communication and human self-offering established in Jesus' own life of faith and sealed with his death on the cross. In the Spirit of Christ's faith, the disciples are able to love the Father as Christ loves the Father, that is, by loving their neighbors in total self-offering because of their overwhelming experience of being loved by the Father.

Sent through the Incarnate Son, the Spirit's presence in the world is modified through the personal history of sacrificial love of Jesus, especially through the experience of the cross. Because of this modification, the Spirit of mutual love of Father and Son is experienced by Christians as the Spirit of the Crucified One. The Spirit's personal action of uniting human persons with the Beloved of the Father takes its particular shape from the Beloved's personal history. Through Jesus' sacrificial actions the Spirit of Christ's faith has also, in a sense, acquired a personal history. As a result of this modification, human persons who receive the Spirit of Christ's faith are necessarily influenced by the temporal sacrificial deeds through which the New Covenant was sealed. They share in the covenant faith and are given the sacrificial attitudes of the One whose sacrifice sealed the covenant.

Establishment of the Heavenly Liturgy

Scriptural and liturgical language looks forward to the heavenly liturgy, the eternal celebration by Christ and the saints of the fullness of God's salvation. The fulfillment of the divine plan for creation is the personal communion of created beings with the Persons of the Trinity; the heavenly liturgy consists in this communion. "The mystery of the Trinitarian communion between Father, Son and Spirit has

---

[30] Kilmartin, "Sacraments as Liturgy," 542.
[31] Kilmartin, *The Eucharist in the West*, 358.
[32] Ibid., 357–358.

now become the heavenly liturgy because it is communicated and shared."[33] The heavenly liturgy is established by the glorification of Christ, which brings his humanity into the fullness of Trinitarian communion. According to ancient tradition, when Christ is glorified, he is joined in glory by the company of those who have lived and died in faith.[34]

In the heavenly liturgy Christ's glorified humanity has communion with the Father by virtue of its hypostatic union with the Word. The saints enter the heavenly liturgy through a sacramental union with the Word; their fully constituted human persons are united with the Person of the Word through the humanity of Christ, sacrament of the divine-human love of humanity and of the divine-human love of God. The Spirit unites the saints, through the humanity of Christ, with the object of the Father's love, the eternal Word. In the Spirit their own personal response of self-offering to receive the Father's love is united with the sacrificial response of Christ, and in this way with the eternal offering of the Word. Thus the saints are given a created personal participation in the life of the Trinity.

Kilmartin insisted that this sacramental participation in the Trinitarian life reveals the true nature of God. God who communicates self in the immanent Trinity is not changed by the fulfillment of the divine plan of self-communication in the economy of grace. The divine Persons, in eternal relationship with each other, express that relationship in the economic modification of Incarnate Word and Spirit through which they bring created persons into the divine life. The divine self is further expressed in the saints, who in union with Christ opened themselves to receive the meaning of their lives from the Father. "The heavenly liturgy is the celebration of life and love in which each of the participants is turned to the others as completely as possible. It is the true life, lived at the heart of the inner-Trinitarian communion."[35]

In the heavenly liturgy Christ and the saints pray for the Church on earth and for the salvation of the world. Their prayer, however, does not involve discrete acts of intercession, for their time of categorial acts has been completed and they are in the divine eternity, which is not parallel to earthly time. Both Jesus Christ and the saints

[33] Kilmartin, *Culture and the Praying Church*, 89.
[34] Ibid., 88.
[35] Ibid., 90–91.

have entered into the beatific vision and are fixed in the vision of God.[36] With their whole beings, Christ and the saints celebrate the divine plan of self-communication, and they ask that the divine plan be fulfilled in the lives of all human persons. Expressing their love for God by their love for their neighbor, they ask for the Spirit to be given to all human persons, so that in the circumstances of their living they experience the Father's love and respond with the sacrificial attitudes of Christ.[37] It is Christ's high priestly prayer, then, that is prayed by Christ and all the saints in heaven.

Sending of the Holy Spirit upon the Church

"With the sending of the Spirit to establish the Church, the heavenly liturgy is extended to earth."[38] The Holy Spirit fulfills the divine plan of self-communication in human history by giving the disciples the gift of Christ's faith, through which they love the Father as Christ does. The Spirit is sent, ultimately from the Father, through the glorified Christ, who continues to love the Father by loving the Father's children. The perfect expression of that love is the sending of the Holy Spirit to bring the Father's children into personal communion with the Father.[39]

Kilmartin identified two moments in the awakening of Christian faith in the disciples and the extension of the heavenly liturgy to the world.[40] The first is the risen Lord's appearances to his disciples, through which he gave them the Spirit of his faith, thus establishing the Church as a community of covenant faith. The action of Christ and the Spirit in these appearances made the disciples the first witnesses of the resurrection. After the resurrection appearances, the faith that the first witnesses received from Christ in the Holy Spirit is mediated by the covenant community. The covenant faith is transmitted through the members of the community as they perform the activities of worship, witness, and service that characterize Christ's life

---

[36] Ibid., 88.

[37] Kilmartin, *Christian Liturgy*, 172.

[38] Kilmartin, *Culture and the Praying Church*, 91.

[39] Ibid., 89.

[40] Kilmartin, "Christ's Presence in the Liturgy," in Paul J. Bernier, ed., *Bread from Heaven* (New York: Paulist Press, 1977) 107; "The Last Supper and the Earliest Eucharists of the Church," in P. Benoit et al., eds., *The Breaking of the Bread*, Concilium 40 (New York: Paulist Press, 1969) 43; "Apostolic Office: Sacrament of Christ," *TS* 35 (1975) 254–255.

of faith. The faith of Christ and the Church, then, is always given to believers in historically and culturally conditioned ways.

In their own lives of faith the disciples actualize the Spirit of that faith which Christ actualized on the cross. "Always it is this one life of faith that is actualized, although this happens in ways that are peculiar to service of the neighbor, preaching and liturgy."[41] In their own histories of living that faith, Christians realize both the Father's love for them as members of Christ and the self-offering response of Christ's love for the Father; they make the spiritual attitudes of Christ their own. The faith that they live comes from a "participation in the Spirit of the faith of Christ," the Holy Spirit who was "the source of the life of faith of the incarnate Lord."[42] That faith is not just a first step on the way to human sanctification; rather, the faith sanctifies by bringing Christians into the covenantal relationship established in Jesus Christ.

The believing community mediates the faith of Christ especially in its liturgy, which is the life of faith under the mode of celebration. "The act of faith by which one accepts the promise recalled in the sacrament under the form of confident prayer of the Church is the realization of the promise of God's self-communication."[43] As prayer, the liturgy not only expresses that faith but is the means by which human persons enter more deeply and consciously into union with God, "letting God be God in our lives."[44] The liturgy is both the prayer of faith and the means by which the gift of faith is grasped.

The celebration of Christian liturgy demonstrates that the faith of Christ is both received and actualized in relationship with other believers, who make up the Body of Christ. This, as Kilmartin commented in his dissertation, entails a change of attitude for the believer. Generally, human persons concentrate on their own individual salvation.

"But with the reception of the grace of Christ [persons] enter into the life of the [Children] of God, the life of the Mystical Body of Christ, which has as a typical mark *Charity*. For it is by charity that we become one with God and the [Children] of God. But if charity unites us to God and our neighbor, it makes us wish the good of God and

---

[41] Kilmartin, "Sacraments as Liturgy," 534; *Culture and the Praying Church*, 70.
[42] Kilmartin, "Catholic Tradition," 455.
[43] Kilmartin, "Sacraments as Liturgy," 538.
[44] Kilmartin, *Culture and the Praying Church*, 76.

our neighbor as our own! It gives us a common heart. . . . It is impossible for a Christian to hope uniquely for himself [or herself]."[45]

Part of the worshipers' "letting God be God" is accepting that their relationship with one another is a constitutive part of their covenantal relationship with the Father. The communion of Trinitarian life celebrated in the liturgy "entails sharing of the life of faith between those who participate in the mystery of the shared Trinitarian life."[46] The liturgy's common prayer and ritual action both manifest and deepen that sharing as the worshipers celebrate the divine self-communication. Expressing Christ's faith as their own through the celebration of the liturgy, they have communion with the Father through Christ in the Holy Spirit. "Sacraments, as acts of worship, enable the communion [of worshipers] and the individual subject to accept God's offer of self-communication."[47] The offer is experienced and responded to through the mediation of other human persons; its acceptance is enfleshed through the worshipers' relationship with one another as they engage in the liturgical celebration.

The liturgy, from this viewpoint, is preeminently the work of the Holy Spirit, Spirit of Christ's faith and bond of union of the divine Persons. Through Christ, the Spirit extends the communion of the Trinity to the earthly Church at prayer. The Spirit creates a communion of persons, uniting the worshipers with Christ and with one another, binding the liturgical assembly together as the Church, the Body of Christ.

The resulting communication of the life of faith among the members of the Church, expressed in the verbal and gestural prayer of the liturgy, surpasses in depth and intimacy any other communication in their human lives. "If one truly enters into the spirit of the liturgy, actively participates according to the real meaning of liturgy, one is necessarily led into commitment to the common action by which the Church grows into the Body of Christ."[48] Active and conscious participation in the earthly liturgy, then, necessarily impels the Christian to that service of other human persons that continues Jesus' proclamation of God's love in deeds of love of neighbor.

---

[45] Kilmartin, "Eschatology and the Evanston Congress," 232.
[46] Kilmartin, "Sacraments as Liturgy," 527.
[47] Ibid., 539.
[48] Kilmartin, *Culture and the Praying Church*, 72.

The earthly liturgy, no less than the heavenly, celebrates the Trinitarian life shared with personal creatures: the Mystery of God in Christ. United with Christ, the object of the Father's love, the worshipers are in communion with the Father; they offer their lives in love of the Father, in union with the self-offering of Christ. The earthly liturgy, however, differs from the heavenly liturgy in the mode in which the life of faith is celebrated. The heavenly liturgy is the liturgy of the glorified Christ, in union with all the saints, celebrating the divine plan of self-communication. They give praise for the fulfillment of this plan in their company and intercede for its final fulfillment through the sending of the Holy Spirit upon all human persons.

The earthly liturgy celebrates the reality that the divine plan is already fulfilled in Christ and the saints but also that it is being fulfilled in the Church on earth. In the sacrificial histories of individual Christians and of the worshiping community, the Church already participates in Christ's *transitus* to the Father.[49] In the earthly liturgy Christ is present as sacrament of the divine love for human persons and of the human response of self-offering, as "worshiper of the Father in the first place, and lover of humanity for the sake of the Father."[50]

LITURGICAL ANAMNESIS

Both in Jewish and in Christian worship, liturgical anamnesis—the proclamation of the *magnalia Dei*—has an epicletic character. Prayerful recognition that God has established covenant relationships with human persons in specific events of human history itself manifests the faith that brings a person into those covenant relationships. The remembrance of God's covenant faithfulness in past time at least implicitly includes a confession of sin of unfaithfulness to the covenant. As they proclaim God's faithfulness in the past, the worshipers are already asking God to renew the covenant by bringing them into the original relationship of covenant faith.

The dynamics of liturgical anamnesis reveal that God uses the covenant people's prayer of memory to renew the covenant. The verbal and gestural prayer remembers the events through which God created a particular community of faith, establishing the covenantal relation-

[49] Kilmartin, *Christian Liturgy*, 348.
[50] Kilmartin, "Sacraments as Liturgy," 536.

ship with them. Praying as the covenant community, the worshipers become present in memory to the events through which their ancestors in faith received and accepted God's offer of covenantal relationship. The verbal and gestural prayer expresses the covenant community's memory of its creation through the gift of covenant faith and of the divine promise to renew the covenant with those who celebrate its memorial. Through their active participation in the prayer, the worshipers receive an accurate memory of the attitudes by which the community's original members participated in the covenant sacrifice. Celebrating together as the covenant community, they actively receive the gift of covenant faith, which renews them in covenantal relationship with God and with one another. Through their active participation, the worshipers appropriate the attitudes in which the original members of the covenant community accepted God's offer. This renewal of the covenant community's faith is the purpose of liturgical anamnesis in both Jewish and Christian traditions.

Celebration in the Holy Spirit of the Covenant Faith of Jesus Christ

Christian liturgical prayer proclaims that in Christ God has established a New Covenant of Trinitarian self-communication with human persons, thus fulfilling the divine plan for creation. Remembering Jesus Christ, the Church praises God for the faith of Christ and the gift of his faith to the Church. Remembering God's past action in Christ, the liturgy asks the Father to send the Holy Spirit to renew the liturgical assembly, and indeed the whole Church, in the faith of Christ. Renewal in the Spirit of Christ's faith restores and strengthens the Church in its covenant relationship with the Father.

Christian liturgy celebrates the one life of faith that Christ shares with Christians through the mediation of the Holy Spirit. The Church's prayer is a participation in Christ's response of faith to the Father's unique love for him and a realization of Christ's life as "person for others." This participation is mediated by the Holy Spirit, whom Christ possesses in fullness. "In the power of the Spirit the [worshiping] communion as such is enabled to respond to the object of Christ's act of faith, and really attain that object, i.e., the mystery of the incarnate fidelity of the Father."[51] The liturgical celebration, made up through the interpersonal communication of Christian worshipers celebrating the one life of faith, both manifests and realizes "the mystery

[51] Ibid., 543.

of the Church, which is the mystery of participation in the response of the faith of Christ."[52]

In the liturgical memorial celebrating Christ's sacrificial openness to the Father and love for the Father's children, Christ is present to join Christians with his covenant sacrifice. The Spirit, mediating the presence of Christ and Christians to one another, animates the liturgy as Spirit of the faith that Christ realized upon the cross. "The Spirit is the source of the life of faith, the life of trust and hope in, and love of, God. Hence the Spirit is source of acts of the life of faith animated by the religious attitudes conformed to those of Christ."[53] Actualizing the Spirit of Christ's faith through their participation in the verbal and gestural prayer of memory, Christian worshipers enter into the covenant sacrifice made in Jesus' flesh, and so are renewed in covenant relationship with the Father.

Covenant renewal, it must be remembered, involves right relationship, renewed intimacy, and shared purpose among the members of the covenant community. The dynamics of liturgical prayer indicate the importance of those interpersonal relationships and are the means by which the covenant community finds its renewal. Christ is present in the Holy Spirit through the personal presence and action of the worshipers as they perform the liturgical celebration; their action is the means by which the faith of Christ is made accessible to their fellow worshipers. "The mystery of Christ . . . employs the worshiping community as the means of its expression, as the concrete representation of itself."[54] According to the divine decision to be bound by the dynamics of human communication, the offer of Trinitarian self-communication is realized in and by the human communication of the faith of Christ that constitutes the Church's liturgy.

The modes of Christ's liturgical presence in the Holy Spirit further emphasize the human mediation of the mystery of Christ. Christ is present by faith in the liturgical assembly, in its song and prayer, in the proclamation of Scripture and the preaching of the Word, in the person of the ministers, and in the performing of sacramental signs, especially in the eucharistic communion. In each of these modes Christ's presence is mediated by those who exercise various roles in the verbal and gestural prayer made in his memory. The devotion

---

[52] Ibid.
[53] Kilmartin, *The Eucharist in the West*, 374.
[54] Kilmartin, *Christian Liturgy*, 332.

and commitment of the worshipers are the means by which the sacrificial attitudes of Christ are communicated and accepted. "The active participation of the assembly is realized by the individual believer's degree of agreement with the religious attitudes expressed verbally and gesturally in the ritual act, and which mirror the sacrificial attitudes of Jesus expressed at the Last Supper and in the event of his historical death on the cross."[55]

Through the interpersonal action by which individual worshipers, and the entire liturgical assembly, celebrate Christ's faith, they are incorporated into the New Covenant sealed in Jesus' sacrificial deeds.[56] Together with Christ and the saints in the heavenly liturgy, the celebrants of the earthly liturgy, by verbal and gestural prayer, proclaim their willingness to receive the meaning of their own lives from God's hand. God's response to their prayer is made explicit in the Holy Communion that Christians eat and drink in the eucharistic liturgy.[57]

The Church's union in Christ's self-offering is made in the unity of the Holy Spirit. As Spirit of Christ's faith, the Holy Spirit unites the assembly of believers to Christ, making Christ and the assembly personally present to each other and making the members of the liturgical assembly present to one another precisely as members of Christ. The liturgical memorial of Jesus Christ gives the worshipers a share in his love of God and neighbor, driving them to action in the rest of their lives of faith. "This recalling of Christ as the 'man for others' makes us realize that his passover is not completed until his relationship to all the just is fully realized by their passing from suffering to glory in his single *transitus* to the Father."[58] Christ's love for the Father was expressed in deeds of love of neighbor and ultimately in the sending of the Holy Spirit; the worshipers who are united in his faith will necessarily express their love of God through deeds of love of neighbor. As Christ's acceptance of the Father's love impelled him to prayer and action on behalf of "the many," so the Christian, living the one life of faith, is driven to works of love for neighbor.

Reception of Jesus' Covenant Faith Through Memory

All the Church's liturgy celebrates the memory of Jesus Christ, especially the deeds through which the New Covenant was sealed.

[55] Kilmartin, *The Eucharist in the West*, 371.
[56] Ibid., 358, 372, 374.
[57] Ibid., 370.
[58] Kilmartin, *Christian Liturgy*, 349.

Manners of celebration will vary according to the rhythm of life of the worshiping assembly as a whole and members of the assembly.

"The accomplishment of the ritual act as performative form of the faith of the Church (ecclesial dimension) evokes the individual believer's response of faith (participants of the liturgy) to the offer of the Trinitarian self-communication appropriate to the human and social situation of the life of faith being lived in the mode of ecclesial celebration of the life of faith."[59]

The Church's liturgy always asks for renewal in the covenant sacrifice of Christ. When a particular sacrament is celebrated, special intercession is made for the person(s) in whose favor the sacrament is celebrated. For the individual recipient and for itself, the assembly asks renewal in the sacrificial attitudes of Christ and deeper entry into the Mystery of God in Christ in the particular circumstances of their lives.

This prayer made in confident memorial of God's self-communication in Jesus Christ brings the worshipers, in the Holy Spirit of Christ's faith, back to the event of Christ's sacrifice on the cross. The Spirit has worked as architect of the Church's liturgy in the historical development of celebrations of the Church's faith, so that the liturgical memorial will transform Christians by giving an accurate memory of Christ's sacrifice. Expressing the attitudes by which he opened himself to the Father, the worshipers will then be transformed, configured to Christ in his sacrifice.

As they actualize the Spirit of Jesus' faith in the liturgy, the worshipers become present in the Spirit to the deeds in which Jesus actualized his faith. Remembering in the Spirit the events in which the covenant was sealed, they are given the sacrificial attitudes that Christ actualized on the cross. Remembering Christ's sacrificial deeds, they meet him in his sacrificial offering of self to the Father, deepening their conscious actualization of the faith and receiving the gifts of covenant renewal in the circumstances of their own lives. The assembly's reception of these gifts

"derives from the psychological aspect of the action of the Holy Spirit which consists in the transmission of the meritorious attitudes of Christ. By this activity of the Spirit the recipient is *rendered capable*

---

[59] Kilmartin, *The Eucharist in the West*, 360.

of uniting freely with Christ in his acceptable response of faith and thereby receives a share in the blessing of the new covenant from the Father of all blessings through grace, the gift of the Holy Spirit."[60]

In the prayer of memory, then, the Holy Spirit makes Christians present to the mysteries of Christ's humanity. Through this prayer the worshipers receive Christ's own attitudes, his love of the Father and of the neighbor, becoming companions joined with Christ in his covenant sacrifice. The Spirit's action in liturgical anamnesis, then, represents the worshipers to Christ's sacrifice as they actualize the faith given them in the Spirit.

Actualization of the Spirit of Christ's Faith

The medium of prayer and action works to transform the worshipers in several ways. The prayer texts praise the Father for the work of self-communication through Christ in the Spirit. They ask for the gift of receiving the mind of Christ, the thankful awareness and dedication that characterized his ministry, and the love with which he offered himself to receive the meaning of his life from the Father.

The various actions of the liturgical assembly express its openness to receive the gift God wants to give. The gathering of individual Christians as assembly witnesses to their understanding that none of them lives for self, but that they mean to share God's gift in love. The ordered nature of the assembly reminds the worshipers that their communion in the Spirit does not obliterate their personal distinctiveness but enhances it.

The liturgical presidency is exercised by one ordained with formal prayer that this person bring Christ to the Church and the Church to Christ. This ordained minister symbolizes to the worshipers that their incorporation into the mystery they celebrate is God's gift, not something to which any individual or group of persons is entitled by natural right. The ordained presidency also serves as symbol of the communion that the assembly shares with other liturgical assemblies around the world, and so should be an impetus for their greater love of all Christians.

The proclamation of the Word reminds the assembly that it exists because of God's call and that its response of faith is one with the response of the original witnesses to Christ's resurrection. The liturgical homily expresses the truth that God is at work in this assembly's

[60] Kilmartin, "Catholic Tradition," 455. Emphasis in original.

life, as certainly as God was at work in the lives of the chosen witnesses of Scripture.

The performance of sacramental actions, with care and reverence, proclaims the mystery of God present and active in creatures in order to bring them to the highest possible reception of the divine self-communication. Sacramental communion above all, in which the worshipers receive the whole Christ, Head and members, through their eating and drinking the transformed bread and wine, expresses their willing reception of the gift of participation in Christ's covenant sacrifice and their resulting communion with the Trinity in company with all the saints.[61] Through their common prayer and action, the assembly and its ministers communicate Christ's attitudes of loving self-offering and thankful praise by their liturgical expression of the Spirit of Christ's faith.[62]

The Church actualizes the Spirit of Christ's faith in gathering for prayer in Jesus' memory, in celebrating the Word proclaimed in their midst, and then in particular sacramental prayers and actions. In this process the Spirit gives the Church an accurate memory of the deeds of Jesus, gives the assembly and its particular members the saving attitudes of Christ, expressed in the official prayer texts and sacramental actions, and thus renews in them the covenant made in Jesus Christ. Those attitudes include trust, self-offering, love for God and neighbor, and thankfulness for God's loving self-communication. It was those attitudes which Jesus Christ expressed in his temporal acts and which were realized in the pinnacle of his personal history of faith and love on the cross.[63]

CONCLUSION: *MYSTERIENGEGENWART* AS PRESENCE IN MEMORY TO CHRIST'S TEMPORAL DEEDS

The Spirit of the faith by which Jesus passed from this world to the Father works in the prayer of the believing Church, making Christ present through the ritual prayer and action of the liturgical assem-

---

[61] According to Kilmartin's friends and colleagues M. Schaefer, T. Koernke, and J. Laurance, *Christian Liturgy*. I: *Theology* was to have been followed by other volumes, in which the systematic theology of the first volume was applied to celebrations of particular sacraments. Considerations of this sort would have been treated there.

[62] Kilmartin, *The Eucharist in the West*, 360, 371.

[63] Kilmartin, *Christian Liturgy*, 346.

bly. The liturgical realization of the Spirit of Christ's faith gives access to the fruits of Christ's *transitus*. Christ's sacrifice is made present in Christian worshipers through their participation in the worship that Christ offers to the Father. United in the sacrifice of Christ, the members of the liturgical assembly have communion with the Father and with all the saints; they participate proleptically in the one *transitus* of Christ, by which they will come at the fulfillment of a personal history of faith into complete personal communion with the Trinity.[64]

Through the prayer of memory, the liturgical assembly is made present to Christ's temporal acts by the Holy Spirit. The Spirit gives the worshipers a participation in Christ's own faith, through which they enter the New Covenant and are in communion with the Father through the Son. This is a properly personal action of the Holy Spirit: mutual love of Father and Son in the Trinity. The Spirit comes to Christians as Spirit of Christ's faith and moves them to actualize that faith especially in liturgical celebration, whose performance is at the same time an act of love of God and of neighbor. Actualizing the faith that Christ actualized on the cross, Christians become present in memory to his covenant sacrifice, and so receive his sacrificial attitudes, which enable them to enter into the New Covenant by faith.

Christ's attitudes are characterized by his self-offering love of the Father and by his love for the Father's children. His sacrificial offering, however, is itself a response to his basic experience of the Father's love for him. The Holy Spirit, mutual love of Father and Son, gives Christians a participation not just in Christ's attitudes of response but in the experience of the Father's love for the Beloved. By making Christians present in memory to the covenant sacrifice of Christ, then, the Holy Spirit brings them by faith into the self-communication of the economic Trinity, which is the mystery of Christ and the Church.

It should indeed, then, be said that the temporal deeds of Christ are present in the members of the liturgical assembly as they celebrate the faith of Christ and the Church. Those deeds have a presence that is metaphysically affirmed as instrumental cause of the faith given to the praying Church by Christ in the Holy Spirit. Christ's deeds are present insofar as they expressed and modified the Spirit of the faith that Jesus actualized in his death on the cross.

---

[64] Kilmartin, *The Eucharist in the West*, 358, 360.

"The effect of the participation of ordinary human beings in the mystery of God in Christ is dependent on the presence of the historical saving acts of Jesus—of Jesus as agent of modification of the sanctifying action of the Holy Spirit.

"This eternal activity of the Spirit is found as a consequent term in the believer. But this divine action, which effects the divinization of the willing subject, is modified by the historical salvific acts of Jesus by which the believer is enabled to respond properly to the offer of divinization and thereby participate proleptically in the single *transitus* of Jesus from the world to the Father."[65]

The metaphysical affirmation of the presence of the temporal deeds of Christ as instrumental cause modifying the action of the Holy Spirit, then, serves to help explain how the Spirit acts in the liturgy to bring the worshipers in memory back to those deeds.[66] Although the temporal acts of Christ themselves remain locked in space and time, they are present in the sacrificial attitudes of Christ given and received by the worshipers. The one sacrifice of Christ is not made present to the believer and then appropriated by faith, as Casel proposed; rather, Christ's sacrifice is made present by faith in the worshiping Christian and in the liturgical assembly as they celebrate their participation in the Mystery of God in Christ in the verbal and gestural prayer of memory that is the Church's liturgy.

---

[65] Kilmartin, "Catholic Tradition," 453–454.
[66] Kilmartin, *The Eucharist in the West,* 358–359.

Chapter Five

Conclusions

This concluding chapter is divided into three sections. The first of these considers whether Kilmartin's proposed approach to describing the *Mysteriengegenwart der Heilstat Christi* succeeds in meeting the criteria for judgment developed in the first chapter. In that chapter the various proposals offered during the controversy over the mystery presence were found to be inadequate on two grounds. First, those theories that postulated a perennialization of Christ's temporal acts had to be dismissed because they did not respect the metaphysical distinction between time and eternity. Second, none of the suggested approaches, as reported by the commentators on the controversy, succeeded in making a strong connection between the deeds of Christ and the action of the Church in its liturgical celebration. Kilmartin's proposed approach is briefly considered in light of these two criteria.

The second section of this chapter addresses Kilmartin's success in articulating a systematic theological approach to the mystery presence. At the end of Chapter 2 a brief listing was made of elements that, according to Kilmartin's interpretation of the content of the *lex orandi*, would have to be included in a truly systematic theology of liturgical celebration. That list provides a framework for a short consideration of whether Kilmartin's system met the criteria that he himself set up.

The third section offers some concluding remarks and a few suggestions of ways in which Kilmartin's insights might profitably be carried forward.

THE QUESTION OF THE *MYSTERIENGEGENWART*

Edward Kilmartin considered the relation of the temporal deeds of Jesus Christ to the Church's liturgical celebration from a broader viewpoint than had Odo Casel and the other theologians who, earlier in the twentieth century, had engaged in the *Mysteriengegenwart* controversy.

Kilmartin set the question of the liturgical presence of the mysteries of Christ's life within the context of the action of the Trinity in the economy of divine self-communication. In this way he attempted to find a more satisfactory way to describe the mystery presence.

When Kilmartin began his career, more than thirty years of discussion and research had yielded no satisfactory description of the relationship between the temporal deeds of Christ and the Church's liturgical memorial of those deeds. In the light of the Thomist revival, the late scholastic *Effektustheorie* proposed by Suarez and Cajetan, and developed by their followers, was seen to be unsatisfactory. It had to be rejected on metaphysical grounds, for it could not provide an unbroken chain of instrumental causes to connect the temporal deeds of Christ with the actions of the Church at prayer.

Odo Casel and many of his interlocutors in the *Mysteriengegenwart* controversy postulated a perennialization of some aspect of Christ's temporal acts. Freed from the confines of time and space, these perennialized acts could be made present and saving by the glorified Christ in the Church's liturgy. This idea, however, also ran afoul of Thomist metaphysics, according to which an action in space and time must be considered a consequent term of the eternal divine knowing and willing. According to this understanding of the structure of reality, a temporal action expressing the eternal divine knowledge and will cannot become perennialized without destroying the distinction between time and eternity. Furthermore, as Casel's critics insisted, an action exists only in space and time; it has no essence that can become eternalized. Both Casel's theory of perennialized acts, then, and the *Effektustheorie* he sought to displace had to be rejected because of the metaphysical contradictions inherent in them.

Gottlieb Söhngen had suggested that the mystery of Christ's *transitus* to the Father, accomplished through his sacrifice on the cross, is represented in the worshipers themselves. Söhngen's proposed approach to describing the liturgical presence of Christ's saving deeds posed no metaphysical contradictions but, according to the secondary literature, did not develop how theologians might clarify the way in which that representation actually takes place.

As was seen in the first chapter, then, the *Mysteriengegenwart* controversy raised, but did not answer, the question of how liturgical anamnesis connects Christian worshipers with the temporal deeds of Christ. The connection was affirmed, and its importance emphasized, by the various theologians who engaged in the discussion and by the

Roman magisterium, from *Mediator Dei* onward. No satisfactory answer to the question, however, appears to have been offered.

Nevertheless, several indications of possibly fruitful directions of inquiry emerged from the theological conversation.

The first of these was the relationship between the sacramental symbol and the imagination of Christians at worship. This connection was noted by both Nicolas and McNamara in their investigation of sacramental causality.

The second indication came from the developing magisterial teaching on the interrelated modes of Christ's presence in the liturgy. *Mediator Dei*, distinguishing among the modes of Christ's liturgical presence, introduced the possibility of differentiation and interrelation of the "liturgical presences" of Christ. *Sacrosanctum Concilium*, repeating *Mediator Dei*'s list of modes of presence, introduced the idea that the liturgical assembly is the active subject of the liturgical event. *Eucharisticum Mysterium* drew out the implication of *Sacrosanctum Concilium*'s teaching, placing Christ's presence by faith in the liturgical assembly as the first of the modes of presence.

The third indication of a possibly fruitful direction of theological inquiry came from the Council's teaching that the liturgy, celebrating God's action in the paschal mystery, is the Church's response to the divine initiative. The mystery of the liturgy, then, according to the conciliar teaching, has a dialogical character. By the time of the Council, as was seen at the beginning of the second chapter, Kilmartin was already describing Christian liturgy using the Greek patristic idea of the divine self-communication as it had been appropriated for Western theology by Karl Rahner. Kilmartin would continue to use the theme of dialogue in his writings on the mystery of human sanctification in and through the Church's liturgy throughout his career.

Kilmartin's Analysis of the Problem

While he rejected the approach to the mystery presence found in Casel's work and, in his opinion, continued in the "modern average Catholic theology" of sacraments, Kilmartin also attempted to understand the reasons behind this approach. In his judgment, Casel and his interlocutors, shaped by the Western tradition of *Trinitätsvergessenheit*, focused too narrowly upon the passion of Christ rather than considering the economy of Trinitarian self-communication revealed in and through Christ's temporal deeds. In Casel's understanding, the mystery is Christ himself; the liturgy represents Christ with his saving deeds, and the Eucharist is described as the "sacramental representation of the historical sacrifice of the cross."[1] It is the essence of that historical sacrifice which, in Casel's theory, is perennialized and which becomes present in the liturgy in order that Christians may participate in the mystery of Christ. Casel's approach, however, does not clearly situate the sacrifice of the cross in its context of Trinitarian self-communication, nor does it clarify the meaning of the sacrifice which Christ offers and which is liturgically represented.

Kilmartin judged that Casel and his contemporaries were hindered by the theological assumption common to their day that all the acts of the Trinity *ad extra* are acts of efficient causality done by the Godhead acting as one principle. They were also hampered by a static understanding of a person's humanity, very different from the more developmental approach that characterizes late twentieth-century philosophy and theology.

In Casel's time, Catholic theology would have hesitated to speak of the development of Christ's humanity through a history of categorial acts; Christ's humanity was treated as a fact given in the hypostatic union, not as a reality that developed and took shape through a personal history. Nor was it conceivable to speak of Christ's life of faith, for the prevailing theological tradition defined faith not in the biblical sense of that trust in God which Jesus preached but as an intellectual assent to truths not seen. Because the Person of Christ, the divine Word, is always in the presence of the Father, it was assumed that in his humanity Christ had the beatific vision; he did not walk by faith but by sight. Given the theological and philosophical assumptions within which he worked, Kilmartin remarked, Casel could not have described Jesus' passion and death on the cross as deeds that expressed and actualized his life of faith.

As a result of these limitations, Kilmartin believed, Casel and his contemporaries formulated the question of the mystery presence incorrectly. Rather than asking about the liturgical presence of the mystery of the economic Trinity revealed in Christ and his saving acts, they inquired only about the mystery presence of Christ and his saving acts. Their question, Kilmartin asserted, was the wrong question; no satisfactory answer could be provided because the question was

---

[1] Edward J. Kilmartin, "The Catholic Tradition of Eucharistic Theology: Towards the Third Millennium," *Theological Studies* (hereafter cited as *TS*) 55 (1984) 420.

incorrectly formulated. Within the assumptions of the neo-scholastic theological tradition, they were not able to consider the mystery revealed and accomplished in Jesus Christ's personal history, proceeding from that question to the Church's sacramental celebration.

Kilmartin's Trinitarian Approach

A more accurate formulation of the question of the mystery presence, Kilmartin argued, is provided by the *lex orandi* expressed in the texts of the classical Eucharistic Prayers. These prayers, considered together, describe Christian liturgy as celebration of the mystery of Trinitarian self-communication experienced in and through human history.[2] As they praise the Father for the New Covenant accomplished in Jesus Christ, these prayers confidently ask for renewal of that covenant by the configuration of the worshipers to Christ in his sacrificial self-offering. The dynamic of these prayers emphasizes the personal activity of the Holy Spirit revealed in Christ and the Church. The prayer texts, Kilmartin argued, teach that the Church's liturgical celebrations are events in which, through the medium of the interpersonal action of the celebration of faith, the Holy Spirit manifests Christ, and therefore manifests the Trinitarian self-communication accomplished and revealed through the history of Christ's humanity. "The one mystery of Christian faith is the Triune God in his self-communication to humanity. All classical liturgies confess this Trinitarian grounding and goal of the economy of salvation. In different ways, the forms of liturgy express the conviction of faith that the Triune God, in their (sic) economic activity, is the mystery of Christian worship."[3]

For Kilmartin, the liturgy celebrates nothing less than the mystery of God's bringing human persons into the communion of the Trinity by the action of Word and Holy Spirit. The liturgical assembly's relationship to the temporal deeds of Christ, he believed, can properly be

[2] Meyer, "Eine Trinitarische Theologie der Liturgie," *Zeitschrift für Katholische Theologie* 113 (1991) 26–27, favorably compares Kilmartin's Trinitarian approach with more popular "encounter with Christ" sacramental theologies. Meyer's review article stresses the importance of Kilmartin's emphasis on the mystery presence of the economic Trinity. Jean Corbon is cited by both Meyer and Kilmartin as author of one of the few other attempts to construct a systematic Trinitarian theology of the liturgy. Ibid., 30; see Kilmartin, "Foreword to the English Edition," in Jean Corbon, *The Wellspring of Worship* (New York/Mahwah, N.J.: Paulist Press, 1988) 1–2.

[3] Kilmartin, *Christian Liturgy* (Kansas City: Sheed and Ward, 1988) 98. *Christian Liturgy* was printed without incorporating Kilmartin's corrections of the proofs. The book is unfortunately replete with typographical errors.

described only in light of the mystery of the economic Trinity, revealed in Christ's death and resurrection. That mystery includes both the divine offer of self-communication and the human response of self-sacrificing acceptance.

The perfect human response to the divine initiative was made by Jesus Christ in his own life of faith. Kilmartin held that Jesus expressed that sacrificial offering in its final and definitive form by his intercession for his disciples as he died. This idea, he claimed, is found in the scriptural accounts of the institution of the Eucharist.

In the New Testament narratives of the Last Supper, Jesus describes his impending death as a sacrifice offered for others, by which God would establish a New Covenant in which the disciples would share. It is this interpretation of Christ's sacrificial offering, Kilmartin insisted, that is preserved and celebrated in the classical Eucharistic Prayers. These prayers, he said, express the Church's understanding of Jesus' own belief; the Church proclaims that Jesus meant his death to be the means through which the Father would send the Spirit of the faith in which he had lived his life upon his disciples so that they would love the Father as he did. From this viewpoint, it may be deduced that Jesus, on the cross, offered himself in sacrificial petition for the sending of the Spirit of love. In this understanding, Jesus' dying prayer was an invocation of the Holy Spirit.

Since human persons express the love of God by discrete acts of love for one another, Jesus' dying intercession for his brothers and sisters was at the same time his expression of love for his Father. It was also a prayer for the fulfillment of the Father's will, for Jesus, as he manifested in his preaching and in his meals with sinners and tax collectors, believed that God desires to receive a response of love from all human persons. Ultimately, then, Jesus' dying intercession expressed that relationship of trust and self-surrender that the Bible calls faith.

There are several senses, then, in which Kilmartin saw the faith of Christ as the means through which Christians enter into the mystery of the economic Trinity. This faith, developed through Jesus' human history, was the way in which he experienced and accepted the mystery of the Trinity that is the mystery of his own Person. This faith, in which he knew the divine plan of self-communication, was the basis of his intercession for the sending of the Holy Spirit upon his disciples so that all human persons might enter into the Trinitarian mystery. It was in this faith that Jesus offered himself in the sacrificial response of love that established the New Covenant of Trinitarian self-communication in space and time. It is this sacrificial faith of Christ, in Kilmartin's understanding, that must be represented in the liturgical celebration, for it is through this faith that Christians participate in the mystery of Trinitarian self-communication.

The faith of Christ, however, is the gift of the Holy Spirit, who acquired a personal history in Jesus' experience of being loved by the Father and of responding to the Father's initiative with a self-offering acceptance expressed in categorial acts of love of God and neighbor. The Holy Spirit, sent through Jesus' intercession at the moment of his death and glorification, comes to Christians as the Spirit of Christ's sacrificial faith. In their liturgical celebration, Christian worshipers actualize the Spirit of Christ's sacrificial faith, receiving Christ's sacrificial attitudes of love of God and neighbor. As they fully, consciously, actively participate in the celebration in memory of the deeds in which Christ expressed his sacrificial faith, the Holy Spirit unites worshipers with Christ, in whose faith they are acting. In this way, the prayer of memory and faith brings Christian worshipers' sacrificial offering of their own lives, celebrated in the liturgy, into sacramental union with the deeds in which Christ offered his own life in sacrifice. The worshipers are made present in memory to Christ's actualization of his faith in order to receive his sacrificial attitudes, which they in turn actualize in the liturgical celebration. This approach, Kilmartin held, offers a more satisfactory explanation of the mystery presence of Christ and his saving deeds.

EVALUATION OF KILMARTIN'S PROPOSAL

Respect for Metaphysical Distinction Between Time and Eternity
In Kilmartin's approach, there is no need to postulate a perennialization of some aspect of the temporal deeds of Christ, an attempted solution that raises more problems than it solves. Kilmartin treats Christ's temporal deeds precisely as temporal and spatial, and as unique in human history. They are the means by which Jesus Christ, in the faith and love of the Holy Spirit, gave a truly human response to the divine offer of self-communication. This response was the perfect, sufficient, once-for-all acceptance of the divine purpose for creation, in which and through which that divine purpose was accomplished in human history.

The discrete categorial actions by which Jesus Christ made his response of sacrificial faith have, from the viewpoint of space and time, ceased to exist. Kilmartin pointed out, however, that there are several senses in which these temporal actions should be thought of as present in the celebration of the liturgy. From the standpoint of a relational ontology, Jesus Christ's temporal actions were the means by which he developed his own personal history; they have become part of his human personality. Wherever he is personally present, in this understanding, his temporal actions may be said to be present as well. From the viewpoint of the eternal divine knowing and willing, Christ's temporal deeds are the means by which the Trinitarian self-communication is accomplished in space and time. They reveal that Christ's *transitus* in the Holy Spirit to the Father is the divinely intended goal for all human persons. These deeds are always present to God in the successionless *nunc stans* of the divine eternity, as the accomplishment of the economic movement of self-communication that includes creation, incarnation, and the *transitus* of Christ and the saints.

These temporal deeds should be considered to be present in the liturgy in the sense that they are the instrumental cause modifying the divinizing action of the Holy Spirit. That is to say, because of these temporal deeds the Holy Spirit comes to Christian worshipers as the Spirit of the faith that Christ actualized in his death on the cross. According to Thomist metaphysics, Christ's deeds, as instrumental cause, are present in their effect in Christian worshipers. These temporal deeds modify the action of the Holy Spirit, sent through Christ's death on the cross, so that the effect of the Spirit's action in the believers is that they are configured to Christ in his sacrificial faith, thus receiving the effect of Trinitarian self-communication. The temporal deeds of Christ, then, are present in the reception by Christian worshipers of Christ's sacrificial attitudes, which they actualize in the liturgical celebration. There is no need, Kilmartin said, to postulate a perennialization of some element of Christ's temporal deeds; those deeds are present and active in the sanctification of Christian worshipers as they celebrate the memorial of Jesus Christ.

Connection Between Deeds of Christ and of Christians
According to the *lex orandi*, Kilmartin held, the divine plan, revealed in Jesus Christ, is that human persons accept the divine offer of self-communication, responding with that loving self-offering by which they enter the New Covenant and have communion with the divine Persons. The Spirit of Christ's faith, invoked in the anamnetic and epicletic dynamic of liturgical prayer, is given to human persons

so that as they perform deeds of self-sacrificing love for God and neighbor, they will actualize the faith of the covenant. In this way, by grace given especially through the thankful memory of Christ, they come into the covenantal relationship with the Father, through the Son, in the Spirit. In Christian liturgy, Kilmartin insisted, believers celebrate the union of their personal histories of lived faith with the faith of Christ; the liturgy is the one life of faith under the mode of celebration.

In their liturgical celebration the worshipers actualize the Spirit of Christ's faith by assembling for the event, by singing and praying, by listening to proclaimed Scripture, by their various ministries, and by their use of particular sacramental symbols. Since it is by their action that the Holy Spirit makes Christ present in various modes, the devotion of each member of the assembly, expressed in active participation in the liturgical action, is of prime importance. Each person's taking part in the celebration both accepts and communicates the Spirit of Christ's faith, and is the means by which Christ in the Spirit becomes personally present to the members of the assembly and to the assembly as a whole. By his consideration of the faith of Christ, then, and by emphasizing the activity of the Holy Spirit as the personal mediation between Christ and the Christian, Kilmartin could make a clearer connection between the deeds of Christ and those of Christians than could either Casel or Söhngen.

Attention to Symbol and Imagination,
Modes of Presence and Dialogical Character

It was remarked in the first chapter that it appeared that a successful approach to the question of the mystery presence should address three areas: the role of the symbol in shaping the Christian imagination, the interrelationship of the modes of Christ's liturgical presence, and the dialogical character of the paschal mystery. A few words are offered here about Kilmartin's attention to these three areas, moving from the last to the first.

Kilmartin's whole theological system is based on the understanding that the Christian life is a response to God's initiative. Like many other theologians, he simply asserts that life itself has a dialogical character: life is received gratuitously and demands some sort of response. In the life of grace, he insisted, the basic dynamic is also one of the divine initiative and the human response. Like Rahner, he believed that in Jesus Christ God reveals that the dynamic of self-communication and answering response are at the heart of God's own life. The dialogical character of liturgy, in his understanding, is part of the liturgical celebration's representation of the mystery of the economic Trinity.

Kilmartin's treatment of the modes of presence of Christ is thoroughly articulated and runs throughout a great many of his writings. He both stresses that these modes are interdependent and insists that Christ's presence by faith in the liturgical assembly is the primary one of these modes. He describes the proclamation of Scripture as the proclamation of faith and considers its role in awakening memory, and therefore enabling the prayer for covenant renewal. Liturgical preaching, he insists, should both point to the action of God in the events of the life of the worshipers and help to frame the appropriate response of faith. Kilmartin sees the sacramental action of the liturgical assembly as the way in which it embodies the prayer of memory and petition contained in official prayer texts. In various places he repeats that the ministers of the assembly represent the faith of the Church, and so represent Christ. Those who exercise liturgical presidency, he argued, must in the normal course of events be ordained, for their ministry symbolizes the belief that Christ's presence to the Church and the Church's presence to Christ is a gift that the Church receives only through prayer. All these modes of presence of Christ in the liturgy are dependent upon each other, he insisted. By their nature they refer to each other and point to the primacy of faith and to the central liturgical symbol of the assembly as gathering of the people of the New Covenant.

In this way, Kilmartin's treatment of the modes of presence of Christ leads directly into the subject of his understanding of the role of the sacramental symbol in the development of the Christian imagination. His development emphasizes that the central symbol in Christian liturgy is the liturgical assembly, and attempts to give some systematic grounding to that assertion. All the other symbols of the liturgy, he argued, should be treated in reference to that central symbol that is the Christian assembly. He set the context for considering the interrelationship of the various liturgical symbols by developing the concept of celebration, an event in which people employ traditional symbolic language to represent themselves within a particular world of meaning.

There are some hints in his writing about liturgical anamnesis that it is by using ritual symbols, especially the great symbol of eucharistic eating and drinking, that Christians develop the emotional resonance with Jesus that is the goal of the contemplation of the mysteries of the life of Christ in Ignatius Loyola's *Spiritual Exercises*. This is an area in which Kilmartin laid a systematic groundwork for development, in which he offered some indications of his thought but which he was not able fully to develop. He made eminently clear that the official prayer texts should be considered along with the use of the sacramental action, using especially the relationship between Eucharistic Prayers and sacramental communion as an example.

His insistence that the action of eucharistic eating and drinking must always be referred back to the faith of Christ embodied by the liturgical assembly similarly gives some indication of his understanding of how the sacramental sign actually works to communicate the sacrificial attitudes of Christ. The second volume of *Christian Liturgy*, as noted earlier, would have been particularly valuable in its further reflections on the symbols employed in particular sacramental celebrations.

INTEGRATION OF BASIC THEMES
IN A SYSTEMATIC THEOLOGY

At the end of the second chapter, a brief listing was made of elements that Kilmartin believed should be addressed by a systematic theology arising from the *lex orandi*. These are repeated here, with a few comments.

In the area of the theology of the Trinity, it was noted that Kilmartin believed that a theological system should constantly refer back to the Church's experience of the mystery of the economic Trinity. Such a system, he held, should take seriously the Trinitarian self-communication and should attend to the personal missions of the Word and the Holy Spirit. Kilmartin assiduously followed his own advice in this area, developing a theological model of bestowal with which to complement the traditional model of the divine processions.

In the area of Christology, Kilmartin held that the descending Logos-Christology that has dominated Western theological history should also be complemented by an ascending Spirit-Christology that can relate the personal development of a history of faith and holiness of Christians with the life of faith of Jesus of Nazareth. He argued that the idea of Jesus Christ as the substantial covenant between God and humankind should be developed in a way that emphasizes Jesus' response, in discrete categorial acts of love of God and of neighbor, to the data of his own consciousness of being uniquely loved by God. Kilmartin's Christology draws out the implications of the classical Christological dogmas for the human experience of Jesus.

In the area of pneumatology, Kilmartin remarked that theologians should be particularly concerned with detailing the relationship of the Holy Spirit to Christ and to the Father. For insight into the personal characteristics of the Holy Spirit, he relied especially on the action for which the Church prays in its liturgical epiclesis. From the Spirit's activity of creating unity of Christians with Christ while preserving a distinction of persons, he moved to the Western tradition of considering the Holy Spirit as the mutual love between Father and Son.

In Kilmartin's bestowal model of the Trinity, the Holy Spirit is described as the personal mediation binding the Father and the Son together. From that personal action of mediation of immediate presence, he moved to considering the action of the Spirit as "mediating immediacy" in the works of the Trinity *ad extra*. In his description, the Holy Spirit mediates the presence of God to the world, making all creation sacramental. The Holy Spirit unites the humanity of Christ, at the moment of its creation, with the divinity of the Word, effecting the union that makes Christ, in himself, the substantial covenant between God and humankind.

The same Spirit, as Spirit of the Father's transcendental love for the Son in the immanent Trinity, is experienced by Jesus as Spirit of the Father's unique love for him. Jesus' response to that gift in discrete acts of love of God and neighbor is the expression in a human history of the transcendental love of the Son for the Father. Thus the Holy Spirit, through Jesus' life of faith, acquires a personal history and becomes personally present in the world as the Spirit of Christ's faith. It is with this mode of personal presence that the Holy Spirit is sent on the Church.

In Kilmartin's relentlessly Trinitarian understanding, Christians' reception of the Spirit, sent by the Father through Christ, is itself a sacrament of the transcendental bestowal of the Spirit on the Son as Spirit of the Father's love. Christians' actions of self-sacrificing love are, in turn, sacraments of the answering return of the Spirit from the Son to the Father within the immanent Trinity. The entire life of the world, for Kilmartin, expresses the activity of the economic Trinity, communicating the divine life in particular human situations that are both sinful and holy.

Within this understanding of the economic Trinity, Kilmartin called for an ecclesiology that would also reflect the data of liturgical celebration, especially of the classical Eucharistic Prayers. He described the Church as the context for conscious, interpersonal encounter with Christ through the actions of worship, witness, and service which, according to the Scriptures, characterized the life of Jesus, and as the covenant people, continually re-created by God through the liturgical prayer of memory and faith. He taught that by living Christ's faith, by actualizing his sacrificial response to the Father's love, the members of the Church, and the Church as a whole, would be sacrament of salvation for the world. Always actualized in particular communities with their own histories of sin and conversion, this Church has communion in the Spirit of Christ's faith with all the saints around the world as well as with the saints united in the heavenly liturgy.

Because it is constituted precisely in particular worshiping communities that celebrate their union in the Spirit of Christ's faith, the Church will always be a localized event, expressing the one faith of Christ in its particular culture, and a communion of Churches around the world, each of which has a responsibility to live in shared faith and action with the others. Each of the characteristics that Kilmartin claimed should be represented in a truly liturgical ecclesiology is represented in his work.

Kilmartin did not claim to offer a full systematic synthesis, like the *Summae* of Thomas Aquinas and other great medieval theologians. He wrote that his systematic theology was no more than an initial attempt to construct a truly Trinitarian theology of Christian worship and did not claim that he had succeeded in fully integrating the *lex credendi* into the *lex orandi*. Instead, he pointed to that reintegration as the task for theologians in the coming millennium and described his own system as indicating some directions that others might profitably follow.[4] It seems to this writer, however, that, in regard to the subject of this dissertation, Kilmartin outlines an acceptable systematic approach to the mystery presence. His approach respects the data of the liturgical sources, emphasizes liturgical celebration as manifestation of the economic Trinity, and is acceptable from the viewpoint of Thomist metaphysics.

[4] Kilmartin, "Catholic Tradition," 457. Kilmartin reported to this author that he was excited and encouraged by Meyer's judgment in the review article of *Christian Liturgy* that Kilmartin's Trinitarian approach to the mystery presence seemed to be correct.

Two interrelated areas of Kilmartin's treatment of the liturgical mystery seem to this author to be especially significant. These are his explication of the meaning of the sacrifice of Christ and his development of the influence that Christians have upon one another in all the activities of the life of faith, especially in the celebration of the liturgy.

Kilmartin's development of the idea of sacrifice carries out Karl Rahner's insight of the divine self-communication and the human response of self-transcendence. Kilmartin writes that for the human person to open his or her self to the Trinity, to receive the meaning of life from God's hand, is the ultimate act of self-transcendence. It is this self-offering, accomplished over a lifetime of categorial actions of love of God and neighbor, that Kilmartin identifies as sacrifice. This definition of the term, he argued, is in line both with the New Testament understanding of the sacrifice of Christ and the Church and with that found in the classical Eucharistic Prayers.

Kilmartin wrote that the sacrifice of Christ, by the action of the Holy Spirit in liturgical anamnesis, is present in the human attitudes of self-offering expressed in the liturgical celebration. By the action of the Holy Spirit, the sacrifice of Christ is represented in the worshipers themselves as they actualize Christ's faith in the celebration of the liturgy. This understanding of the sacrifice of Christ allows the concept of sacrifice to be reappropriated, freed from its history of popular misunderstanding and from images of an angry God whose vengeance is satisfied only by the blood of his dearly Beloved. Kilmartin's recovery of the scriptural understanding of covenant sacrifice and his interpretation of traditional sacrificial images within the patristic/Rahnerian framework of the eternal divine plan of loving self-communication are a major contribution to Christian theology.

Kilmartin's theology of liturgy is particularly valuable because of its strong connection between the deeds of Christ and those of Christian worshipers. His treatment of the one life of faith, given by the Holy Spirit, with its elements of witness, worship, and service, helps to relate liturgical prayer to the rest of the Christian life. His insistence that the presence of Christ and the Spirit of Christ's faith is mediated through the action of the members of the liturgical assembly gives a clear basis for understanding the importance of the full, conscious, active participation urged by *Sacrosanctum Concilium*, while also providing theological grounds for the inculturation of the faith in liturgical celebration. Finally, by defining the sacrifice of Christ as something that can be participated in not only by intention but by a life of self-offering, he opens a door for understanding how the Christian life may truly be lived in union with Christ. In these ways Kilmartin's approach to liturgical anamnesis enables preaching and teaching that clarify the connection between liturgy and life.

Kilmartin's insistence that the celebration of the liturgy should be used as a matrix for systematic theology is also an important contribution. Many Christians' only contact with the official Church, and with the Church's theology, is the celebration of liturgy. All too often Christians exclaim that they find theology abstract or unhelpful, while they experience God's salvation in the liturgy. Kilmartin argues that liturgical celebration connects the truths of faith with one another, thereby presenting a truly systematic theology. His work indicates how teachers and preachers may help Christian worshipers connect their active participation in the liturgical celebration of the divine self-communication with the rest of their lives of faith.

At the same time, Kilmartin's description of the liturgy as a celebration of the economic Trinity, in which the gift of the Holy Spirit is mediated through the devotion of the members of the liturgical assembly, presents a stiff challenge to the Church. The understanding that the Holy Spirit acts through the instrumentality of the members of the liturgical assembly calls for a new level of conscious participation in the liturgy by all members of the assembly.[5] This degree of awareness implies a commitment to building a society of justice and love that is far greater than that exhibited by all but a few liturgical assemblies. Similarly, many Christians who regularly celebrate the liturgy together would be surprised to hear that, as Kilmartin noted before the Vatican Council, one of the necessary dispositions for worthy reception of the Church's sacraments is the openness to receiving saving grace through the mediation of other members of the liturgical assembly.

The theme of covenant renewal through the liturgy presents similar challenges to the Church. In Kilmartin's understanding, sacramental communion expresses an awesome level of personal commitment to living the sacrifice of Christ. In the popular mind, the link between baptismal commitment and eucharistic communion is

[5] The challenge of recovering liturgical celebration as a truly communal act is frequently acknowledged by liturgical theologians. The Consilium for the Reform of the Liturgy commented on this challenge in 1978 in an answer to a question on the posture of the liturgical assembly during the Eucharistic Prayer: *DOL* no. 1411, p. 474, n. R2.2. See Adolf Adam, *Corso di Liturgia* (Brescia: Queriniana, 1988) 68–71.

a tenuous one. Kilmartin's reconnection of Eucharist and covenant renewal demonstrates that the Eucharist is a sacrament of commitment to Christ and his sacrificial response to the Father's love continued in the covenant community of the Church.

CONCLUDING REMARKS:
ANAMNESIS, EPICLESIS, AND THE FUTURE

According to Kilmartin's understanding, the celebration of the one life of faith in Christian liturgy is an event of both anamnesis and epiclesis. The liturgical memory of Christ is not just a subjective recall, for anamnesis is not just a human work. It is also the work of the Holy Spirit, personally present in the faith of Christ and the faith of the Christian assembly. In the liturgy the Spirit acts in the memory of the Church, expressed in word and action developed through history to communicate the saving attitudes of Christ's faith.

Kilmartin's study led him to understand liturgical anamnesis as the performative form of the act of faith, involving both verbal and gestural language handed down by historically and culturally conditioned communities. This description points to the need for systematic theology to give serious treatment to the role of symbols in forming imagination and to the ways in which human celebration helps build communities of shared purpose that can transmit their common life from one generation to another. In this regard, Kilmartin's treatment of human celebration as an event of the expansion of human consciousness might be enriched by consideration of Bernard Lonergan's reflection on conversion as well as on the mediation of Christ in prayer.[6] Kilmartin's connection of the engagement of the members of the liturgical assembly in common symbolic activity with the transmission of the faith of Christ highlights the importance of such considerations.

Kilmartin's treatment of Jesus as "man for others" and his acknowledgment of the influence of sinful history in the development of the Church's liturgy can be enriched by interaction with the feminist theological effort both to recover lost history and to break out of the patterns of oppression reflected in the historical development of

[6] These concepts are applied to liturgical celebration by Stephen Happel, "The Sacraments: Symbols that Redirect Our Desires," in *The Desires of the Human Heart: An Introduction to the Theology of Bernard Lonergan*, ed.Vernon Gregson (New York: Paulist Press, 1988) 237–254. See Margaret Mary Kelleher, "Liturgy: An Ecclesial Act of Meaning," *Worship* 59 (1985) 482–497.

liturgical celebration.[7] Here again, the broad outline of his thought needs to be filled in with more practical details, some of which he indicated in articles touching on the relationship between Christians' liturgical celebration and their work for justice in the world.

That these areas for further development arise from a study of Kilmartin's contribution to the theology of the liturgy seems particularly poignant in light of his own effort to make the thought of German and French theologians accessible to Americans. His major conversation partners, as has been seen, were Germans, not Americans. His systematic theology stresses that liturgical praxis is the means of communication of the grace of the Holy Spirit; the analysis of liturgical praxis through the study of ritual performance, however, is a particular concern of American theologians.[8] Had Kilmartin had the time, energy, and health to act as a bridge not only from Europe to America but also from America to Europe, his work might be seen as even more significant.

As has been remarked above, one of Kilmartin's achievements is his integration of Trinitarian theology with Karl Rahner's transcendental Thomist treatment of the divine self-communication. Critics of Rahner's transcendental theology will, then, find the same weaknesses in Kilmartin's system that they do in Rahner's. Indeed, these weaknesses highlight the inability of any theological system to explain the mystery that the Church celebrates in the liturgy. The mystery which is manifested in the liturgy can never be grasped in its entirety, nor confined by discursive examination. Nevertheless, Christians struggle to express their experience of the mystery in comprehensive fashion, in systems of theology.

With this in mind, Kilmartin's Trinitarian reworking of Rahner's theological system offers an important service for other theologians. Kilmartin was careful to show his respect for the Thomist tradition and to present a theology of liturgy that is clearly within the Catholic theological tradition. In this way he demonstrated how Catholic theologians might preserve much of the clarity that scholastic theology and Thomist metaphysics shed upon the Christian mystery,

---

[7] An introduction to this stream of theological thought is provided in Mary Collins, *Renewal to Practice* (Washington, D.C.: Pastoral Press, 1987).

[8] Both a description of the importance of ritual studies and an initial bibliography are given by Margaret Mary Kelleher, "Ritual Studies and the Eucharist: Paying Attention to Performance," in *Eucharist: Toward the Third Millennium*, ed. Martin F. Connell (Chicago: Liturgy Training Publications, 1997) 51–64.

while moving into a theological world which is more explicitly Trinitarian and which re-emphasizes the *lex orandi*.

Kilmartin's work, like that of every life, is incomplete. When he died at the age of seventy, he left unfinished manuscripts and notes for articles that were never written. He also left a body of work that indicated how Catholic theology might reintegrate the *lex orandi* and the *lex credendi* using an ascending Christology incorporating the Eastern insight of the proper personal mission of the Holy Spirit. This reintegration, he believed, would assist Christians in their attempt to live the one life of faith with integrity and joy. It would also contribute to restored communion between the Churches of East and West and between Catholicism and the Reformation traditions. As future generations of theologians take up this work where Edward Kilmartin left off, it will become increasingly clear how much he accomplished.

Bibliography

PRIMARY SOURCES

Kilmartin, Edward J. "The Active Role of Christ and the Holy Spirit in the Divine Liturgy." *Diakonia* 17 (1982) 95–108.

_____. "The Active Role of Christ and the Holy Spirit in the Sanctification of the Eucharistic Elements." *Theological Studies* 45 (1984) 225–253.

_____. "Apostolic Office: Sacrament of Christ." *Theological Studies* 35 (1975) 243–264.

_____. "The Basis of the Sunday Mass Obligation." *Emmanuel* 81 (1975) 298–303.

_____. "Bread from Heaven." In *Bread from Heaven*. Ed. Paul J. Bernsier, 1–7. New York: Paulist Press, 1977.

_____. "The Catholic Tradition of Eucharistic Theology: Towards the Third Millennium." *Theological Studies* 55 (1994) 405–457.

_____. *Christian Liturgy I: Theology and Practice*. Kansas City: Sheed and Ward, 1988.

_____. "Christ's Presence in the Liturgy." *Emmanuel* 82 (1976) 237–243.

_____. *Culture and the Praying Church*. Ottawa: CCCB, 1990.

_____. "Development in the Post-Caselian Period." Diskette file, 1992. Kilmartin Archives, Jesuit Community at Boston College.

_____. "Ecclesiological Implications of Some Classical Eucharistic Prayers." *Wort und Wahrheit: Supplementary Issue No. 5: Fifth Ecumenical Consultation Between Theologians of the Oriental Orthodox Churches and the Roman Catholic Church, Vienna-Lainz, September 18–25, 1988*, 85–99. Vienna: Herder, 1989.

_____. "Epiclesis." *New Catholic Encyclopedia* 18: Supplement. New York: McGraw-Hill, 1988: 76–78.

_____. "Eschatology and the Evanston Congress: A Study of Developments in Eschatology in the Twentieth Century, and Its Influence on the Theology of the World Council of Churches." S.T.D. Dissertation. Rome: Pontifical Gregorian University, 1958.

_____. "Eucharist and Community." In *Bread from Heaven*. Ed. Paul J. Bernier, 34–44. New York: Paulist Press, 1977.

_____. "Eucharist as Sacrifice." *New Catholic Encyclopedia* 5. New York: McGraw-Hill, 1967: 609–615.

_____. *The Eucharist in the Primitive Church.* Englewood Cliffs, N.J.: Prentice-Hall, 1965.

_____. *The Eucharist in the West.* Ed. Robert J. Daly. Collegeville: The Liturgical Press, 1999.

_____. "The Eucharistic Prayer: Content and Function of Some Early Eucharistic Prayers." In *The Word in the World.* Ed. Richard J. Clifford and George MacRae, 117–134. Cambridge: Weston, 1973.

_____. "History of the Theology of the Eucharist in the Western Church." Diskettes, 1992. Kilmartin Archives, Jesuit Community at Boston College.

_____. "The Last Supper and Earliest Eucharists of the Church." In *The Breaking of Bread.* Concilium 40. Ed. P. Benoit, R. Murphy, B. van Iersel, 19–25. New York: Paulist Press, 1969.

_____. "Liturgical Influences on John 6." *Catholic Biblical Quarterly* 22 (1960) 183–191.

_____. "A Modern Approach to the Word of God and Sacraments of Christ: Perspectives and Principles." In *The Sacraments: God's Love and Mercy Actualized.* Proceedings of the Theological Institute 11. Ed. F. A. Eigo, 59–109. Villanova, Pa.: Villanova University Press, 1979.

_____. "Office and Charism: Reflections on a New Study of Ministry." *Theological Studies* 38 (1977) 547–554.

_____. "The One Fruit and the Many Fruits of the Mass." In *Proceedings of the Catholic Theological Society of America* 21 (1966) 37–69.

_____. "Pastoral Office and the Eucharist." In *Bread from Heaven.* Ed. Paul Bernier, 138–150. New York: Paulist Press, 1977.

_____. "Patristic Views of Sacramental Sanctity." In *Proceedings of the Catholic College Teachers of Sacred Doctrine* 8 (1962) 59–82.

_____. "Paul VI's References to the Holy Spirit in Discourses and Writings on the Second Vatican Council, 1963–1965." In *Paolo VI e i problemi ecclesiologici al Concilio,* 399–406. Brescia: Istituto Paolo VI, 1989.

_____. "Pope Gelasius on the Subject of Eucharistic Theology." Diskette. Kilmartin Archives, Jesuit Community at Boston College.

_____. "Reflections on Modern Eucharistic Theology." *New Catholic World* 224 (1981) 178–181.

_____. Review of *Eucharistie,* by H. B. Meyer. *Theological Studies* 52 (1991) 150–151.

_____. "Sacramental Theology: The Eucharist in Recent Literature." *Theological Studies* 32 (1971) 233–277.

_____. *The Sacraments: Signs of Christ, Sanctifier and High Priest.* Glen Rock: Paulist Press, 1962.

_____. "Sacraments as Liturgy of the Church." *Theological Studies* 50 (1989) 527–547.

_____. "The Sacred Liturgy: Reform and Renewal." In *Remembering the Future: Vatican II and Tomorrow's Liturgical Agenda.* Ed. Carl A. Last, 33–47. New York: Paulist Press, 1983.

_____. "The Sacrifice of Thanksgiving and Social Justice." In *Liturgy and Social Justice.* Ed. Mark Searle, 53–71. Collegeville: The Liturgical Press, 1980.

_____. "Sacrificium Laudis: Content and Function of Early Eucharistic Prayers." *Theological Studies* 35 (1974) 268–287.

_____. "Spirit and Liturgy: Notes for lectures at Creighton University, June, 1992." Kilmartin Archives, Jesuit Community at Boston College.

_____. "A System of Organic Synthesis." M.A. thesis, Boston College, 1948.

_____. "Summary of Bibliography." Diskette. Kilmartin Archives, Jesuit Community at Boston College.

_____. "Theology of the Sacraments: Toward a New Understanding of the Chief Rites of the Church of Jesus Christ." In *Alternative Futures for Worship.* Vol. 1, *General Introduction.* Ed. Regis A. Duffy, 115–167. Collegeville: The Liturgical Press, 1987.

_____. "Two Thermodynamic Relations of the System: Sucrose and Water." M.S. thesis, Holy Cross College, 1950.

_____. "When Is Marriage a Sacrament?" *Theological Studies* 34 (1973) 275–286.

Kilmartin, Edward J., and Andrew Van Hook. "Heats of Crystallization of Sucrose from Water Solutions." *Sugar* (London, England) 45, no. 10 (October 1950).

Van Hook, Andrew, and Edward J. Kilmartin. "The Surface Energy of Sucrose." *Zeitschrift für Elektrochemie.* Berichte der Bundesgesellschaft für physikalische Chemie, Band 56, Heft 4 (1952) 302–305.

SECONDARY SOURCES

Adam, Adolf. *Corso di Liturgia.* Brescia: Queriniana, 1988. Original German publication 1985.

Alberigo, Giuseppe, et al., eds. *Une École de théologie: Le Saulchoir.* Paris: Cerf, 1985.

Aquinas, Thomas. *Summa Theologiae* III. New York: Blackfriars, 1963.

Bellet, Maurice. "Anamnèse I: La mémoire du Christ." *Christus* 76 (1972) 520–532.

Betz, Johannes. *Die Eucharistie in der Zeit der griechischen Väter.* Vol. I/I, *Die Aktualpräsenz der Person und des Heilswerkes Jesu im Abendmahl nach der vorephesinischen griechischen Patristik.* Fribourg: Herder, 1955.

_____. "Eucharist I. Theological." In *Sacramentum Mundi.* Ed. Karl Rahner, 447–459. New York: Seabury, 1975.

_____. "Die Gegenwart der Heilstat Christi." In *Wahrheit und Verkündigung: Festschrift M. Schmaus*. Ed. L. Scheffczyk et al., 1807–1826. Munich: Schöningh, 1967.

Bouley, Allan. "Anamnesis." In *The New Dictionary of Theology*. Ed. Joseph A. Komonchak, Mary Collins, and Dermot Lane, 16–17. Wilmington, Del.: Michael Glazier, 1987.

Bouyer, Louis. *Eucharist: Theology and Spirituality of the Eucharistic Prayer*. Notre Dame: Notre Dame University Press, 1968.

_____. "Le salut dans les religions à mystères." In *Revue des Sciences Religieuses* 28 (1953) 1–16.

Casel, Odo. *Das Christliche Kultmysterium*, 3rd ed. Regensburg: Pustet, 1948.

_____. *Die Liturgie als Mysterienfeier*. Freiburg i. B.: Herder, 1922.

_____. "Mysteriengegenwart." *Jahrbuch für Liturgiewissenschaft* 8 (1928) 145–224.

Chauvet, Louis-Marie. *Symbol and Sacrament*. Collegeville: Pueblo, 1995.

Coffey, David. *Deus Trinitas: The Doctrine of the Triune God*. New York: Oxford, 1999.

_____. *Grace: The Gift of the Holy Spirit*. Manly, N.S.W.: Catholic Institute of Sydney, 1979.

_____. "The Holy Spirit as the Mutual Love Between the Father and the Son." *Theological Studies* 51 (1990) 193–229.

_____. "The Incarnation: Fact, Not Myth." *Faith and Culture* 1 (1978) 13–29.

_____. "The 'Incarnation' of the Holy Spirit in Christ." *Theological Studies* 45 (1984) 466–480.

_____. "The Palamite Doctrine of God: A New Perspective." *St. Vladimir's Theological Quarterly* 32 (1988) 334–342.

_____. "The Pre-existent and the Incarnate Word." *Faith and Culture* 5 (1983) 62–76.

_____. "A Proper Mission of the Holy Spirit." *Theological Studies* 47 (1986) 227–250.

_____. "The Resurrection of Jesus and Catholic Orthodoxy." *Faith and Culture* 3 (1980) 27–37.

Collins, Mary. *Renewal to Practice*. Washington, D.C.: Pastoral Press, 1987.

Corbon, Jean. *The Wellspring of Worship*. With a foreword by E. J. Kilmartin. New York: Paulist Press, 1988.

Cowburn, John. *Love and the Person*. London: Chapman, 1966.

Daly, Robert J. *The Origins of the Christian Doctrine of Sacrifice*. Philadelphia: Fortress Press, 1978.

Dekkers, Eloi. "La liturgie, mystère Chrétien." *La Maison-Dieu* 14 (1948) 30–64.

De Lubac, Henri. *Corpus Mysticum*. Paris: Aubier, 1949.

Del Colle, Ralph. *Christ and the Spirit: Spirit-Christology in Trinitarian Perspective*. New York: Oxford, 1994.

Denzinger, Henricus, and Adolfus Schönmetzer, eds. *Enchiridion Symbolorum*. 26th ed. Barcelona: Herder, 1976.

Documents on the Liturgy, 1963–1979. Collegeville: The Liturgical Press, 1982.

Eisenbach, Franziskus. *Die Gegenwart Jesu Christi im Gottesdienst: Systematische Studien der Liturgiekonstitution des II. Vatikanischen Konzils*. Mainz: Grünewald, 1982.

Faivre, B. "Eucharistie et mémoire." *Nouvelle Revue Theologique* 90 (1968) 278–290.

Filthaut, Theodor. *Die Kontroverse über die Mysterienlehre*. Warendorf: Schnellsche, 1947.

Flannery, Austin, ed. *Vatican II: The Conciliar and Post Conciliar Documents*. Collegeville: The Liturgical Press, 1975.

Gaillard, Jean. "Chronique de Liturgie: La théologie des mystères." *Revue Thomiste* 57 (1957) 510–551.

Garvey, Colin. Review of *Love and the Person*, by John Cowburn. *Philosophical Studies* 17 (1968) 338–342.

Gerken, Alexander. "Kann sich die Eucharistie ändern?" *Zeitschrift für Katholische Theologie* 97 (1975) 415–429.

Giraudo, Cesare. *La struttura letteraria della preghiera eucaristica. Saggio sul genesi letteraria di'una forma. Tôdâ veterotestamentaria, berakâ giudaica, anafora cristiana*. Analecta Biblica 92. Rome: Biblical Institute, 1981.

_____. *Eucaristia per la Chiesa*. Rome: Gregorian University Press, 1989.

Giuliani, Maurice. "Présence actuelle du Christ." *Christus* 1.1 (1954) 102–110.

_____. "Présence actuelle du Christ." *Christus* 1.2 (1954) 97–123.

Gleeson, Philip. "Mystery." In *The New Dictionary of Theology*. Ed. Joseph A. Komonchak, Mary Collins, and Dermot Lane, 688–692. Wilmington, Del.: Glazier, 1987.

Gurrieri, John. "Catholic Liturgical Sources of Social Commitment." In *Liturgical Foundations of Social Policy in the Catholic and Jewish Traditions*. Ed. Daniel Polish and Eugene Fisher, 19–38. Notre Dame: Notre Dame University Press, 1983.

Happel, Stephen. "The Sacraments: Symbols that Redirect Our Desires." In *The Desires of the Human Heart: An Introduction to the Theology of Bernard Lonergan*. Ed. Vernon Gregson, 237–254. New York: Paulist Press, 1988.

Häussling, Angelus. "Odo Casel—noch von Aktualität?" *Jahrbuch für Liturgiewissenschaft* 28 (1986) 357–387.

Hild, J. "L'encyclique 'Mediator Dei' et le mouvement liturgique de Maria-Laach." *La Maison-Dieu* 14 (1948) 15–29.

Irwin, Kevin. *Context and Text: Method in Liturgical Theology*. Collegeville: The Liturgical Press, 1994.

_____. *Liturgical Theology*. Collegeville: The Liturgical Press, 1990.

Jasper, Ronald C., and Geoffrey Cuming. *Prayers of the Eucharist: Early and Reformed*. New York: Pueblo, 1992.

John Paul II. *Dominum et Vivificantem: On the Holy Spirit in the Life of the Church and the World*. May 30, 1986. Washington, D.C.: USCC, 1986.

Jungmann, Joseph. *The Mass of the Roman Rite*. New York: Benziger, 1951.

Kasper, Walter, and G. Sauter. *Kirche—Ort des Geistes: Kleine ökumenische Schriften*. Freiburg: Herder, 1976.

Kelleher, Margaret Mary. "Liturgy: An Ecclesial Act of Meaning," *Worship* 59 (1985) 482–497.

_____. "Ritual Studies and the Eucharist: Paying Attention to Performance." In *Eucharist: Toward the Third Millennium*. Ed. Martin F. Connell, 51–64. Chicago: Liturgy Training Publications, 1997.

Kennedy, D. J. "Sacraments." *The Catholic Encyclopedia*, 1912.

Lafont, Ghislain. "Permanence et Transformations des intuitions de Dom Casel." *Ecclesia Orans* 4 (1987) 261–284.

Lennerz, H. *Sacramentis Novae Legis in Genere*, 2nd ed. Rome: Gregorian University Press, 1939.

Lies, Lothar. "Trinitätsvergessenheit gegenwärtiger Sakramententheologie?" *Zeitschrift für Katholische Theologie* 105 (1983) 290–314.

_____. "Verbalpräsenz—Aktualpräsenz—Realpräsenz: Versuch einer systematischen Begriffbestimmung." In *Praesentia Christi: Festschrift Johannes Betz zum 70. Geburtstag dargebracht von Kollegen, Freunden, Schülern*. Ed. Lothar Lies, 79–100. Düsseldorf: Patmos, 1984.

Mazza, Enrico. *The Eucharistic Prayers of the Roman Rite*. New York: Pueblo, 1986.

McCool, Gerard, ed. *A Rahner Reader*. New York: Crossroad, 1981.

McKenna, John H. "Eucharistic Epiclesis: Myopia or Microcosm?" *Theological Studies* 36 (1975) 265–284.

McNamara, Brian. "*Christus Patiens* in Mass and Sacraments: Higher Perspectives." *Irish Theological Quarterly* 42 (1975) 17–35.

Meyer, Hans Bernhard. *Eucharistie*. Regensburg: Pustet, 1989.

_____. "Casels Idee der Mysteriengegenwart in neuer Sicht." *Archiv für Liturgiewissenschaft* 28 (1986) 388–395.

_____. "Eine Trinitarische Theologie der Liturgie." *Zeitschrift für Katholische Theologie* 113 (1991) 24–38.

Monden, Louis. *Het Misoffer als Mysterie: Een studie de heilige mis als sacramenteel offer in het licht van de mysterieleer van Dom Odo Casel*. Roermond-Maaseik: Romen & Zonen, 1948.

Nicolas, Jean-Hervé. "Réactualisation des mystères rédempteurs dans et par les sacrements." *Revue Thomiste* 58 (1958) 20–54.

O'Donnell, John J. "In Him and Over Him: The Holy Spirit in the Life of Jesus." *Gregorianum* 70 (1989) 25–45.

Oeing-Hanhof, Ludger. "Trinitarische Ontologie und Metaphysik der Person." In *Trinität: Quaestiones Disputatae 101*. Ed. W. Breuning, 143–181. Freiburg: Herder, 1984.

Pius XII. *Mediator Dei. Acta Apostolicae Sedis* 39 (1947) 521–595. Vatican Library translation. Boston: Daughters of St. Paul, 1947.

_____. *Mystici Corporis. Acta Apostolicae Sedis* 35 (1943) 193–248.

Rahner, Karl. *The Church and the Sacraments*. New York: Herder and Herder, 1963.

_____. "The Eucharist and Suffering." *Theological Investigations* 3, 161–170. Trans. Karl-H. and Boniface Kruger. London: Darton, Longman and Todd, 1967.

_____. *Foundations of Christian Faith*. New York: Crossroad, 1989.

_____. "The Experience of the Holy Spirit." *Theological Investigations* 18, 189–210. Trans. Edward Quinn. New York: Crossroad, 1983.

_____. "The New Image of the Church." *Theological Investigations* 10, 3–29. Trans. David Bourke. New York: Crossroad, 1977.

_____. "The Oneness and Threefoldness of God in Discussions with Islam." *Theological Investigations* 18, 105–121. Trans. David Bourke. London: Darton, Longman and Todd, 1984.

_____. "Personal and Sacramental Piety." *Theological Investigations* 2, 109–131. Trans. Karl-H. Kruger. London: Darton, Longman and Todd, 1963.

_____. "The Presence of the Lord in the Christian Community at Worship." *Theological Investigations* 10, 71–83. Trans. David Bourke. New York: Herder and Herder, 1977.

_____. "Remarks on the Dogmatic Treatise *De Trinitate*." *Theological Investigations* 4, 77–102. Trans. Kevin Smyth. Baltimore: Helicon Press, 1966.

_____. "Some Implications of the Scholastic Concept of Uncreated Grace." *Theological Investigations* 1, 319–346. Trans. Cornelius Ernst. Baltimore: Helicon Press, 1961.

_____. *Theology of Pastoral Action*. New York: Herder and Herder, 1968.

_____. "The Theology of the Symbol." *Theological Investigations* 4, 221–252. Trans. Kevin Smyth. Baltimore: Helicon Press, 1966.

_____. *The Trinity*. New York: Crossroad, 1977.

_____. "The Word and the Eucharist." *Theological Investigations* 4, 253–386. Trans. Kevin Smyth. Baltimore: Helicon Press, 1966.

Rahner, Karl, and Angelus Häussling. *The Celebration of the Eucharist*. New York: Herder and Herder, 1968.

Russo, Gary. "Rahner and Palamas: A Unity of Grace." *St. Vladimir's Theological Quarterly* 32 (1988) 157–180.

Ryan, John Barry. *The Eucharistic Prayer: A Study in Contemporary Liturgy*. New York: Paulist Press, 1974.

Sagne, Jean-Claude. "La mémoire du coeur." *La Vie Spirituelle* 60 (1978) 184–199.

Schaefer, Mary M. *Twelfth Century Latin Commentaries on the Mass: Christological and Ecclesiological Dimensions*. Ann Arbor: University Microfilms, 1983.

Schillebeeckx, Edward. *Christ the Sacrament of the Encounter with God*. New York: Sheed and Ward, 1963.

_____. *De Sakramentele Heilseconomie: Theologische bezinning op Sint-Thomas' sacramentenleer in het licht van de traditie en van de hedenaagse sacramentsproblematiek*. Antwerp: 't Groeit, 1952.

Schilson, Arno. *Theologie als Sakramententheologie*. Mainz: Grünewald, 1982.

Sesboüé, Bernard. "Bulletin de théologie dogmatique: Pneumatologie." *Recherches de Science Religieuse* 76 (1988) 123–124.

Skelly, Michael. *The Liturgy of the World: Karl Rahner's Theology of Worship*. Collegeville: The Liturgical Press, 1991.

Smulders, Pieter. "Tractatus de Sacramentis in Genere." Editio altera emendata. Course notes for distribution, 1949. Kilmartin Archives, Jesuit Community at Boston College.

Sobrino, Jon. *Christology at the Crossroads*. Maryknoll: Orbis, 1978.

Söhngen, Gottlieb. "Christi Gegenwart in uns durch den Glauben." *Die Messe in der Glaubensverkündigung*. Ed. F. X. Arnold, 14–28. Regensburg: Pustet, 1953.

_____. "Die Kontroverse über die kultische Gegenwart des Christus mysteriums." *Catholica* 7 (1938) 114–149.

_____. "Le rôle agissant des mystères du Christ dans la liturgie." *Questions Liturgiques et Paroissiales* 24 (1939) 79–107.

_____. *Das sakramentale Wesen des Messopfers*. Essen: Wibbelt, 1946.

_____. *Symbol und Wirklichkeit im Kultmysterium*. Bonn: 1940.

Staniloae, Dumitru. *Theology and the Church*. Crestwood, N.Y.: St. Vladimir's, 1980.

Van Roo, William. *De Sacramentis in Genere*. Editio secunda. Rome: Gregorian University Press, 1960.

Von Balthasar, Hans Urs. "*Fides Christi*. An Essay on the Consciousness of Christ." *Explorations in Theology*. Vol. 2, *Spouse of the Word*. San Francisco: Ignatius, 1991. German original: *Skizzen zur Theologie*. Vol. 2, *Sponsa Verbi*, 45–79. Einsiedeln: Johannes, 1961.

Vonier, Anscar. *A Key to the Doctrine of the Eucharist*. New York: Benziger, 1925.

Warnach, Victor. *Agape. Die Liebe als Grundmotif der neutestamentlichen Theologie*. Düsseldorf: Patmos, 1951.

Winzen, Damasus. "Note complémentaire et réponse à quelques critiques." *Questions Liturgiques et Paroissiales* 24 (1939) 108–113.

Index

eucharistic incarnation, 62, 70
Eucharisticum Mysterium, 47

faith of Christ, 77, 90–92, 106–108,
    129, 134–135
faith of Christ and Church, 93, 129,
    141, 145–146
faith as context of liturgical cele-
    bration, 42, 43, 90
Faivre, B., 113–115
    memory as presence, 114

Guitton, Jean, 112

heavenly liturgy, 135–137
Holy Spirit
    and accurate memory of
        Christ, 110, 123, 146
    and contemplation, 112–113,
        114, 116
    as agent of encounter of
        Christian with Christ,
        117–118, 123
    and incarnation, 62, 102
    and Jesus' life of faith,
        129–131, 134–135
    as mediation, 93, 96–97, 119,
        131, 142, 160
    as mutual love, 83, 84, 102,
        131, 147, 160
    mediated immediacy, 118
    mediated through interper-
        sonal activity of liturgical
        assembly, 163
    personal activity of, 62–63,
        82, 116, 131
    proper mission of, 77, 81, 94,
        99, 101, 104, 113, 116

incarnation, historical and euchar-
    istic, 62, 70
institution narrative, 53, 57, 59–60,
    62-63, 67–69, 72

Kasper, Walter, 116–118
    Spirit as memory and creative
        desire, 116
    Church as sacrament of
        Spirit, 117

Lex Orandi, 39, 50–52, 70–72, 99
    and Eucharistic Prayer, 52–54
linguistic community, formation of,
    89
liturgical assembly, 10, 36, 43, 49,
    53, 158
    and covenant renewal,
        121–122
    and eucharistic prayer,
        64–66, 69
    and heavenly liturgy, 74
    and mediation of faith of
        Christ and Church, 41–42,
        137–140, 156–157, 162
    and representation of Christ,
        119
    as sacrament of communion,
        129
    communal interpersonal
        action and sacramental
        grace, 42, 43, 49
    epiclesis for sanctification of,
        69
liturgical year, 11, 33
liturgy as self-actualization of
    Church, 41, 81, 97
love of God and love of neighbor,
    55, 132, 137, 143

McNamara, Brian, 23, 25, 28–31, 35
    efficient causality, 29–30
    intelligibility of divine plan,
        29, 31
    participation in Christ's
        attitudes, 31
    time and eternity, 25–26
mediated immediacy, 83–84,
    96–97, 118
Mediator Dei, 4, 32–34, 36
memory and petition, 58–60, 67
Modes of presence of Christ, 33–34,
    46–47, 49, 119–120, 142–145, 158
models of Trinity
    from procession of Word and
        Spirit, 78–79, 97–99
    from bestowal of Spirit on
        incarnate Word, 99–100

"More than just a comment on an aspect of Kilmartin's theology, this book is itself a major contribution to liturgical theology at the outset of the new millennium. Kilmartin spoke about the liturgical tasks of the new millennium: recovering the forgotten insights of the first millennium, identifying and appropriating the valid developments of the second millennium, and establishing the right balance between *Lex Orandi* and *Lex Credendi*. Hall's achievement is to lay open in an accessible way the magnificent theological vision of Edward J. Kilmartin, and to show that its realization may be much more within reach than we had previously thought."

Robert J. Daly, S.J.
Boston College

"*We Have the Mind of Christ* is a lucid presentation of a key truth we have all forgotten—our active participation in the work of God. . . . Hall not only summarizes Kilmartin's work, but provides an effective synthesis of the field of liturgical theology in the process. A must read for every student of liturgy."

Rev. Virgil C. Funk
President
National Association of Pastoral Musicians